I0234576

38407
Dress
75

DRESS REGULATIONS

FOR

THE OFFICERS OF THE ARMY

(Including the Militia).

1891.

LONDON:
PRINTED FOR HER MAJESTY'S STATIONERY OFFICE,
BY HARRISON AND SONS, ST MARTIN'S LANE,
PRINTERS IN ORDINARY TO HER MAJESTY.

And to be purchased, either directly or through any Bookseller, from
EYRE & SPOTTISWOODE, East Harding Street, Fleet Street, E.C.; or
JOHN MENZIES & Co., 12, Hanover Street, Edinburgh, and
88 and 90, West Nile Street, Glasgow, or
HODGES, FIGGIS, & Co., 104, Grafton Street, Dublin.

Price One Shilling and Sixpence.

First published in 1891 by
Her Majesty`s Stationery Office.

HORSE GUARDS, WAR OFFICE,

1st April, 1891.

THE following Regulations for the Dress of the Officers of the Army having received Her Majesty's approval, His Royal Highness the Commander-in-Chief enjoins on all Officers the strictest conformity thereto, and he holds General Officers and Commanding Officers of Corps responsible for any deviations from the authorized patterns in the uniform of the Officers under their respective commands.

By Command,

Redvers Buller

A.G.

Hand-written amendments

The volume (original edition) used to produce this facsimile contains a number of hand-written amendments. These have been included and are as follows:-

Pages120
The line crossed through reads - ....to be worn at Levée, Balls, and State Occasions.... Just below this the additional words - to be worn at Balls etc. (see left margin) are to follow the word *Pouch.*

Page 121
The heading - INSPECTING VETERINARY SURGEON has been crossed through and amended to read - VETERINARY LIEUT. COLONEL.

TABLE OF CONTENTS

III.—Personal Staff of the Sovereign and of the Royal Family.

IV.—Personal Staff of General Officers and Governors.

III. Cavalry.

IV. Artillery.

I.—Royal Artillery.

III.—Artillery Militia.

V. Engineers.

I.—Royal Engineers.

VI. Infantry.

VII. Army Service Corps 97

VIII. Departments.

IX. Reserve of Officers 123

X. Lieutenants and Deputy Lieutenants of Counties 124

XI. Miscellaneous.

I.—GENERAL INSTRUCTIONS.

ORDINARY CLOTHING.

Badges of Rank—The rank of officers is shown by badges as under :—

Field-Marshal—Crossed batons on a wreath of laurel, with a crown above.

General—Crossed sword and baton, with crown and star above.

Lieutenant-General—Crossed sword and baton, with crown above.

Major-General—Crossed sword and baton, with star above.

Brigadier-General—Crossed sword and baton.

Colonel—Crown and two stars below.

Lieutenant-Colonel—Crown and one star below.

Major—Crown.

Captain—Two stars.

Lieutenant—One star.

Second Lieutenant—No badge.

Badges of rank, except when otherwise ordered, will be worn on shoulder straps, and in certain cases, specially provided for, on saddle cloths. They may be in metal or embroidery. In metal, the stars and crowns on shoulder straps are ¾ inch high ; in embroidery 1 inch high. On saddle cloths, stars and crowns, whether in metal or embroidery, will be 2½ inches high. The badge of crossed sword and baton on shoulder straps is 2 inches long ; on saddle cloths 4 inches.

Regimental Officers having Brevet Rank wear the badges of their army rank ; Departmental Officers having honorary rank, the badges of that rank ; and Departmental Officers not having honorary rank the badges of the combatant grade with which they rank.

Badges, Special—No badges of a special character are allowed to be worn, except those authorized by these Regulations. A.O. 250, 1889.

Boots and Spurs—Mounted Officers, except where otherwise specified, wear, when on mounted duties, knee boots with jack spurs fastened with straps and buckles. Officers who are not mounted wear Wellington, or ankle, boots. The knee boots must be, as regards shape, in accordance with the sealed pattern, but the height will depend upon the length of the leg and the relative height of the calf. The boot, which is sloped down at the back, should reach in front to about 4 inches from the top of the knee and at the back just to the top of the calf.

Braid, Buttons, &c.—Unless otherwise specified, loops, frogs, and buttons on the front of tunics, &c., will be at equal distances. Buttons, generally, will be an inch in diameter ; small buttons ¾ of an inch. When loops of lace or cord are worn across the breast, the top loops will reach to the sleeve seams, and those at the waist will be 4 inches long.

Cocked-Hats—Cocked-hats will be of black beaver, or silk ; and of the following dimensions :—

The left side 7 inches high, the right side 6¼ inches, each corner 4¾ inches long.

On the right side, a black silk cockade with a loop and button over it ; and, at each corner, a bullion tassel, 1¾ inches long, exclusive of the head.

Collars—The collars of tunics, frock-coats, and jackets will, unless
01002/3832 otherwise stated, be rounded at the top in front and the height
is not to exceed 2 inches.

Depth of Skirts—The skirts of tunics for officers 5 feet 9 inches high will be—

For Field Marshals, General Officers and Colonels on the Staff, Artillery, Engineers, Foot Guards, Infantry Regiments, Army Service Corps and Departments generally—10 inches.

For General Staff, Cavalry, and Rifle Regiments—9 inches.

The skirts of frocks will be 17 inches deep for all Officers 5 feet 9 inches high.

The proportionate variation for each inch of difference in height is about ¼ inch in the skirts of frocks and ⅛ inch in the skirts of tunics.

Forage Caps—Round forage caps with peaks will be 3 inches high ; without peaks 2⅝ inches.

Gloves—Gloves, except as under, or where otherwise stated, will be of white leather.

Brown dogskin or brown buckskin gloves will be worn as directed in the Queen's Regulations and Orders for the Army.

Great-Coats and Capes—Great-coats will be made according to the following description :—

Milled cloth, double-breasted, to reach within a foot of the ground. Stand and fall collar, 4½ inches deep with a fly to cover the band of the cape when buttoned on. Loose round cuffs, 6 inches deep. 2 pockets with flaps at the waist in front, 2 openings behind, at the side-seams, with pointed flaps 11 inches long ; a pocket inside the left breast. A slit in the left side for hilt of sword to pass through. An opening behind, 19 inches long, with a fly. 2 rows of buttons down the front, 6 in each row, the top buttons 6 inches apart, the bottom ones 4 inches ; 3 buttons on each skirt-flap, the centre one to close the pocket; 4 small buttons at the opening behind; and 5 flat buttons under the fly at the collar. A cloth back-strap, attached to the top button of the skirt-flap, to confine the coat at the waist; 2 hooks and eyes to the collar. Shoulder-straps on the coat, of the same material as the garment; a small button of the pattern authorized for the respective services at the top. Badges of rank in gold; in bronze for Rifle Regiments. Cape of the same cloth as the coat, and long enough to cover the knuckles; 4 small buttons in front; to fasten at the neck with a leather strap, runner and buckle. Four cloth tabs with button-holes in the lining at the bottom, one on either side in front and two in the rear, so as to secure the cape to the bottom buttons of the coat in front and to the top buttons on the flaps behind.

In the case of the Mounted Officers for whom the above pattern of coat is authorized, the following modifications will be made:—The opening of the coat behind will be long enough to reach to the cantle of the saddle, and a gusset will be introduced commencing at the top of the slit and extending downwards to about 24 inches, with about 19 inches' width at the bottom. A tab with button-hole at the bottom of the gusset to close it when the coat is worn on foot. A small pocket with a flap at the back of the left sleeve. On the inside of each skirt a cloth band with button to secure the skirts over the knees when the coat is worn on mounted duties. The four buttons at the opening behind are omitted. The coat to reach to the ankles when worn on foot.

*Haversacks.** Black for Rifles; white for all other services. Two large pockets, the rear one containing a metal enamelled plate. At the back of the front pocket, two smaller pockets, and a loop with portable knife and fork. Flap fastened with a small button of Regimental or Departmental pattern. White web strap with white metal fittings; for Rifles, black strap with black metal fittings.

Helmets—

Helmet—Home Pattern, with fittings.

(*a*) Cork, covered with blue cloth in four seams, two on each side; peaks, front and back, stiffened and covered with cloth without a seam; the front peak bound with gilt metal $\frac{3}{16}$ inch wide, the back peak with patent leather $\frac{1}{8}$ inch wide. Above the peaks and going round the helmet a cloth band $\frac{3}{4}$ inch wide, and stitched top and bottom. Back peak to centre of crown $10\frac{1}{2}$ inches; front peak to centre of crown $10\frac{1}{4}$ inches; side to centre of crown 8 inches. Gilt curb-chain chin strap, the links $\frac{3}{4}$ inch wide and the strap lined with black velvet. Gilt rose fastenings at the sides; gilt convex bar, $\frac{1}{4}$ inch wide, down the centre of the back, and to the bottom of the back peak. The bar is in one piece, and is fastened to the helmet by means of two studs and a flattened prolongation of the bar under the back peak. At the top of the helmet, a gilt spike mounted on a cross-piece base.

* Haversacks need not be worn as a general rule, except on service in the field or at extended manœuvres. G.O. 16, 1885.

G.O. 109, 1880.

61002
4076

Helmet—Home Pattern, with fittings—(continued).

The dimensi ns of the spike are—

Height of spike from place of insertion in the top rose of the cross-piece base ... ... 2¾ inches.

Total height of spike and base ... ... 3¼ inches.

Diameter of spike at point of contact with the top rose of base ... ... ⅞ inch.

The cross-piece base is of gilt metal; there is a rose at the top into which the spike is screwed, and a smaller rose on each of the four terminations of the base. A gilt hook at the back of the base, to which the chin strap is attached when not required to be worn under the chin. The width of the base from the point of the front termination to the point of the rear termination, measured in a straight line underneath, 4⅞ inches, that from side to side 3½ inches. The base is attached to the helmet by four screws and nuts. For ventilation, the base is perforated with four holes. A gilt collet inserted in the crown of the helmet.

(*b.*) In Field Batteries and Garrison Brigades of the Royal Artillery, in the Army Service Corps, the Medical Staff, and the Army Veterinary Department, a gilt ball in a leaf cup is substituted for the spike. Height of ball and cup 1¾ inches.

(*c.*) In Light Infantry, the helmet is covered with dark green cloth.

(*d.*) In Rifle regiments the helmet is covered with rifle-green cloth, and bronze is substituted for gilt metal in the fittings. Bronze curb-chain chin strap on Morocco leather of the colour of the regimental facings. The leather lined with black velvet.

(*e.*) A description of the plates worn with this pattern of helmet is included in the Dress of the Services for which it is regulation. The plates are also worn on the white pattern of helmet at stations for which puggarees are not authorized.

Patrol-Jackets—Patrol-jackets, except those otherwise specified, will be made according to the following description :—

Blue cloth, serge for warm stations, 28 inches long from the bottom of the collar behind, for an officer 5 feet 9 inches in height, with a proportionate variation for any difference in height, rounded in front, and edged with inch black mohair braid all round and up the openings at the sides. On each side in front, 4 double drop loops of ½ inch flat plait, with eyes in the centre of each loop ; the top loops extend to the shoulder seams, and the bottom to 4 inches ; 4 netted olivets on the right side, to fasten through the loops on the left. On each sleeve, an Austrian knot of flat plait 7 inches high from the bottom of the cuff. Double flat plait on each back seam, with crow's foot at top and bottom, and 2 double eyes at equal distances. Pockets fitted with flaps in and out. Hooks and eyes in front. Shoulder straps of the same material as the garment, edged with ⅛ inch black mohair braid, except at the base ; black netted button at the top. Badges of rank in gold.

Sabretaches—Staff Officers will wear, when mounted, Russia leather sabretaches with three slings of Staff pattern.

Officers of Household Cavalry, Dragoon Guards, Dragoons and Lancers, Mounted Officers of Royal Engineers, Foot Guards, Rifles, and Departments, wear, when on mounted duties, black leather sabretaches of similar pattern, with three slings, ¾ inch wide, of patterns to match their sword-belts. Metal ornaments of regimental patterns, or of departmental patterns, will be worn on the flaps.

Mounted Officers of Infantry will also wear sabretaches of the pattern above described, but without metal ornaments.

Saddle—General Officers, Officers of the General, Divisional, and Brigade Staff, and other officers for whom a hunting saddle is approved, may use, instead, a saddle as briefly described hereunder—

The seat and flaps are similar to those of a hunting saddle, but with fans as in a Cavalry saddle. The pannel is lined with soft leather and stuffed with curled horse-hair. Regulation wallets are fastened in front; no surcingle. The regulation waterproof cloak can be carried resting on the fans behind. A brown leather waterproof pocket can be fastened to the off side, and a spare horse-shoe carried in a case which is on the near side under the flap.

Sashes.—Sashes are worn by Field Marshals, General Officers, and Equerries to H.R.H. the Prince of Wales, round the waist, the tassels hanging from the left side. By other officers sashes are worn diagonally over the left shoulder under the left shoulder-strap and over the sword belt: the ends are crossed through a runner at the waist. Sashes will be of such length that the ends of the tassels shall just reach the bottom of the skirt of the tunic.

Shoulder-Straps—Shoulder-straps, except when otherwise provided, are worn on tunics, stable-jackets, shell-jackets, frock-coats, patrol-jackets, cloaks, and great-coats. A description of the shoulder-straps is included in that of the articles on which they are worn.

Straps—Whenever spurs are worn with trousers, straps are to be worn also.

Swords— Swords unless otherwise described, will be made according to the following description :—

Half-basket hilt and back-piece of steel or gilt metal, black fish-skin grip, bound with silver wire when the hilt is of steel, or with gilt wire when the hilt is of gilt metal; slightly-curved blade, grooved and spear-pointed. Full size—blade 35 inches long and inch wide at the shoulder; extreme length, including the hilt, 41 inches; weight, without scabbard, 2 lbs. Second size—blade 33 inches long and an inch wide at the shoulder; extreme length, including hilt, 38½ inches; weight without scabbard 1 lb. 12 ozs.

Sword-Belts—The sword-belt will be worn as follows :—

Over the tunic by Colonels on the Staff, by the Personal Staff of the Sovereign and Royal Family, and by officers of all arms except those mentioned below.

Under the tunic by Field-Marshals, General Officers, the General Staff, the Personal Staff of General Officers, and officers of Lancers, Hussars, and Rifle Regiments. Over the blue frock-coat and infantry serge patrol-jacket (except in Rifle Regiments) and under all other jackets.

Tunics and Jackets—All tunics, and jackets, will be single-breasted, unless otherwise stated.

Waterproof Cloak—For all ranks in accordance with the patterns for mounted and dismounted Services respectively, deposited* in the pattern room, Horse Guards, War Office. Length of the cloak to vary according to height of wearer. This cloak may be worn by the Staff, and in camp and quarters off parade by all other officers.

Whistle, for Officers of Infantry, except Officers of Rifle Regiments—
G.O. 201, 1887. White metal, pattern as for sergeants. To be attached by means of a crimson silk cord passed through a brass eyelet in the lining at the top of the inside breast pocket of the tunic or patrol jacket, and carried in the pocket.

CLOTHING IN HOT AND COLD CLIMATES, &c.

Great-Coat (Dominion of Canada). Milled cloth of the colour author-
G.O. 81, 1884. ized for the ordinary great-coats for each service; double-breasted, with lappels, $4\frac{1}{2}$ inches wide at the top, and $2\frac{1}{2}$ inches at the bottom ; the shape as for frock-coat ; to reach within a foot of the ground. For Mounted Officers the coat will reach to the ankles. The body, skirts, and sleeves lined with real or imitation fur ; the collar and cuffs on the outside and the lappels on the inside lined, in the case of blue great-coats, with black Astrachan fur ; in that of grey, with Astrachan fur of that colour. The Astrachan forms an edging 1 inch wide on the inside of the collar and down the lappels, on the outside, to the waist. Four loops of $\frac{1}{4}$-inch black flat cord down the front on each side. Each loop forms an eye in the centre at the top and bottom and a crow's foot at the end ; a black netted olivet on each loop near the crow's foot, two olivets at the waist behind. Pocket inside the left breast. Pockets in the plaits of the skirts behind. Three hooks and eyes on the collar. Shoulder-straps of the same material as the garment ; a black netted button at the top. Badges of rank in gold.

Kamarband—During a voyage through the Red Sea or Indian Ocean, and in the West Indies, Bermuda, Mauritius, Ceylon,

* Present patterns sealed 1890.

China, Straits Settlements, and Egypt, at the discretion of General Officers Commanding, officers may be allowed to wear at mess a kamarband instead of the mess waistcoat.

The colour of the kamarband will be :—

For the Staff	Red.
" " Royal Artillery	Blue.
" " Scottish Rifles	Green.
" " King's Royal Rifle Corps	Red and green.
" " Royal Irish Rifles	Green.
" " Rifle Brigade	Black and green.
" " Army Service Corps ...	Blue and White.
For every other regiment, corps, or department	Red.

With the kamarband a white collar and black tie will be worn, and the mess jacket will be fastened at the neck by a loop of gold or black braid, according to the regulation for the respective services.

WHITE CLOTHING. 61002 3478

White clothing for China, Straits Settlements, Ceylon, Mauritius, West Indies, and Malta (off parade only at the last-named station, and then at the option of the wearer):—

Patrol-jackets—Plain drill, blue patrol-jacket shape, without braid, fastened by five gilt buttons of patterns for respective services; cuffs pointed; the collar rounded off in front; velvet or silk shoulder straps, according to detail annexed, fastened at top by a small gilt button. Badges of rank in gold.

Shoulder-Straps for above Patrol-Jackets.

A.O. 3. 1897.

Service.	Material.	Colour.
General Officers, Colonels on the Staff, Divisional and Brigade Staff.	Velvet	Dark blue.
Dragoon Guards and Dragoons	Silk	Scarlet.
Lancers	"	Scarlet, edged with white.
Hussars	"	Light blue.
Royal Artillery	"	Blue, edged with scarlet.
Royal Engineers	"	Scarlet, edged with blue.
Infantry of the Line, Royal Regiments	"	Blue.
Infantry of the Line	"	White.
Scottish Rifles	"	Rifle green.
Highland Regiments, Royal	"	Blue.

Service.	Material.	Colour.
Highland Regiments, except Royal and Highland Light Infantry.	Silk	Yellow.
King's Royal Rifle Corps...	"	Rifle green, edged with scarlet.
Royal Irish Rifles....	"	Dark green.
Rifle Brigade	"	Rifle green, edged with black velvet.
Army Service Corps	"	Blue, edged with white.
Medical Staff	"	Black, edged with yellow.
Ordnance Store Department	" ...	Blue, edged with black.
Veterinary Department	"	Maroon.
Army Pay Department	"	Orange.
Chaplain's Department*	"	Black.
Royal Malta Artillery	"	Blue, edged with scarlet

Mess-jacket†—Plain drill, without buttons down the front, upright collar, fastened in front with a loop of white braid, pocket inside the left breast, cuffs pointed. Shoulder-straps as for patrol-jacket, but with badges of rank in silver.

Mess Trousers—Plain drill.

Mess Waistcoat—Plain drill, without lappels, and fastened with four buttons of patterns authorized for respective services.

Trousers—Plain drill.

White Helmet, with fittings, for India and the other Stations specified.—Cork, covered with white cloth in six seams, bound with buff leather at the bottom; above the peak, and going round the helmet, a buff leather band, 1 inch wide, stitched top and bottom. The head-piece let in with zigzag ventilator; back peak to centre of crown 12 inches, front peak to centre of crown 10¾ inches, side to centre of crown 9 inches, gilt side hooks, gilt curb-chain chin-strap, the links ⅝ inch wide, the strap lined with white leather. At top of helmet a gilt collet, riveted on to a gilt collar, ¾ inch wide, to receive spike and base.

Rifle regiments will have a bronze curb-chain chin-strap on Morocco leather of the colour of the regimental facings, lined with black velvet.

61002/4029 * Chaplains will wear collar badges in embroidery and badges of rank in embroidery as on the frock. Buttons of Staff pattern, but in bronze.

61002/3533 † In China a red mess-jacket with rolled collar may be worn in place of white, under local regulations.

White Helmet, with fittings, for India and the other Stations specified.—(continued).

Ornaments.

(1) General, Staff, and Departmental Officers, except Officers of the Medical Staff and Veterinary Department, *when plumes are not worn.* G.O. 109, 1886. 61002/4076

(*a*.) A spike of bright gilt metal, on a dead gilt base,—leaf pattern.

The dimensions are:—

Height of spike from base 3⅞ inches.
Total height of spike and base 4⅜ inches.
Diameter of spike at point of contact with leaf base 1 inch.
Diameter of base 3¼ inches full.

The base has eight principal points, with an interval of about 1¼ inches between each point.

(2) Cavalry.

(*b*.) Spike and base as at (*a*.).

Royal Engineers, Infantry, and Ordnance Store Corps G.O. 109, 1886.

(*c*.) Spike of bright gilt metal, mounted on a bright gilt dome base. G.O. 16,

The dimensions of this spike and the dome base are:— 1885.

Height of spike from place of insertion in dome 2¾ inches.
Total height of spike and dome 3¼ inches.
Diameter of spike at point of contact with dome 1 inch.
Diameter of dome 1⅞ inches full.
Circumference of dome at point of contact with helmet 5⅞ inches.

(3) Rifles.

In Rifle regiments the spike and base are of bronze. Dimensions as for Infantry. G.O. 109, 1886.

(4) Royal Artillery, Army Service Corps, and Medical Staff.

In the Royal Horse Artillery in India, Field Batteries of the Royal Artillery, Army Service Corps, Medical Staff, Veterinary Department, a gilt ball in a leaf on the cup, pattern of base as at (*a*.). The height of the ball and cup is 1⅞ inches. In Garrison Brigades the gilt ball in leaf cup is mounted on the dome base as at (*c*.). 61002/4076

Zinc Button.

A zinc button, covered with white cloth, is worn on all occasions when the spike is not used.

Plumes.

(*a*.). General and Staff Officers—White swan feathers, 10 inches long, drooping outwards, with red feathers under, reaching to the end of the white ones. Officers under the rank of Brigadier 7 inches long, instead of 10 inches. Military Secretaries and Aides-de-Camp wear the smaller plume, but with the red feathers outside the white. Officers of Royal Engineers (other than Staff) not performing regimental or garrison duty, a plume of white cock's feathers 7 inches long. The leaf pattern of base is to be worn with the plume. G.O. 60, 1885.

Regimental Staff Officers do not wear plumes. By Regimental Staff Officers is meant those officers who are borne on the establishments of regiments, not Departmental Officers attached to regiments for duty.

(*b*.). Departmental Officers who wear the cocked hat at home—Plumes of the description and colour laid down in these Regulations for their respective services. The plumes for officers ranking as Major-Generals will be 10 inches long, under that rank 7 inches. 39407/Q.R./778

The leaf pattern of base will be worn with the plumes.

(*c*.). Plumes are attached to the helmet by means of a screw passing through a dead gilt socket, 1½ inches high, leaf pattern, and fastened by a nut.

Puggarees.

White puggarees are worn with helmets in India, Ceylon, Hong Kong, the Straits Settlements, Mauritius, Malta, and Cyprus.

Plates.

At stations for which puggarees are not regulation, plates are worn in front of the helmets. For General, Staff, and Departmental Officers, the plate is gilt, and represents the Royal Arms. The dimensions of the plate are as follows:—

From top of crest to end of scroll, back measurement ... ... 3½ inches.
Extreme horizontal width, back measurement ... ... 2⅞ inches.

(D.R.)

White Helmet, &c.—(Contd.).

For other officers, including officers attached to the Ordnance Store Corps and Veterinary Department, plates are worn of the patterns approved for the Home pattern of Helmet.

STATIONS AT WHICH THE ABOVE DESCRIPTION OF HELMET IS WORN BY ALL OFFICERS.

India, West Indies, Mauritius, Mediterranean, Bermuda, Cape of Good Hope, Ceylon, Hong Kong, Straits Settlements, St. Helena, Dominion of Canada (when fur caps are not worn), and in the West African Settlements.

KHAKI CLOTHING.

Khaki uniform may be worn under local regulations at the following stations :—

61002/4044 Egypt.
Straits Settlements (with brown leather belts).
61002/4040 West African Settlements.

BROWN BELTS.

61002/4101/4040 *Brown belts* may be worn by officers on active service, and with Khaki uniform at the Straits Settlements.

SHIRT COLLARS.

61002/3155 *Shirt Collars* are worn in undress uniform in the 7th Hussars, and in the Oxfordshire Light Infantry. They are also worn in India by all services in undress uniform. The collar is not to show more than ¼ of an inch above the uniform.

DECORATIONS AND MEDALS.

38407/Dress/74 Military decorations and medals are to be worn with the tunic or dress jacket only, and on the left breast. They are to be worn in a horizontal line, suspended from a single bar, of which the buckle is not to be seen. The bar is to be placed between the first and second buttons from the bottom of the collar of the tunic ; in Hussar regiments, immediately below the top bar of lace on the left breast. The riband is not to exceed one inch in length, unless the number of clasps require it to be longer. The buckles attached to the ribands of the third class of the Orders of the Bath and of St. Michael and St. George should be seen. When the decorations and medals cannot, on account of the number, be suspended from the bar so as to be fully seen, they are to overlap. They are to be worn over the sash and under the pouch-belt.

61002/3995 Military medals will be worn in the order of the dates of the campaigns for which they have been conferred; the first decoration or medal obtained being placed farthest from the left shoulder.

The following is the order of arrangement :—

1. English decorations.*
2. English medals.†
3. Foreign decorations.
4. Foreign medals.

38407 / Q.R. / 816

The Victoria Cross, when suspended from the bar, will come immediately after the badge of the Order of the Indian Empire.

On all occasions when the Sovereign, or the representative of the Sovereign, is present, on the parade in celebration of the birthday of the Sovereign, and on all State occasions, including levées, drawing-rooms, and balls, Officers of the Army who are Knights Grand Cross of the Order of the Bath, or Knights Grand Commanders of the Order of the Star of India, or Knights Grand Cross of the Order of St. Michael and St. George, will, when in full dress uniform, wear the riband of the Order, or the ribands of the Orders to which they belong, over the right shoulder and under the sash or belt. Knights-Commanders will wear the riband of the Order, or the ribands of the Orders to which they belong, inside the collar of the tunic, the badge being suspended 2 inches below the lower edge of the collar.

Stars of Orders will never be worn with the patrol jacket, the stable jacket, or the mess jacket, and only with the frock-coat when the cocked hat is also worn. A.O. 341 / 1890

Abroad, Officers of the Army will wear their stars when foreign Officers wear theirs.

On the same occasions as those specified above, Officers of the Army, who may be members and honorary associates of the Order of the Hospital of St. John of Jerusalem, in England, will wear the badge of the Order. 38407 / Q.R. / 788b.

These regulations extend to officers who have retired from the service, or from the Indian Army, provided that under the regulations they be allowed to wear uniform.

Ribands of medals and decorations will be worn with undress or mess-dress uniform by Officers. These ribands should be sewn plain on to the cloth of the coat or jacket, without intervals. They should not, like medals, be made to overlap, and when there is not sufficient room to wear the ribands in one row, they should be worn in two rows, the lower being arranged directly under the upper. The riband of a Knight Grand Cross, or Knight Commander of any Order, is not to be worn, A.O. 341 / 1890

---

* The Queen's Jubilee Medal will be worn after English decorations. 38407 / Q.R. / 816

† The Badges of the Order of St. John of Jerusalem, in England, will be worn after English medals.

the riband of the Companion of the Order being in these cases substituted. Officers in uniform will not wear miniature orders or medals.

Stars of Orders and miniature decorations and medals will be worn in evening dress (plain clothes) in the presence of members of the Royal Family, or of Viceroys and Governors General, and on public and official occasions.

Retired Officers are authorised to wear Stars of Orders and miniature decorations and medals in evening dress on all public and official occasions.

The bar for the suspension of decorations and medals is in all cases to be provided at the expense of the wearer. It may be of any metal or material, and of any pattern consistent with the above instructions, provided the bar and the buckle are wholly concealed by the ribands.

SECOND LIEUTENANTS.

G. O. 26, 1887. Second Lieutenants will wear the same dress as Lieutenants, except that they will not wear badges of rank (see page 1).

SEALED PATTERNS.

Sealed patterns of buttons, lace, embroidery, badges of rank, special badges, devices, horse furniture and appointments, are deposited, for reference and guidance, at the pattern room, Horse Guards, War Office.

II.—STAFF.

1. FIELD MARSHALS, GENERAL OFFICERS, AND COLONELS ON THE STAFF.

1. FIELD MARSHAL.

Tunic—Scarlet cloth, with blue cloth collar and cuffs. The collar embroidered in gold. The cuffs round, 3 inches deep, with gold embroidery 2¼ inches deep round the top; a scarlet flap on each sleeve, 6½ inches deep and 2¼ inches wide, embroidered in gold. A similar flap on each skirt behind, ½ inch shorter than the length of the skirt and 2½ inches wide; 8 buttons down the front: 3 on each flap; 2 at the waist behind. The front, collar, cuffs, and flaps edged with white cloth, $\frac{3}{16}$ inch wide. An aiguillette of gold wire cord, ¼ inch in diameter, with gilt embossed tags will be worn. The aiguillette is attached to a plaited strap, on the right shoulder, of round gold cord $\frac{3}{16}$ inch in diameter, intertwined with a small dead gold cord. A similar strap on the left shoulder. On each strap, crossed batons of crimson velvet and gold, on a wreath of laurel embroidered in silver, with a crown in silver above; a small gilt button at the top.

Embroidery—Oak-leaf pattern, in dead and bright gold.

Lace—Gold, oak-leaf pattern.

Buttons—Gilt, with crossed batons and crown, encircled with laurel.

Pantaloons—White buckskin. *Boots*—Jacked. *Spurs*—Gilt, with straps and buckles.	To be worn at Drawing-Rooms, and on other State occasions.
Dress Trousers—Blue cloth, with 2½ inch lace down the side seams. *Boots*—Wellington, with brass spurs.	To be worn on other occasions.

Cocked-Hat—As described at page 2, with loop of double gold bullion; gold purl netted button; tassels, flat gold worked head, 6 gold bullions, with 5 crimson bullions under them.

Plume—White swan feathers, drooping outwards, 10 inches long, with red feathers under them long enough to reach the ends of the white ones; feathered stem three inches long.

Helmet, White—See pages 8 to 10.

Sword—Mameluke gilt hilt, with device of crossed batons encircled with oak-leaves; ivory grip; scimitar blade.

Scabbard—Brass, ridged, with cross lockets and rings.

Sword-Knot—Gold and crimson cord, with gold and crimson acorn.

Sword-Belt—Russia leather $1\frac{1}{2}$ inches wide, with slings 1 inch wide, gold oak-leaf embroidery on belt and slings. The belt to be worn under the tunic, but over the frock coat, and in the latter case, under the sash.

Waist-Plate—Round gilt clasp: on the centre-piece, crossed batons and crown, in a wreath of oak and laurel leaves, all in silver; on the outer cicle, a laurel wreath in dead and bright gold.

Sash—Gold and crimson silk net, $2\frac{1}{4}$ inches wide; 2 crimson stripes $\frac{3}{8}$ inch wide, the rest gold; tassels of loose gold bullion fringe, 9 inches long. The sash fastened with gilt buckles, round the waist, the tassels hanging from the left side.

Frock—Blue cloth, double-breasted, with blue velvet collar and cuffs; the cuffs round, 3 inches deep. Plain flaps at the plaits behind, 11 inches long and $1\frac{1}{2}$ inches wide; 2 rows of buttons down the front, 8 in each row, the rows 8 inches apart at the top and 4 inches at the waist; 2 buttons at the waist behind, and 1 at the bottom of each skirt flap. The skirts lined with black. Shoulder-straps, with badges of rank as for tunic.

Patrol-Jacket, to be worn on Service in the Field—Blue cloth, blue velvet lay-down collar, square in front, inch mohair braid at bottom of collar, with black Russia tracing at top of braid, showing $\frac{1}{8}$ inch blue light and forming an eye at either corner. 1-inch mohair braid traced with Russia braid all round up the slits, and along the back seams. The tracing forms an eye at each angle of the braid, except at the top of the slits and back seams where it forms a crow's foot, 1 inch in length, and at the bottom in the centre, where it forms a long crow's foot $1\frac{1}{2}$ inches in length. Five loops of inch mohair braid at equal distances down the front on each side, with two olivets on each loop, the top loops extend to the shoulder seams, and the bottom to 4 inches. Blue velvet pointed cuffs, with inch mohair braid traced with black Russia braid forming an Austrian knot above and below the mohair braid. The mohair braid reaches to 7 inches from bottom of cuff, and the Austrian knot at the top to 9 inches. Pockets in front edged at the bottom with inch mohair braid, black silk lining; pocket inside left breast Shoulder-straps of the same material as the garment, edged with $\frac{1}{2}$ inch black mohair braid, except at the base; black netted button at the top. Badges of rank in gold.

Undress Trousers—Blue cloth, with scarlet stripes, $2\frac{1}{2}$ inches wide and welted at the edges, down the side seams.

Pantaloons, &c., for Mounted Duties—Oxford mixture cloth, with scarlet stripes as on the trousers. Knee boots, as described at page 1, with brass jack spurs.

Forage Cap—Blue cloth, with gold embroidered drooping peak and band of 2 inch lace; gold purl button and braided figure on the crown.

Forage Cap, for Active Service and Peace Manœuvres—Blue cloth folding cap 5 inches high, with scarlet cloth top, and blue side flaps 4 inches deep, to turn down when required. Gold French braid welts on cap and flaps, and at front and back seams. Badge on the left side, the Royal Crest, with crossed batons.

Great-Coat and Cape—Blue milled cloth, of the pattern described at page 2, lined with scarlet rattinett; the collar lined with blue velvet. Shoulder-straps of the same material as the garment; a small gilt button at the top. Badges of rank in gold.

Horse Furniture.

Saddle—Hunting, with gilt metal cantle, or the saddle described at page 6; blue girths.

Stirrups—Gilt, square-set, with oval bottoms; the sides engraved with oak-leaves; the top to cover the eye, and to have crossed batons and crown in relief.

Saddle-Cloth—Blue cloth, 3 feet 2 inches long at the bottom, and 2 feet 2 inches deep, laced all round with 2 stripes of 1½ inch lace, ¼ inch apart; at each hind corner, crossed batons of crimson velvet and gold with a crown in gold above on a laurel wreath embroidered in silver.

Holsters—Brown leather, with gilt caps to the pipes, chased with a double row of pointed leaves; covers of blue cloth, with lace and badges as on the saddle-cloth, and cloth flounces similarly laced. With undress, the holsters are to be covered with black bear-skin, except abroad, where they are to have brown leather covers.

Bridle—Brown leather, with chased gilt whole buckles; bent branch bit, with pads; gilt bosses, with Royal Cypher in the centre, and crossed batons under, encircled with laurel, and surmounted by a crown; cheeks of the shell pattern; open tails with bolts and rings; gilt water chain.

Head-Stall and Bridoon Rein—Gold lace, an inch wide, lined with red Morocco leather; blue front and rosettes.

Breast Plate—Brown leather, with device in gilt metal of crossed bátons, with crown above, and oak branches below.

2. GENERAL.

Tunic—Scarlet cloth, with blue cloth collar and cuffs. The collar embroidered in gold. The cuffs round, 3 inches deep, with gold embroidery 2¼ inches deep round the top; a scarlet flap on each sleeve, 6½ inches deep and 2¼ inches wide, embroidered in gold. A similar flap on each skirt behind, ½ inch shorter than the length of the skirt and 2½ inches wide; 8 buttons down the front; 3 on each flap; 2 at the waist behind. The front, collar, cuffs and flaps edged with white cloth, $\frac{3}{16}$ inch wide. Shoulder-straps of round gold cord $\frac{3}{16}$ inch in diameter, intertwined with a small dead gold cord. On each strap, crossed sword and baton with crown and star above in silver; a small gilt button at the top.

Embroidery—Oak-leaf pattern, in dead and bright gold.

Lace—Gold, oak-leaf pattern.

Buttons—Gilt, with sword and baton crossed, encircled with laurel.

Dress Trousers—Blue cloth, with $2\frac{1}{2}$ inch lace down the side seams.

Dress Pantaloons—Blue cloth; gold lace as for dress trousers.

Boots—Wellington. Knee-boots for mounted duties, as described at page 1.

Spurs—Brass.

Cocked-Hat—As described at page 2, with loop of double gold bullion; gold purl netted button; tassels, flat gold worked head, 6 gold bullions, with 5 crimson bullions under them.

Plume—White swan feathers, drooping outwards, 10 inches long, with red feathers under them long enough to reach the ends of the white ones; feathered stem 3 inches long.

Helmet, White—See pages 8 to 10.

Sword—Mameluke gilt hilt, with device of sword and baton crossed, encircled with oak leaves; ivory grip; scimitar blade.

Scabbard—Brass, ridged, with cross lockets and rings.

Sword-Knot—Gold and crimson cord, with gold and crimson acorn.

61002/4063 *Sword-Belt*—Plain leather or web, $1\frac{1}{2}$ inches wide, with buckle, and loops for slings, to be worn under the tunic and over the frock coat. Slings, 1 inch wide, with gold oak-leaf embroidery.

Sash—Gold and crimson silk net, $2\frac{1}{4}$ inches wide; 2 crimson stripes $\frac{5}{8}$ inch wide, the rest gold; tassels of gold fringe, 9 inches long. Web or leather lining with loops for sword
61002/4063 slings, when worn over the frock coat. The sash fastened with gilt buckles, round the waist and over the sword belt when worn with the frock coat, the tassels hanging from the left side.

Frock—Blue cloth, double-breasted, with blue velvet collar and cuffs; the cuffs round, 3 inches deep. Plain flaps at the plaits behind, 11 inches long and $1\frac{1}{2}$ inches wide; 2 rows of buttons down the front, 8 in each row, the rows 8 inches apart at the top and 4 inches at the waist; 2 buttons at the waist behind, and 1 at the bottom of each skirt-flap; the skirts lined with black. Shoulder-straps with badges of rank as for tunic.

Patrol Jacket to be worn on Service in the Field—Blue cloth, blue velvet lay-down collar, square in front, inch mohair braid at bottom of collar, with black Russia tracing at top of braid, showing $\frac{1}{8}$ inch blue light, and forming an eye at either corner. 1 inch mohair braid traced with Russia braid all round, up the slits, and along the back seams. The tracing forms an eye at each angle of the braid, except at the top of the slits and back seams, where it forms a crow's-foot, 1 inch in length, and at the bottom in the centre, where it forms a long crow's-foot, 1½ inches in length. Five loops of inch mohair braid at equal distances down the front on each side, with two olivets on each loop, the top loops extend to the shoulder seams, and the bottom to 4 inches. Blue velvet pointed cuffs, with inch mohair braid traced with black Russia braid, forming an Austrian knot above and below the mohair braid. The mohair braid reaches to 7 inches from bottom of cuff, and the Austrian knot at the top to 9 inches. Pockets in front, edged at the bottom with inch mohair braid; black silk lining; pocket inside left breast. Shoulder-straps of the same material as the garment, edged with ½-inch black mohair braid, except at the base; black netted button at the top.. Badges of rank in gold.

Serge Patrol-jacket to be worn in South Africa, and at all warm Stations, under local regulations—Blue serge, with collar and cuffs of the same material, and ½-inch braid. In other respects the jacket will be of the same pattern as described in the preceding paragraph. 61002/3440 61002/4023 61002/4070

Undress Trousers—Blue cloth, with scarlet stripes, 2½ inches wide and welted at the edges, down the side seams.

Pantaloons, &c., for Mounted Duties—Blue cloth, with scarlet stripes as on the trousers. Knee-boots, as described at page 1, with brass spurs.

Forage Cap—Blue cloth, with gold embroidered drooping peak and band of 2-inch lace; gold purl button and braided figure on the crown.

Forage Cap for Active Service and Peace Manœuvres—Blue cloth folding cap 5 inches high, with scarlet cloth top, and blue side flaps 4 inches deep, to turn down when required. Gold French braid welts on cap and flaps, and at front and back seams. Badge on the left side, the Royal Crest, with sword and baton crossed.

Mess-Jacket—Scarlet cloth, edged all round, including the collar, with 1 inch oak-leaf lace forming barrels at the bottom of the back seams. Blue cloth collar and cuffs, the collar square in front, with a loop of gold braid at the bottom to fasten across the neck. A tracing of ⅜ inch gold chain gimp along the bottom of the collar. A row of gilt studs in front on the left side. The cuffs pointed and edged with 1 inch oak-leaf lace, the lace extending to 6¼ inches from the bottom of the cuff. Shoulder-straps of blue cloth, edged with ⅜ inch oak-leaf lace, except at the base. A small gilt button at the top. Badges of rank as for tunic, except that they are smaller, and that the hilt of the sword is in gold. Scarlet silk lining. 61002/4137

6'002 / 4137

*Mess-Waistcoat**—Blue cloth, to close at the neck. Edged with ½ inch oak leaf lace at the top of the collar, down the front and along the bottom to the side seams; at ⅛ inch from the gold lace, a tracing of gold Russia braid. The braid forms eyes 2¾ inches from each end of the collar, down the front and at the bottom to the side seams. The pockets edged with eyes in gold Russia braid with a crow's foot at each end. A row of gilt studs and hooks and eyes down the front.

Kamarband—See page 6 and 7.

Great-Coat and Cape—Blue milled cloth, of the pattern described at page 2, lined with scarlet rattinett; the collar lined with blue velvet. Shoulder-straps of the same material as the garment, a small gilt button at the top. Badges of rank in gold.

Horse Furniture.

Saddle—Hunting, or the saddle described at page 5; plain stirrups and blue girths.

Saddle-Cloth—Blue cloth, 3 feet 2 inches long at the bottom, and 2 feet 2 inches deep, laced all round with two stripes of 1½ inch lace, ¼ inch apart; at each hind corner, crossed sword and baton, with crown and star above. Crown, star and baton, and hilt of sword in gold, blade of sword in silver.

Wallets—Brown leather; covers of blue cloth, with lace and badges as on the saddle-cloth, and cloth flounces similarly laced. With undress, the wallets are to be covered with black bear-skin, except abroad where they are to have brown leather covers.

Bridle—Brown leather, with chased gilt whole buckles; blue front and rosettes, bent branch bit, with pads; cheeks of the shell pattern; open tails, with bolts and rings: steel water chain; link and tee bridoon; gilt bosses, with Royal Cypher in the centre, and crossed sword and baton under, encircled with laurel, and surmounted by a crown.

Breast-Plate—Brown leather, with gilt buckles and gilt metal ornament, as on bit, but larger.

3. LIEUTENANT-GENERAL, MAJOR-GENERAL, BRIGADIER-GENERAL.

Uniform and horse furniture as for a General, except that the badges of rank are:—

For a Lieutenant-General—Crossed sword and baton, with crown above.

* Mess-Tunics and Waistcoats of old pattern may continue to be worn until they are required to be replaced.

For a Major-General—Crossed sword and baton, with star above.
For a Brigadier-General—Crossed sword and baton.
For Officers Commanding Infantry Volunteer Brigades uniforms and horse furniture as for a Brigadier-General, except in the case of Officers Commanding regiments who are *ex officio* Brigadiers of Volunteer Brigades, who will wear their regimental uniform. Officers holding rank, honorary or otherwise, higher than that of Brigadier-General will wear the badges of the higher rank. A.O. 441, 1888.

4. COLONEL ON THE STAFF.

Tunic—Scarlet cloth, with blue cloth collar and cuffs. The collar laced round the top and bottom with ½ inch lace; the cuffs round, 3 inches deep, with two bars of ½ inch lace round the top, showing ⅛ inch of blue cloth between the bars. A scarlet flap on each sleeve, 6 inches long and 2½ inches wide, edged with ½ inch lace; and a similar flap, as long as the depth of the skirt, 2½ inches wide, on each skirt behind. The back-skirts edged with ½ inch lace. Eight buttons down the front; three on each flap, two at the waist behind. The front, collar, cuffs, and flaps edged with white cloth, ¼ inch wide, and the skirts lined with white. Shoulder-straps of twisted round gold cord, universal pattern, lined with scarlet; a small button at the top. Badges of rank in silver.
Lace—Gold, staff pattern.
Buttons—Gilt, frosted, with burnished laurel round the edge.
Dress Trousers—Blue cloth, with 1¾ inch lace down the side seams.
Dress Pantaloons—Blue cloth, gold lace as for dress trousers.
Boots—As described at page 1.
Spurs—Brass.
Cocked-Hat—As described at page 2, with loop of ¾ inch lace; gold purl netted button; tassels, netted gold purl head, eight small gold bullions, with seven crimson bullions under them.
Plume—White swan feathers, drooping outwards, 8 inches long, with red feathers under them, long enough to reach the ends of the white ones; feathered stem, 3 inches long.
Helmet, White—See pages 8 to 10.
Sword—As described at page 5; the hilt of gilt metal, with device of sword and baton crossed, encircled with laurel leaves, and surmounted by a crown.
Scabbard—Brass.
Sword-Knot—Gold and crimson cord, with gold and crimson acorn.
Sword-Belt—Russia leather, 1¼ inch wide, with slings an inch wide; two stripes of gold embroidery on belt and slings; a gilt hook to hook up the sword.

Waist-Plate—Gilt rectangular burnished plate; on the plate, in silver, a device of the Royal Cypher, surmounted by the Crown; an oak branch on each side, and below, a scroll inscribed "Dieu et mon droit."

Sash—Gold and crimson net, 2½ inches wide, in ½ inch stripes of gold and crimson silk alternately; runner of plaited gold and crimson; tassels of gold and crimson fringe, 9 inches long.

Frock—Blue cloth, double-breasted. Rolling collar; the front and collar edged with ¾ inch black mohair braid. An Austrian knot of black Russia braid on each sleeve, reaching to 6 inches from the bottom of the cuff; 5 loops of black Russia braid on each side of the breast, fastening with black olivets; two olivets at the waist behind. The skirts lined with black. Shoulder-straps of the same material as the garment, edged with ½ inch black mohair braid, except at the base; black netted button at the top. Badges of rank in gold.

Waistcoat—Scarlet cloth, without collar, edged with gold Russia braid, and fastening with hooks and eyes. A pocket on each side.

Patrol Jacket for Service in the Field—Blue cloth, blue cloth stand-up collar, height not to exceed 2 inches, rounded in front; ½ inch mohair braid at top and bottom of collar; 1 inch mohair braid traced with Russia braid all round, up the slits, and along the back seams. The tracing forms an eye at each angle of the braid, except at the top of the slits and back seams, where it forms a crow's-foot, 1 inch in length, and at the bottom in the centre, where it forms a long crow's-foot 1½ inches in length. Five loops of inch mohair braid at equal distances down the front on each side, with two olivets on each loop, the top loops extend to the shoulder seams, and the bottom to 4 inches. Blue cloth cuffs, pointed with inch mohair braid traced with black Russia braid, forming an Austrian knot above and below the braid. The mohair braid reaches to 7 inches from bottom of cuff, and the Austrian knot at the top to 9 inches. Pockets in front edged at the bottom with inch mohair braid; black silk lining; pocket inside left breast. Shoulder-straps of the same material as the garment, edged with ½ inch black mohair braid, except at the base; black netted button at the top. Badges of rank in gold.

61002/3440 *Serge Patrol Jacket to be worn in South Africa and at all warm Stations, under local regulations*—Blue serge, with collar and
61002/4023 cuffs of the same material, and ½ inch braid. In other respects, the jacket will be of the same pattern as described in the
61002/4070 preceding paragraph.

Undress Trousers—Blue cloth, with scarlet stripes 1¾ inches wide, down the side seams.

Pantaloons, &c., for Mounted Duties—Blue cloth, with scarlet stripes as on trousers. Knee boots as described at page 1, with brass spurs.

Forage Cap—Blue cloth, with gold embroidered drooping peak, and band of $1\frac{3}{4}$ inch lace; gold purl button and braided figure on the crown.

Forage Cap for Active Service and Peace Manœuvres—Blue cloth folding cap 5 inches high, with scarlet cloth top, and blue side flaps 4 inches deep, to turn down when required. Gold French braid welts on cap and flaps, and at front and back seams. Badge on the left side, the Royal Crest.

Mess-Jacket—Scarlet cloth, edged all round, including the collar, with $\frac{1}{2}$ inch lace forming barrels at the bottom of the back-seams. Blue cloth collar and cuffs; a line of gold braid along the bottom of the collar with an eye in the centre; the cuffs pointed, 3 inches deep, with 2 bars of $\frac{1}{2}$ inch lace, $\frac{1}{4}$ inch apart, above the cuffs. A row of gilt studs in front, on the left side. Scarlet silk lining. Hooks and eyes in front, and a loop of gold braid at the bottom of the collar, to fasten across the neck. Shoulder-straps* of blue cloth, edged (except at the base) with $\frac{3}{8}$ inch lace. Badges of rank as for the tunic. 61002/4136

Mess-Waistcoat—Blue cloth; gold Russia braid edging round the top, down the front, and along the bottom to the side seams; at $\frac{1}{2}$ an inch from the edging, gold Russia braid forming eyes down the front and along the bottom to the side seams. The pockets edged with eyes in gold Russia braid, with a crow's foot at each end. A row of gilt studs and hooks and eyes down the front.

Kamarband—See pages 6 and 7.

Great-Coat and Cape—Blue milled cloth, of the pattern described at page 2, lined with scarlet rattinett; the collar lined with blue velvet. Shoulder-straps of the same material as the garment, a small button at the top. Badges of rank in gold.

Horse Furniture.

Saddle—Hunting; or the saddle described at page 5; with plain stirrups and blue girths.

Saddle-Cloth—Blue cloth, 3 feet long at the bottom and 2 feet deep, with gold lace an inch wide and scarlet cloth beading all round; the badges of rank, embroidered in silver, on the hind corners.

Bridle and Breast-Plate—Brown leather, according to sealed pattern; bent branch bit, with gilt bosses, bearing the Royal Cypher within a garter, and a crown above; blue front and rosettes; steel chain reins.

---

* Shoulder-straps in possession may be worn until they require to be replaced.

Wallets—Brown leather, with black bear-skin covers, except abroad, where they are to have brown leather covers.

Colonels on the Staff, if belonging to the Royal Artillery, wear their regimental uniform, but with the cocked-hat and plume described above, and with Staff embroidered peak to forage-cap.

Commanding Royal Engineers, when Colonels on the Staff, wear their regimental uniform, but with the plume described above, and with Staff embroidered peak to forage-cap.—See also page 64.

II. GENERAL STAFF.

1. ADJUTANT-GENERAL, QUARTERMASTER-GENERAL, DEPUTY ADJUTANT-GENERAL, DEPUTY QUARTERMASTER-GENERAL, INSPECTOR-GENERAL OF FORTIFICATIONS AND OF ROYAL ENGINEERS,* AND DIRECTOR OF ARTILLERY, WITH THE RANK OF GENERAL OFFICER.*

61002/4140 *Tunic*†—Scarlet cloth, edged all round, except the collar, with round-back gold cord. Blue cloth collar and cuffs; the collar ornamented with inch lace round the top and bottom; the cuffs pointed, with inch lace round the top, and a rich tracing in double gold braid above and below the lace, extending to 11 inches from the bottom of the cuffs for an Adjutant-General or Quartermaster-General, and to 7 inches for a Deputy Adjutant-General or Deputy Quartermaster-General. On each side of the breast, 4 loops of round-back gold cord, with caps and drops, fastening with gold worked olivets. On each back-seam, a line of the same cord forming 3 eyes at the top, passing under a netted cap at the waist, below which it is doubled, and ending in an Austrian knot reaching to the bottom of the skirt. The skirt rounded off in front, closed behind, and lined with white. Shoulder-straps of round gold cord, $\frac{3}{16}$ inch in diameter, intertwined with a small dead gold cord; a small gilt button at the top. On each strap, the badges of rank in silver.

Lace—Gold, oak-leaf pattern.

Buttons—Gilt, with sword and baton crossed, encircled with laurel.

Dress Trousers—Blue cloth, with 2½ inch lace down the side seams.

Dress Pantaloons—Blue cloth; gold lace as for trousers.

Boots—As described at page 1.

Spurs—Brass.

---

* Uniform in possession may continue to be worn until required to be replaced.

† For Deputy Adjutant-General, Royal Artillery, see page 56.

Cocked-Hat—As described at page 2; with loop of double gold bullion; gold purl netted button; tassels, flat gold worked head, 6 gold bullions with 5 crimson bullions under them.

Plume—White swan feathers, drooping outwards, 10 inches long, with red feathers under them long enough to reach the ends of the white ones; feathered stem, 3 inches long.

Helmet, White—See pages 8 to 10.

Sword—Mameluke gilt hilt, with device of sword and baton crossed, encircled with oak-leaves; ivory grip; scimitar blade.

Scabbard—Brass, ridged, with cross lockets and rings.

Sword-Knot—Gold and crimson cord, with gold and crimson acorn.

Sword-Belt—Russia leather, 1½ inches wide, with slings 1 inch wide, gold oak-leaf embroidery on belt and slings; a gilt hook to hook up the sword. The belt to be worn under the tunic, but over the frock coat.

Waist-Plate—Round, gilt clasp; in gilt metal on a burnished gilt centre, the Royal Cypher surmounted by the Crown; on the outer circle, a laurel wreath.

Shoulder-Belt—Gold lace, 2½ inches wide, with crimson morocco leather lining and edging; gilt ornamented buckle, tip, and slide

Binocular-case—Black patent leather, to hold a binocular field glass; solid leather flap, reaching to the lower edge of the case, ornamented with Royal Cypher and Crown in gilt metal.

Frock—Blue cloth, double-breasted. Rolling-collar; the front and collar edged with ¾ inch black mohair braid. An Austrian knot of black Russia braid on each sleeve, reaching to 6 inches from the bottom of the cuff; 5 loops of black Russia braid on each side of the breast, fastening with black olivets; 2 olivets at the waist behind. The skirts lined with black. Shoulder-straps of the same material as the garment, edged with ½ inch black mohair braid, except at the base; black netted button at the top. Badges of rank in gold.

Waistcoat—Scarlet cloth, without collar, edged with gold Russia braid, and fastening with hooks and eyes. A pocket on each side.

Patrol Jacket for Service in the Field—Blue cloth, blue velvet lay-down collar, square in front, inch mohair braid at bottom of collar, with black Russia tracing at top of braid, showing an ⅛ inch blue light and forming an eye at either corner. One inch mohair braid traced with Russia braid all round, up the slits, and along the back seams. The tracing forms an eye at each angle of the braid, except at the top of the slits and back seams, where it forms a crow's foot 1 inch in length, and at the bottom in the centre, where it forms a long crow's foot 1½ inches in length. Five loops of inch mohair braid at equal distances down the front on each side, with two olivets on each loop, the top loops extend to the shoulder seams, and the bottom to 4 inches. Blue velvet pointed cuffs, with inch mohair braid traced with black Russia braid forming an Austrian knot above and below the mohair braid. The mohair braid reaches to 7 inches from bottom of cuff, and the Austrian knot at the top to 9 inches. Pockets in front, edged at the bottom with inch mohair braid; black silk lining; pocket inside left breast. Shoulder-straps of the same material as the garment, edged with ½ inch black mohair braid, except at the base; black netted button at the top. Badges of rank in gold.

61002/3440 61002/4023 61002/4070 *Serge Patrol Jacket to be worn in South Africa, and at all warm Stations, under local regulations*—Blue serge with collar and cuffs of the same material, and ½ inch braid. In other respects the jacket will be of the same pattern as described in the preceding paragraph.

Undress Trousers—Blue cloth, with scarlet stripes 2½ inches wide and welted at the edges, down the side seams.

Pantaloons, &c., for Mounted Duties—Blue cloth, with scarlet stripes as on the trousers. Knee boots as described at page 1, with brass spurs.

Forage Cap—Blue cloth, with gold-embroidered drooping peak, and band of 2 inch lace; gold purl button and braided figure on the crown.

Forage Cap for Active Service and Peace Manœuvres—Blue cloth folding cap 5 inches high, with scarlet cloth top, and blue side flaps 4 inches deep, to turn down when required. Gold French braid welts on cap and flaps, and at front and back seams. Badge on the left side, the Royal Crest, with sword and baton crossed.

*Mess-Jacket**—Scarlet cloth, edged all round, including the collar with 1 inch lace forming barrels at the bottom of the back-seams. Blue cloth collar and cuffs; a tracing of ⅜ inch gold chain gimp along the bottom of the collar; the cuffs pointed, with lace and braiding of the same pattern as on the cuffs of the tunic. A row of gilt studs in front, on the left side. Scarlet lining. Hooks and eyes in front, and a loop of gold braid at the bottom of the collar, to fasten across the neck. Shoulder-straps with badges of rank as for tunic.

*Mess-Waistcoat**—Blue cloth; ½ inch gold lace round the top, down the front, and along the bottom to the side seams; the lace traced down the front and along the bottom with gold Russia braid, forming eyes. The pockets edged with eyes in gold Russia braid, with a crow's foot at each end. A row of gilt studs and hooks and eyes down the front.

* For Deputy Adjutant-General, Royal Artillery, see page 56.

Kamarband—See pages 6 and 7.

Great-Coat and Cape—Blue milled cloth, of the pattern described at page 2, lined with scarlet rattinett; the collar lined with blue velvet. Shoulder-straps of the same material as the garment; a small gilt button at the top. Badges of rank in gold.

Horse Furniture.

Saddle—Hunting, or the saddle described at page 5; plain stirrups and blue girths.

Saddle-Cloth—Blue cloth, 3 feet 2 inches long at the bottom, and 2 feet 2 inches deep, laced all round with 2 stripes of 1½ inch lace, ¼ inch apart; at each hind corner, badges of rank in gold, except the blade of the sword in the badge of crossed sword and baton, which is in silver.

Wallets—Brown leather, with covers of blue cloth, with lace and badges as on the saddle-cloth, and cloth flounces similarly laced. With undress, the wallets are to be covered with black bear-skin, except abroad, where they are to have brown leather covers.

Bridle—Brown leather, with chased gilt whole buckles; blue front and rosettes; bent branch bit, with pads; gilt bosses, with Royal Cypher in the centre, and crossed sword and baton under, encircled with laurel, and surmounted by a crown; cheeks of the shell pattern; open tails, with bolts and rings; steel water chain; link and tee bridoon.

Breast-Plate—Brown leather, with gilt metal ornament as on bit.

2. ADJUTANT-GENERAL, AND QUARTERMASTER-GENERAL. UNDER THE RANK OF GENERAL OFFICER.

Tunic—Scarlet cloth, edged all round, except the collar, with round-back gold cord. Blue cloth collar and cuffs; the collar ornamented with ½ inch lace* round the top, gold Russia braid along the bottom, and a rich tracing in double gold braid below the lace; the cuffs pointed with ½-inch lace round the top, and a rich tracing in double gold braid above and below the lace, extending to 9 inches from the bottom of the cuffs. On each side of the breast, 4 loops of round-back gold cord, with caps

* Pattern ½ inch Staff lace, sealed, 1890.

and drops, fastening with gold worked olivets. On each back-seam, a line of the same cord forming 3 eyes at the top, passing under a netted cap at the waist, below which it is doubled, and ending in an Austrian knot reaching to the bottom of the skirt. The skirt rounded off in front, closed behind, and lined with white. Shoulder-straps of twisted round gold cord, universal pattern, lined with scarlet; a small button at the top. Badges of rank in silver.

Lace—Gold, Staff pattern.

Buttons—Gilt, frosted, with burnished laurel round the edge.

Dress Trousers—Blue cloth, with 1¾ inch lace down the side seams.

Dress Pantaloons—Blue cloth; gold lace as on trousers.

Boots—As described at page 1.

Spurs—Brass.

Cocked-Hat—As described at page 2; with loop of ¾-inch lace; gold purl netted button; tassels, netted gold purl head, 8 small gold bullions, with 7 crimson bullions under them.

Plume—White swan feathers, drooping outwards, 6 inches long, with red feathers under them long enough to reach the ends of the white ones; feathered stem, 3 inches long.

Helmet, White—See pages 8 to 10.

Sword—As described at page 5; the hilt of gilt metal, with device of sword and baton crossed, encircled with laurel leaves, and surmounted by a crown.

Scabbard—Brass.

Sword-Knot—Gold and crimson cord, with gold and crimson acorn.

Sword-Belt—Russia leather, 1¼ inch wide, with slings an inch wide;
61002/3317 2 stripes of gold embroidery on belt and on sword and sabretache slings, with gilt lion's head buckles and flat billets; a gilt hook to hook up the sword.

Waist Plate—Round, gilt clasp, with Royal Cypher and Crown in the centre, and a laurel wreath on the outer circle.

Sabretache—See pages 4 and 5.

Shoulder-Belt—Gold lace, 1¾ inches wide, with crimson Morocco leather lining and edging; gilt ornamented buckle, tip, and slide.

Binocular-Case—Black patent leather, to hold a binocular field glass; solid leather flap, reaching to the lower edge of the case, ornamented with Royal Cypher and Crown in gilt metal.

Frock—Blue cloth, double-breasted. Rolling collar; the front and collar edged with ¾ inch black mohair braid. An Austrian knot of black Russia braid on each sleeve, reaching to 6 inches from the bottom of the cuff; 5 loops of black Russia braid on each side of the breast, fastening with black olivets; 2 olivets at the waist behind. The skirts lined with black. Shoulder-straps of the same material as the garment, edged with ½-inch black mohair braid except at the base; black netted button at the top. Badges of rank in gold.

Waistcoat—Scarlet cloth, without collar, edged with gold Russia braid, and fastening with hooks and eyes. A pocket on each side.

Patrol-Jacket for Service in the Field—Blue cloth, blue cloth stand-up collar, height not to exceed 2 inches, rounded in front; ½-inch mohair braid at top and bottom; inch mohair braid traced with Russia braid all round, up the slits, and along the back seams. The tracing forms an eye at each angle of the braid, except at the top of the slits and back seams, where it forms a crow's foot, 1 inch in length, and at the bottom in the centre, where it forms a long crow's foot, 1½ inches in length. Five loops of inch mohair braid at equal distances down the front on each side, with two olivets on each loop, the top loops extend to the shoulder seams, and the bottom to 4 inches. Blue cloth cuffs, pointed with inch mohair braid traced with black Russia braid forming an Austrian knot above and below the mohair braid. The mohair braid reaches to 7 inches from bottom of cuff, and the Austrian knot at the top to 9 inches. Pockets in front edged at the bottom with inch mohair braid: black silk lining; pocket inside left breast. Shoulder-straps of the same material as the garment, edged with ½-inch black mohair braid, except at the base; black netted button at the top. Badges of rank in gold.

Serge Patrol Jacket to be worn in South Africa and at all warm Stations, under local regulations—Blue serge with collar and cuffs of the same material, and ½ inch braid. In other respects the jacket will be of the same pattern as described in the preceding paragraph.

Undress Trousers—Blue cloth, with scarlet stripes 1¾ inches wide, down the side seams.

Pantaloons, &c., for Mounted Duties—Blue cloth, with scarlet stripes as on the trousers. Knee boots as described at page 1, with brass spurs.

Forage Cap—Blue cloth, with gold-embroidered drooping peak, and band of 1¾ inch lace; gold purl button and braided figure on the crown. No chin strap. 61002/146

Forage Cap for Active Service and Peace Manœuvres—Blue cloth folding cap 5 inches high, with scarlet cloth top, and blue side flaps 4 inches deep, to turn down when required. Gold French braid welts on cap and flaps, and at front and back seams. Badge on the left side, the Royal Crest.

Mess-Jacket—Scarlet cloth, edged all round, including the collar, with ½-inch lace* forming barrels at the bottom of the back-seams. Blue cloth collar and cuffs, a line of gold braid along

* Pattern sealed, 1890.

the bottom of the collar, with an eye in the centre; the cuffs pointed, with lace and braiding of the same pattern as on the cuffs of the tunic. A row of gilt studs in front, on the left side. Scarlet lining. Hooks and eyes in front, and a loop of gold braid at the bottom of the collar, to fasten across the neck. Shoulder-straps* of blue cloth, edged (except at the

61002/4136 base) with ⅝ inch lace. Badges of rank as for tunic.

Mess-Waistcoat—Blue cloth; gold Russia braid edging round the top, down the front, and along the bottom to the side seams; at ½ an inch from the edging, gold Russia braid forming eyes down the front and along the bottom to the side seams. The pockets edged with eyes in gold Russia braid, with a crow's foot at each end. A row of gilt studs and hooks and eyes down the front.

Kamarband—See pages 6 and 7.

Great-Coat and Cape—Blue milled cloth, of the pattern described at page 2, lined with scarlet rattinett, the collar lined with blue velvet. Shoulder-straps of the same material as the garment; a small gilt button at the top. Badges of rank in gold.

HORSE FURNITURE.

Saddle—Hunting, or the saddle described at page 5; plain stirrups and blue girths.

Saddle-Cloth—Blue cloth, 3 feet long at the bottom and 2 feet deep, with gold lace, an inch wide, and scarlet cloth beading all round: the badges of rank, embroidered in silver, on the hind corners.

Bridle and Breastplate—Brown leather, according to sealed pattern; bent branch bit, with gilt bosses, bearing the Royal Cypher within a garter and a crown above; blue front and rosettes; steel chain reins.

G.O. 93 1886. *Wallets*—Brown leather; with black bear-skin covers, except abroad, where they are to have brown leather covers.

3. DEPUTY ADJUTANT-GENERAL AND DEPUTY QUARTERMASTER-GENERAL. UNDER THE RANK OF GENERAL OFFICER.

Uniform and horse furniture as laid down for an Adjutant-General and Quartermaster-General, under the rank of General Officer, except that the braided figures on the collar and sleeves are smaller, the braiding on the sleeves extending to 7 inches from the bottom of the cuffs.

* Shoulder-straps in possession may be worn until they require to be replaced.

4. ASSISTANT ADJUTANT-GENERAL, ASSISTANT QUARTERMASTER-GENERAL, ASSISTANT DIRECTOR OF ARTILLERY, INSPECTING OFFICER FOR AUXILIARY CAVALRY, ASSISTANT-DIRECTOR OF MILITARY EDUCATION, AND INSPECTOR OF GYMNASIA. 61002/4141 ... 4187

The uniform, &c., are the same as those of a Deputy Adjutant-General, except that on the tunic there is only a tracing of small eyes in single braid on the collar, and above and below the lace on the cuff, the braid on the sleeve extending to 6 inches from the bottom of the cuff.

5. DEPUTY ASSISTANT ADJUTANT-GENERAL,* DEPUTY ASSISTANT QUARTERMASTER-GENERAL, BRIGADE-MAJOR, ASSISTANT TO THE DIRECTOR OF ARTILLERY, ASSISTANT INSPECTOR OF GYMNASIA, DEPUTY ASSISTANT ADJUTANT-GENERAL FOR INSTRUCTION, DEPUTY ASSISTANT-DIRECTOR OF MILITARY EDUCATION, DISTRICT INSPECTOR OF MUSKETRY, INSPECTOR OF ARMY SIGNALLING, STAFF CAPTAIN.* 61002/4141 ... 4187

The uniform, &c., are the same as those of an Assistant Adjutant-General, except that there is only a line of single braid above and below the lace on the cuff of the tunic and shell-jacket, the braid on the sleeve extending to 5 inches from the bottom of the cuff.

In the case of a Captain, the collar of the tunic has a plain line of single braid below the lace; the shoulder belt is of white patent leather; and there are no badges of rank on the saddle-cloth.

N.B.—Officers whose appointment to the Staff of the Army may be limited to a period of three years, will not be required to provide themselves with the following articles of full dress Staff uniform and horse furniture:— G.O. 25, 1887.

Tunic.
Dress trousers.
Dress pantaloons.
Shell-jacket.
Mess-waistcoat.
Saddle-cloth.

* Officers appointed to the Staff of the Intelligence Division may wear Staff dress or Regimental dress at their option, 7606/9833

On occasions when these officers have, in accordance with the Regulations, to wear full dress uniform, they may wear the full dress of the regiment or corps to which they belong, or to which they last belonged, substituting the Staff shoulder-belt and sword-belt for the regimental belts or sashes. In this order the full regimental head-dress will be worn.

6. JUDGE ADVOCATE-GENERAL IN INDIA.

The uniform, &c., are the same as those of a Deputy Adjutant-General under the rank of General Officer, but without shoulder-belt and telescope-case.

7. DEPUTY JUDGE ADVOCATE-GENERAL IN INDIA. DEPUTY JUDGE ADVOCATE.

The uniform, &c., are the same as those of an Assistant Adjutant-General, but without shoulder-belt and telescope-case.

8. MILITARY ATTACHÉ AT A FOREIGN COURT.

If a General, the uniform, &c., of his rank.

Under the rank of General the uniform, &c., are the same as those of an Assistant Adjutant-General.

III.—PERSONAL STAFF OF THE SOVEREIGN, AND OF THE ROYAL FAMILY.

1. AIDE-DE-CAMP TO THE QUEEN.

Full Dress.

Tunic—Scarlet cloth, with blue cloth collar and cuffs, the skirt 12 inches deep for an officer 5 feet 9 inches in height, with a proportionate variation for any difference in height. On each side in front, eight embroidered frog-drop loops, 4 inches long exclusive of the drops, five of them above the waist on the left side with buttons, the rest without. A similar loop on each side of the collar. Round cuffs, 3 inches deep. A scarlet flap on each sleeve, with three embroidered loops and buttons, each loop $1\frac{3}{4}$ inches long exclusive of the drop. A scarlet flap on each back skirt, 10 inches long and 2 inches wide, with two loops and buttons similar to those on the sleeve ; two buttons at the waist behind. A gold aiguillette, the cord $\frac{13}{40}$ of an inch in thickness, on the right shoulder, and a gold cord loop, with a small button, on the left. The collar, cuffs, flaps, and back skirts edged with white cloth, $\frac{1}{4}$ inch wide, and the skirts lined with white. A pocket inside the left breast and inside each skirt behind. Hooks and eyes in front. Shoulder-straps with badges of rank are *not* worn.

Embroidery—Gold, frog-drop device.

Lace—Gold, oak-leaf pattern.

Buttons—Gilt, burnished, with the Royal Cypher in a garter bearing the motto of the Garter, and the Crown above.

Trousers—Blue cloth, with $1\frac{3}{4}$ inch lace down the side seams.

Dress Pantaloons for Mounted duties—Blue cloth, gold lace, as on trousers.

Boots—As described at page 1.

Spurs—Brass.

Cocked-Hat—As described at page 2, with loop of $\frac{3}{4}$-inch lace ; tassels, netted gold purl head, eight small gold bullions, with seven crimson bullions under them.

Plume—Red and white upright swan feathers, 5 inches long.

Sword—Mameluke gilt hilt, with device of the Royal Cypher and Crown ; ivory grip, scimitar blade.

Scabbard—Steel, with gilt mountings.

Sword-Knot—Gold and crimson lace strap, with gold acorn.

Sword-Belt—Russia leather, $1\frac{1}{2}$ inches wide, with slings an inch wide ; three stripes of gold embroidery on belt and slings ; a gilt hook to hook up the sword.

Waist-Plate—Gilt, rectangular burnished plate ; on the plate, in silver, a device of the Royal Cypher, surmounted by the Crown ; an oak branch on each side, and below, a scroll, inscribed "Dieu et mon droit."

Sash—Gold and crimson silk net : plaited runner and fringe, tassels of gold and crimson silk.

Scarlet Undress.

Tunic—The same as the dress tunic, except that instead of the frog-drop loops there are straight loops of scarlet mohair cord, and on the collar, a straight blue cord loop with a small button at each end.

All the other articles as in Full Dress.

Blue Undress.

Frock—Blue cloth, single-breasted, eight loops of blue silk twist on each side of the breast; a similar loop, 5 inches long, with a small button, at each side of the collar. Plain cuffs, with two holes and buttons to each. A flap on each skirt behind, with a button at the bottom. A gold aiguillette, the cord $\frac{1}{4}\frac{8}{0}$ of an inch in thickness, on the right shoulder, and a gold cord, with a small button, on the left; two buttons at the waist behind. The skirts lined with black. A pocket inside each skirt behind. Shoulder-straps with badges of rank are *not* worn.

Trousers—Blue cloth, with scarlet stripes $1\frac{3}{4}$ inches wide down the side seams.

Pantaloons for Mounted duties—Blue cloth, with scarlet stripes as on trousers.

Boots—As described at page 1.

Forage Cap—Blue cloth, with gold embroidered drooping peak, and band of $1\frac{3}{4}$ inch lace, gold purl button and braided figure on the crown.

Scabbard—Steel.

Great-Coat and Cape—Blue milled cloth, of the pattern described at page 2, lined with scarlet rattinett; the collar lined with blue velvet. Shoulder-straps with badges of rank are *not* worn.

Horse Furniture.

Saddle—Hunting; with plain stirrups and blue girths.

Saddle-Cloth—Blue cloth, cut with a sweep behind, 3 feet 2 inches long at the bottom, and 2 feet 2 inches deep; with two stripes of gold lace all round, the outer one $\frac{3}{4}$ inch wide, the inner one an inch wide: $\frac{1}{4}$ inch of scarlet cloth between the stripes. A device, in gold embroidery, on each hind corner, of the Royal Cypher in a garter bearing the motto of the Garter, with a crown above, and oak branches below.

Wallets—Brown leather, with blue cloth covers, laced and embroidered like the saddle-cloth, and black bearskin tops.

Bridle and Breast-Plate—Brown leather, with chased gilt whole buckles; bent branch bit, with gilt bosses bearing the same device as the buttons; blue front and rosettes; steel chain reins.

General Regulations.

The Queen's Aides-de-Camp are to be in full dress on all occasions
when Her Majesty is present in State; in the scarlet undress at
61002/4082 Levées, and when on duty as Queen's Aides-de-Camp at field days
and other military ceremonies when Her Majesty is present.

Aides-de-Camp to the Queen, if on full pay of the Royal Artillery, are to wear *blue* tunics, with scarlet collar and cuffs, and blue flaps, and with blue cord loops on the undress tunic.

The uniform and horse furniture of Aides-de-Camp to the Queen appointed from the Militia are the same as for those appointed from the Regular Forces.

The embroidery, lace, &c., of Yeomanry Aides-de-Camp are of silver, instead of gold, except the sash, which is as above described.

The aiguillette will not be worn with regimental uniform by officers appointed from the Regular Forces, Militia, and Yeomanry, nor by those appointed from the Volunteers when doing duty with their corps. This regulation does not apply to members of the Royal Family. G.O. 127, 1884.

The uniform and horse furniture of Volunteer Officers who may be appointed Aides-de-Camp to the Queen will either be of regimental patterns, with silver aiguillettes, or the uniform and horse furniture prescribed for Aides-de-Camp to Her Majesty appointed from the Regular Forces, with the exception that silver will be substituted for gold in the aiguillettes, embroidery, lace, buttons, cocked-hat, sword-knot, sword-belt and slings, waist-plate and horse furniture. The sash will be of gold and crimson silk net, with plaited runner and fringe, tassels of gold and crimson silk.

2. EQUERRY TO THE QUEEN.

The uniform and horse furniture of the Queen's Equerries are the same as those described for Her Majesty's Aides-de-Camp, except that there are four loops and buttons on the sleeve-flaps of the dress and undress tunics, instead of three.

Equerries, if General Officers, may wear the uniform of their rank with aiguillette on the right shoulder.

3. HONORARY PHYSICIANS AND HONORARY SURGEONS TO THE QUEEN.

Uniform of the Medical Staff, and horse furniture according to rank, but on state occasions, as a mark of the distinction conferred on them, they will wear instead of the dress pouch-belt and pouch, a gold and black sash of special pattern. G.O. 16, 1885.

4. EQUERRY TO THE PRINCE OF WALES.

The uniform and horse furniture are the same as those of the Queen's Equerries, with the following exceptions:—

There is a Prince of Wales's Plume on the sword hilt and on the buttons, instead of the Royal Cypher.

The sash is worn round the waist over the sword-belt, and is
61002/4147 made of gold web $2\frac{1}{8}$ inches wide, with 7 crimson stripes $\frac{1}{8}$ inch wide, gold and crimson tassels with round heads, fastened at the side with gilt wire buckles. The two shoulder straps are of the same pattern.

5. EQUERRIES TO THE ROYAL FAMILY.

The uniform and horse furniture are the same as those of the Queen's Equerries, with the following exceptions :—

Tunic—The same as the full dress tunic of Queen's Equerries, but without loops of embroidery, or cord, on the breast, and with eight buttons down the front; three loops and buttons on each skirt flap, instead of two; the front edged with white cloth; the cord of the aiguillette two-thirds the thickness of that of Queen's Equerries.

Lace—Gold, staff pattern.

Buttons—Gilt, burnished, with a crown in the centre.

Sword—Special device on the hilt.

Sword-Belt—Only two stripes of embroidery on belt and slings.

Frock—Without loops on the breast or collar; the cord of the aiguillette is $\frac{8}{40}$ of an inch in thickness.

6. AIDES-DE-CAMP TO THE LORD-LIEUTENANT OF IRELAND, AND TO THE VICEROY OF INDIA.

The uniform and horse furniture are the same as those of Aides-de-Camp to the Queen, except that instead of the frog-drop loops on the tunic Aides-de-Camp to the Lord-Lieutenant wear a device of shamrocks in gold embroidery, and those to the Viceroy of India, a device of lotus leaves in gold embroidery.

IV.—PERSONAL STAFF OF GENERAL OFFICERS AND GOVERNORS.

1. MILITARY SECRETARY AND ASSISTANT MILITARY SECRETARY TO THE COMMANDER-IN-CHIEF.

WITH THE RANK OF GENERAL OFFICER.

Uniform and horse furniture of their rank.

Under the rank of General Officer.

Uniform and horse furniture as described in sub-section 2 for Field Officers.

2. MILITARY SECRETARY AND ASSISTANT MILITARY SECRETARY.

If Field Officers.

The uniform and horse furniture are the same as those for officers of the General Staff under the rank of General Officer, with the following exceptions :—

Tunic—The collar has a vandyked figure, of special pattern, in gold braid, within the lace; and a similar figure on the sleeve, above and below the lace, extending to 9½ inches from the bottom of the cuff.

Plume—Red and white upright swan feathers, 5 inches long. 61002/3497

N.B.—An officer appointed to be Assistant Military Secretary and Aide-de-Camp (both appointments in one) will, if a Field Officer, be dressed as an Assistant Military Secretary; if below the rank of Field Officer, as an Aide-de-Camp.

If under the Rank of Field Officer.

Uniform and horse furniture as for Military Secretaries who are Field Officers, with the following exceptions :—

Tunic—The collar, which is edged round the top only, and the cuffs, have round-back gold cord instead of lace, with vandyked braided figures of special pattern, those on the sleeves extending to 7½ inches only from the bottom of the cuffs.

Shoulder-Belt—White patent leather, 2 inches wide.

3. AIDES-DE-CAMP TO GENERAL OFFICERS AND TO GOVERNORS.

The uniform and horse furniture are the same as those described for officers of the General Staff, under the rank of General Officer, with the following exceptions :—

Tunic—Field Officers have ½ inch lace round the top of the collar, gold Russia braid along the bottom, and a row of eyes in double braid, below the lace; an Austrian knot of round-back gold cord on each sleeve, $7\frac{1}{4}$ inches deep, with figured braiding round the knot, extending to 11 inches from the bottom of the cuff.

Captains have $\frac{1}{2}$ inch lace round the top of the collar, gold Russia braid along the bottom, and a tracing of plain braid below the lace. The sleeve ornament is the same as for Field Officers, except that the braid is a tracing of eyes round the knot, extending to 8 inches from the bottom of the cuff.

Lieutenants have the collar and sleeve similarly ornamented, except that there is only a plain tracing in single braid round the knot, extending to $7\frac{1}{2}$ inches only from the bottom of the cuff.

Buttons—Gilt, frosted, with a crown in the centre, and burnished edge.

Plume—Red and white upright swan feathers, 5 inches long.

Waist-Plate—Gilt rectangular burnished plate; on the plate, in silver, a device of the Royal Cypher, surmounted by the Crown; an oak branch on each side, and below, a scroll, inscribed "Dieu et mon droit."

Scabbard—Steel.
Shoulder-Belt—White patent leather 2 inches wide. } For all ranks.

Spurs—Steel, except at Levées, and in evening dress, when brass spurs will be worn.

Officers appointed Aides-de-Camp to General Officers are governed, as to dress, by the regulations given in N.B. page 29.

Aides-de-Camp to the Commander-in-Chief do not wear shoulder-belts and telescope-cases. When the Commander-in-Chief or Officer Commanding-in-Chief is a Prince of the Blood Royal, his Aides-de Camp wear with the tunic and frock-coat, an aiguillette and shoulder-
61002/3641 straps. The aiguillette, which is suspended from the right shoulder-strap, is of the pattern for Equerries to the Royal Family, but the gold cord is only $\frac{5}{16}$ of an inch in diameter. Badges of rank, in silver, on the straps. The sword has a Mameluke gilt hilt, with device of the Royal Cypher and Crown, ivory grip, scimitar blade; the scabbard is of steel, ridged, with steel cross lockets and rings. Brass spurs. Officers who may be in possession of the pattern of aiguillette, which at the time of their appointment, was allowed to be worn with a twisted gold cord loop on the left shoulder may continue to wear the same together with the gold cord loop.

Aides-de-Camp appointed from the Militia.

Uniform and horse furniture as for Aides-de-Camp appointed from the Line, except that they will wear the letter M below the badges of rank on shoulder-straps, as laid down for Officers of Militia Battalions, at page 94.

III.—CAVALRY.

1.—HOUSEHOLD CAVALRY.

Full Dress.

Tunic—First Life Guards—Scarlet cloth, with blue velvet collar and cuffs, and blue cloth edging.

Second Life Guards—Scarlet cloth, with blue velvet collar, cuffs, and edging.

Royal Horse Guards—Blue cloth, with scarlet cloth collar, cuffs, and edging.

On the collar, an embroidered device on each side, 5½ inches long and 2 inches wide. Gauntlet cuffs, embroidered like the collar; and three loops of similar embroidery on each back-skirt. 9 buttons in front and 2 at the waist behind. The skirt rounded off in front, and lined with blue cassimere, in the 1st Life Guards; with scarlet silk, in the 2nd Life Guards; and with scarlet cassimere, in the Royal Horse Guards. An aiguillette of gold cord, with gilt engraved tags, on the right shoulder; and a plaited gold cord strap, on each shoulder, with badges of rank in silver.

The Field Officers are further distinguished by a stripe of embroidery, ½ inch wide, round the top of the collar and cuffs.

Embroidery—Gold, oak and laurel leaf pattern.

Lace—Gold, oak-leaf pattern.

Buttons—Of regimental patterns.

Pantaloons—White leather.

Boots—Jacked.

Spurs—Steel; with chains and buckles, in the 1st Life Guards and Royal Horse Guards; with straps and buckles, in the 2nd Life Guards.

Gloves—White leather gauntlets.

Helmet—German silver, with gilt ornaments, and silver Garter star in front.

Plume—White horsehair, in the 1st and 2nd Life Guards; red horsehair, in the Royal Horse Guards.

Sword—Half-basket steel hilt, with brass ornaments; black fish-skin grip; straight cut and thrust blade, 39 inches long, and fully an inch wide at the shoulder. Extreme length of the sword, 45 inches.

Scabbard—Steel, with plain brass mountings.

Sword-Knot—White leather strap, in 1st Life Guards; embroidered crimson leather strap, in 2nd Life Guards and Royal Horse Guards; gold and crimson tassel.

Sword-Belt—Gold lace, 2 inches wide, with slings an inch wide lined with blue Morocco leather for Life Guards, and scarlet Morocco leather for Royal Horse Guards. Waist-plate of regimental pattern.

Pouch-Belt—Gold lace, 2½ inches wide, lined with blue Morocco leather for Life Guards, and scarlet Morocco leather for Royal Horse Guards; gilt mountings, and a silk cord in the centre, red in 1st Life Guards and Royal Horse Guards, and blue in 2nd Life Guards.

61002/3602 *Pouch*—Black patent leather, with gilt mountings, and an ornament on the centre, as follows:—

1st and 2nd Life Guards—In gilt metal, an oval having for pattern the collar of the Order of St. George. On the oval the star of the Order. The oval surmounted by a Crown and flanked on either side by the monogram L.G. on a crimson velvet ground. Below the monograms a scroll inscribed on the right "Waterloo," and on the left "Peninsula."

Royal Horse Guards—The Royal arms, in gilt metal.

Cuirass—Front and back of polished steel, ornamented with brass studs; bound with brass ½ inch wide in the Royal Horse Guards; Morocco leather lining, and velvet edging of the same colour as the facings; gilt scales of regimental patterns, lined with Morocco leather; straps and buckles of regimental patterns.

Trousers—Blue cloth, with 2½ inch lace down the side seams. Red cord down the centre of the lace in 1st Life Guards; blue cord in 2nd Life Guards.

Boots and Spurs—Wellington; with gilt metal spurs.

UNDRESS

Frock—Blue cloth, single-breasted. Stand-up collar, ornamented with figured braiding; and figured braiding on each sleeve, extending to 12 inches from the bottom of the cuff. 6 loops of ¾ inch black braid down the front on each side, with 2 olivets on each loop, the top loops reaching to the shoulder seams, those at the waist 4 inches long; ¾ inch braid on the outer seams of sleeves and back seams, with eyes and fringe at the waist, and tassels on the back-skirts. Hooks and eyes in front The skirt lined with black silk. Shoulder straps of the same material as the garment, edged with ½ inch black mohair braid, except at the base ; black netted button at the top. Badges of rank in gold.

Trousers—Blue cloth, with scarlet cloth stripes, of regimental patterns, down the side seams, viz. :—

1st Life Guards—two stripes, welted, 1¼ inches wide and ½ inch apart ; a scarlet welt between the stripes.

2nd Life Guards—As for 1st Life Guards.

Royal Horse Guards—Single stripe, 2½ inches wide.

Pantaloons, &c.—Blue cloth, with stripes as on trousers ; knee boots as described at page 1.

Spurs—Steel.

Sword-Knot—White leather.

Sword Belt—White leather, 2 inches wide, with slings an inch wide waist-plate of regimental pattern.

Pouch-Belt—White leather, 2½ inches wide, with gilt mountings, and a silk cord in the centre, as on the dress belt.

Sword, Scabbard, and Pouch—As in full dress.

Forage Cap—Blue cloth, with scarlet cloth band, and scarlet welt round the crown ; gold embroidered peak and chin-strap of regimental patterns.

Stable-Jacket—For 1st and 2nd Life Guards—Scarlet cloth, with blue velvet collar, cuffs, and edging ; For Royal Horse Guards —Blue cloth, with scarlet cloth collar, cuffs, and edging.

Gold lace an inch wide all round the jacket, within the edging, and round the top of the cuffs, which are pointed and 5 inches deep. The 2nd Life Guards have a row of gilt studs down the front. Shoulder straps with badges of rank as for tunic.

Field Officers are further distinguished by gold gimp round the collar and cuffs.

Serge Patrol-Jacket—1st Life Guards—Blue. Collar and shoulder-straps of the same colour and material as the rest of the jacket, with small regimental button at top of shoulder-straps. Badges of rank in gold. Stand-up collar with black silk tab, and two hooks and eyes. Six small regimental buttons down the front. A detachable band round the waist to button in 61002/4138
front. A patch pocket with box pleat and shaped flap and button on each breast, and two other pockets below the band. A box pleat running down the back from collar to skirt.

2nd Life Guards—Blue. Full in the chest ; collars and shoulder-straps of the same colour and material as the rest of the jacket, with small regimental button at the top of the shoulder-straps. Badges of rank in gold. Stand-up collar, slightly rounded in front with black silk tab and hook and eye. Five regimental buttons down the front. Gathered at the waist behind and two pleats at each side in front, buttoning over a pocket. A band round the waist to button in front. A patch pocket with flap and button on each side below the band. No cuffs. An opening at the wrist extending to 2 inches, fastened with small regimental button.

Royal Horse Guards—As described on page 45. Blue.

Cloak—1st Life Guards—Scarlet cloth, with blue cloth collar and cape, and scarlet serge lining.

2nd Life Guards—Scarlet cloth, with blue cloth cape, scarlet collar, and scarlet shalloon lining.

Royal Horse Guards—Blue cloth, with scarlet cloth collar, and scarlet rattinett lining.

Shoulder straps of the same material as the garment, with a small button of regimental pattern at the top, and badges of rank, in gold, are worn on the cloaks.

Regimental Staff Officers.

The Adjutant and Riding-Master wear the same uniform as the other officers of their rank.

The Medical Officers, the Veterinary Surgeon, and the Quartermaster wear the same uniform as other officers of corresponding rank, with the following exceptions :—

Cocked-Hat (instead of the Helmet for Medical Officers and Veterinary Surgeons)—As described at page 2 ; the Medical Officer's, with black silk loop, gold tassels, and plume of black cock's-tail feathers ; the Veterinary Surgeon's, with black silk loop, gold tassels, and plume of red feathers.

The cuirass is not worn.

Shoulder-Belt and Instrument Case for Veterinary Surgeon—White patent leather belt and instrument case of departmental patterns. If the Veterinary Surgeon have relative rank above that of Lieutenant, he will wear in Review Order, at Levées, and on State occasions, a dress pouch and pouch-belt of regimental pattern.

Horse Furniture—1st Life Guards.

Shabracque—Blue cloth, 41 inches long at the bottom and 28 inches deep, with the fore and hind corners pointed ; 3 stripes of gold lace all round, showing ¼ inch of scarlet cloth between the stripes, the centre stripe 2½ inches wide, the others ⅝ inch. On each hind corner, a crown, scrolls bearing the word "Dettingen," "Peninsula," "Waterloo," "Egypt, 1882," and "Tel-el-Kebir ;" and reversed cypher L.G. embroidered in gold, and a Garter star below. Holster covers of blue cloth, 23 inches deep and 15 inches wide, laced to match the shabracque, with crown and regimental cypher, with one above, embroidered in gold; black bear-skin caps. Doe-skin seat. White web surcingle.

Saddle—High mounting saddle, with brass cantle, shoe cases, and white web girths. White leather cover with full dress.

Stirrups—Large, square-set, steel; with plain brown stirrup-leathers.

Slides and Tips—Brass, with steel studs.

Holsters—Brown leather, with black plain leather straps.

Bridle—Plain black leather, with brass whole buckles. Chain head-piece and front, brass plates with steel stars in the centres, and a boss at each end. Plain black leather collar. Steel bit, with bar and water chain; Russian hooks and steel loops for cheeks of bridle; brass bosses, with crown and regimental cypher. Plain ring bridoon, with gold lace reins for full dress.

Breast-Plate—Plain black leather, with brass whole buckles, and boss.

Crupper—Turn-back, with brass boss.

Chain—Steel.

Undress Shabracque—Black bear-skin, plain brown leather surcingle.

HORSE FURNITURE—2ND LIFE GUARDS.

Shabracque—Blue cloth, 48 inches long at the bottom and 32 inches deep, with the fore and hind corners rounded; a scarlet cloth border 4¾ inches wide, 1¼ inch from the edge of the shabracque; a stripe of gold lace 2½ inches wide ¾ inch from the outer edge of the scarlet border. On each hind corner, the Royal Crest, scrolls with the words "Dettingen," "Peninsula," "Waterloo," "Egypt, 1882," and "Tel-el-Kebir;" and a laurel wreath embroidered in gold; within the wreath, a Garter star and 2 below. On each fore corner, as on each hind corner, except that the number 2 is omitted. Brown leather surcingle.

Saddle—High mounting saddle, with brass cantle, fan-tails, shoe-cases and white web girths.

Stirrups—Oval pattern, steel, with plain brown stirrup leathers.

Slides—Brass, with steel centres.

Holsters—Brown leather, with holster and cloak strap in one.

Bridle—Plain black leather, with brass buckles. Brass scale head-piece, with white buff front for full dress. Black leather collar, steel bit with bar, and brass bosses bearing the Royal Crest encircled with the words "Peninsula" and "Waterloo." Ring bridoon, with gold lace head and reins, for full dress.

Breast-Plate—Black patent leather, with silver Garter star, for full dress; plain black leather, with boss as on bit, for undress.

Crupper—Turn-back, with boss as on breast-plate.

Chain—Steel.

Undress Shabracque—Black bearskin, with black leather seat.

Horse Furniture—Royal Horse Guards.

Shabracque—Scarlet cloth, 50 inches long at bottom and 35 inches deep, with the fore corners rounded and the hind corners pointed; 2 stripes of gold lace all round, showing ¼ inch of blue cloth between the stripes, the outer lace ¾ inch, the inner an inch wide. On each fore and hind corner, a crown, scrolls with the words "Dettingen," "Peninsula," "Waterloo," "Egypt, 1882," "Tel-el-Kebir;" and laurel leaves embroidered in gold, with a Garter star below. Black patent leather surcingle.

Saddle—High mounting saddle, with Prince's metal cantle, fantails, brass nails with regimental cypher, and white web girths.

Stirrups—Large, square-set, steel; with plain brown stirrup leathers.

Slides—Brass.

Holsters—Brown leather, with brown leather straps.

Bridle—Plain black leather. Head-chain, 2 rows of brass plates with cut steel studs, and a large plate at each end with similar studs. Plain leather front, with a brass shield. For undress, a similar bridle, but with plain leather head-piece and front. Plain leather collar. Steel bit, with twisted beard, bent bar, and brass bosses with cut steel centres. Plain ring bridoon.

Breast-Plate—Plain black leather, with boss as on bit.

Crupper—Turn-back, with brass boss.

Chain—Steel.

Undress Shabracque—Black lambskin.

II. DRAGOON GUARDS AND DRAGOONS.

Full Dress.

Tunic (except for the 6th Dragoon Guards)—Scarlet cloth; with collar and cuffs of the colour of the regimental facings, in the 1st, 3rd, 4th, 5th, and 7th Dragoon Guards, of velvet; in the 2nd Dragoon Guards and the 1st, 2nd, and 6th Dragoons, of cloth. The collar ornamented with ¾ inch lace, all round for Field Officers, but round the top only for Captains and Lieutenants. The cuffs pointed, and edged with round-back gold cord, forming, for Field Officers, a triple Austrian knot traced round with gold Russia braid, and extending to 11 inches from the bottom of the cuffs; for Captains, a double Austrian knot similarly traced, 9 inches deep and, for Lieutenants, a single Austrian knot, 7 inches deep. 8 buttons in front, and 2 at the waist behind; a scarlet flap on each skirt behind, with 3 buttons, and edged with round-back gold cord, traced inside and out with gold Russia braid. The front edged with the same material and colour as the facings, and the skirts lined with white. Shoulder straps of plaited flat gold cord, lined with scarlet; a small button at the top. Badges of rank in silver. In the 4th Dragoon Guards the Star of the Order of St. Patrick is worn on the collar; in the 1st Dragoons the badge of an Eagle is worn on the collar. G.O. 44 & 187 1887.

Tunic, for 6th Dragoon Guards—Blue cloth, edged all round, including the top and bottom of the collar, with round-back gold cord. Collar and cuffs of white cloth; the collar laced, within the cord, like those of the other regiments, the cuffs pointed, with 1½ inch lace round the top, and figured braiding extending to 11 inches from the bottom of the cuff, for Field Officers with an Austrian knot of round-back gold cord, and a tracing of braid in the form of eyes, 8 inches deep, for Captains—and with a similar knot and a tracing of plain braid, 7½ inches deep, for Lieutenants. 8 buttons in front, and 2 at the waist behind; a blue cloth flap on each skirt behind, with three buttons, and edged with round-back gold cord. Shoulder straps of plaited flat gold cord, lined with blue; a small button at the top. Badges of rank in silver.

Lace—Gold, of regimental patterns.

Buttons—Gilt, of regimental patterns.

Trousers, &c.—Blue cloth, with 1¾ inch lace down the side seams; Wellington boots; steel spurs, except at Levées and in the evening in mess or full dress when brass spurs will be worn. The 6th Dragoon Guards have 2 stripes of ¾ inch lace, ¼ inch apart, down each side seam.

Pantaloons, &c., for Mounted Duties—Blue cloth, with stripes as on trousers; knee boots and steel spurs, as described at page 1, except that there is a V cut at the top in front of the knee boots.

Helmet for Dragoon Guards—Gilt brass, bound round the edge. At the top, a cross-piece base and a gilt plume socket, 4 inches high from point of insertion in base. A laurel wreath above the front peak, and an oak-leaf band up the back. A diamond cut silver star in front; on the star in gilt metal, a garter, pierced with the motto, "Honi soit qui mal y pense," or the designation of the Regiment. In the 4th Dragoon Guards, the garter is pierced with the motto "Quis separabit." Within the garter, the regimental device or number. Plain gilt burnished chain, ¾-inch wide, mounted on black patent leather, and fastened on each side with a gilt rose ornament.

Helmet for 1st and 6th Dragoons—Of the same pattern as for Dragoon Guards, but of white metal, with gilt ornaments.

Plume—Horsehair, of the colour stated below for each regiment. The plume rises 2 inches from point of insertion in socket, and falls as far as the bottom of the helmet. A gilt rose at the top, screwed on to the metal stem of the plume.

Regiment.	Colour of Plume.
1st Dragoon Guards ...	Red.
2nd "	Black.
3rd "	Black and Red.
4th "	White.
5th "	Red and White.
6th "	White.
7th "	Black and White.
1st Dragoons	Black.
6th "	White.

Cap for 2nd Dragoons (*Scots Greys*)—Black bearskin, 10 inches high; with a gilt thistle in front; and a gilt grenade on the left side, as a plume socket, bearing the badge of St. Andrew, with the Royal Arms above, and the word "Waterloo" below. Plain gilt burnished chain, lined with black leather.

Plume—White hackle feather, 9 inches long.

Helmet, White—See pages 8 to 10.

Sword—Three-quarter-basket steel hilt with pierced scroll-work guard; black fish-skin grip bound with silver wire; slightly curved blade 36 inches long, grooved and spear-pointed.

Scabbard—Steel, with a large shoe at the bottom, and a trumpet shaped mouth.

Sword-Knot—White leather strap with gold acorn.

Sword-Belt—Gold lace, 1½ inches wide, with slings an inch wide; Morocco leather lining, and velvet edging of the same colour as the facings.

Waist-Plate—Gilt rectangular plate, frosted, with burnished rim; in the centre the Royal Cypher and Crown, encircled with oak leaves in silver.

Sabretache—See pages 4 and 5.

Pouch-Belt—Gold lace, 2½ inches wide, with the same lining and edging as the sword-belt; gilt buckle, tip, and slide. The 6th Dragoon Guards have silver buckle, tip, and slide, and breast ornament.

Pouch—Black leather, with gold embroidered edging round the top; solid silver flap, 7½ inches long and 2¾ inches deep, engraved round the edges; in the centre, the Royal Cypher and Crown, in gilt metal.

Gloves—White leather gauntlets.

UNDRESS.

Frock—Blue cloth, single-breasted. The collar edged with $\frac{3}{4}$ inch black braid, and with figuring in narrow braid. A braided figure on each sleeve, extending to 10 inches from the bottom of the cuff. 6 loops of inch braid across the breast, with 4 rows of olivets. The back-seams and back skirts trimmed with inch braid, traced round with narrow braid, and with olivets and tassels. The skirts lined with black. Shoulder-straps of the same material as the garment; edged with $\frac{1}{2}$ inch black mohair braid, except at the base; black netted button at the top; badges of rank in gold.

Patrol-Jacket, instead of Blue Frock Coat—2nd, 5th, and 6th Dragoon Guards—Blue cloth, stand-up collar, rounded in front, half-inch mohair lace at top and bottom of collar, figured braiding in centre. Inch mohair braid, traced with Russia braid, all round, up the slits, and along the back seams. Five loops of inch mohair braid, at equal distances, down the front on each side with two olivets on each loop, the top loops extend to the shoulder seams and the bottom to 4 inches. The cuffs pointed with inch mohair braid, traced with Russia braid, and figured braiding at the top and bottom. The mohair braid reaches to 5 inches from bottom of cuff, and the figured braiding at the top to 8 inches. Pockets in front edged all round with inch mohair braid. Figured braiding at the top of slits, and at the top of the shoulder seams. Figured braiding in the centre of the back, at the bottom of the collar; and at the bottom of the jacket figured braiding on the right, left, and between the back seams. Hooks and eyes in front. Black lining. Pocket inside left breast. Shoulder straps of the same material as the garment, edged with $\frac{1}{2}$-inch black mohair braid, except at the base; a black netted button at the top. Badges of rank in gold.

Serge Patrol-Jacket—Scarlet; blue in the 6th Dragoon Guards. Full in the chest; collars and cuffs of the same colour and material as the rest of the jacket. Shoulder-straps* of cloth of the colour of the regimental facings, with small regimental button at the top. Badges of rank in gold. Stand-up collar, slightly rounded in front with black enamelled leather tab and 61002/4091
hook and eye. Three small regimental buttons down the front. Four pleats at the waist behind and two pleats at each side in front. A band round the waist to button in front. A patch pocket with flap and small button on each breast; a patch pocket with flap on each side below the band. Wrist-bands $1\frac{1}{2}$ inches deep with an opening at the back extending to 3 inches.

* Cords will be worn in regiments in which the men wear cords on their frocks.

The wrist-band fastened with small regimental button. A box pleat in front at the top of the band.

61002/3140 *Trousers and Pantaloons and Knee Boots for Mounted Duties*—The same as in full dress, except that in the 2nd Dragoon Guards the stripe is of white cloth, and in the 6th Dragoon Guards the double stripes on the trousers and pantaloons are of white cloth instead of gold lace.

Forage Cap—Blue cloth; with $1\frac{3}{4}$ inch gold lace; gold purl button and braided figure on the crown; black patent leather chin-strap. The 2nd Dragoons (Scots Greys) wear a band of thistle pattern, with vandyked edges.

Forage Cap for Active Service and Peace Manœuvres—Blue cloth folding cap, 5 inches high with blue side flaps, 4 inches deep, to turn down when required. Gold French braid welts on cap and flaps, and at front and back seams. Regimental badge on left side.

G.O. 81, 1884. *Stable Jacket*—Blue cloth in the 6th Dragoon Guards, scarlet in the other regiments; edged all round, including the collar, with inch gold lace ($1\frac{1}{4}$ inches for Field Officers) of the same pattern as that on the tunic. The gold lace forms a pear-shaped eye at the bottom of each back seam, except in the 6th Dragoon Guards, in which regiment it forms dummies. Collar and cuffs of the regimental facings; the cuffs pointed with inch lace round the top. Shoulder-straps and badges of rank as for tunic.

Sword-Belt—White leather, $1\frac{1}{2}$ inches wide, with slings an inch wide, gilt mountings; waist-plate as in full dress. The undress sword-belt is not worn in the 6th Dragoon Guards.

Pouch-Belt—White leather, $2\frac{1}{2}$ inches wide, with brass buckle, tip, and slide. The undress pouch-belt is not worn in the 6th Dragoon Guards.

Mess Waistcoat—According to regimental patterns.

Kamarband—See pages 6 and 7.

The other articles, except the gauntlets, as in full dress.

Cloak and Cape—Blue cloth, of the same pattern as for rank and file; to reach to the ankles when worn on foot. White shalloon lining in the 6th Dragoon Guards; scarlet in other regiments. Collar of cape of white cloth in the 6th Dragoon Guards; of blue cloth in the other regiments. Gilt buttons of regimental patterns. Shoulder-straps of the same material as the garment; a small button at the top. Badges of rank in gold.

Regimental Staff Officers.

The Adjutant and Riding-Master wear the same uniform as the other officers of their rank.

The Quartermaster wears the same uniform as the other officers of his honorary rank.

Horse Furniture.

Shabracque—Of authorized regimental pattern in regiments in which the shabracque is retained as an article of equipment. The shabracque must not be re-introduced in regiments which have discontinued or may discontinue its use. The shabracque is not worn by officers in India.

Saddle—Hussar pattern, with brass head and cantle; stirrups according to sealed pattern; blue girths; brown leather wallets.*

Bridle—Brown leather, with brass whole buckles; bent branch bit, with pads and plain bent bar; link-and-tee bridoon; plain leather head-collar; bit-head and bridoon rein sewn on; bosses on bit and ear bosses, of authorized regimental patterns.

Throat Ornament — Horse hair, 18 inches long. For the 1st Dragoons, black; in the 2nd Dragoons, black and red.

Chain—Steel, with swivel, rings, and spring hook.

Breast-Plate and Crupper—Brown leather, with brass whole buckles and bosses as on bit.

Surcingle and Shabracque Strap—Brown leather.

Dress Lambskin—Black Ukraine Lambskin, 3 feet 6 inches long and 13 inches deep, edged with scarlet cloth, and lined with moleskin. Not worn in India.

Undress Lambskin—Black Ukraine lambskin, with black leather seat and large flap to open for wallets, edged and lined as the dress lambskin. Not worn in India.

In the 6th Dragoon Guards the lambskin is edged with white cloth.

III. HUSSARS.

Full Dress.

Tunic—Blue cloth, edged all round with gold chain gimp, except the collar, which has ¾ inch lace round the top. On each side of the breast, 6 loops of gold chain gimp, with caps and drops, fastening with gold worked olivets. On each back-seam, a double line of the same gimp, forming 3 eyes at the top, passing under a netted cap at the waist, and ending in an Austrian knot reaching to the bottom of the skirt; with a tracing of gold braid all round the gimp. An Austrian knot of gold chain gimp on each sleeve, reaching to 8 inches from the bottom of the cuff. The skirt rounded off in front, closed behind and lined with black. Shoulder-straps of plaited gold chain gimp, lined with blue; a small button at the top; badges of rank in silver.

---

* New pattern sealed, 1890.

Field Officers have figured braiding below the lace on the collar, and figured braiding on the sleeve, round the Austrian knot, extending to 11 inches from the bottom of the cuff.

Captains have a row of braided eyes on the collar, below the lace; and a tracing of braided eyes round the knot on the sleeve 9 inches deep.

Lieutenants have a tracing of plain braid only below the lace on the collar; and round the knot on the sleeve 8 inches deep.

The 3rd Hussars have scarlet cloth collars; and the 13th, buff.

Lace—Of regimental patterns.

Trousers, &c.—Blue cloth, with two stripes of $\frac{3}{4}$ inch lace, $\frac{1}{4}$ inch apart, down each side seam; Wellington boots; steel spurs, except at Levées, and in the evening in mess or full dress, when brass spurs will be worn.

G.O. 81, 1884. *Pantaloons, &c., for Mounted Duties*—Blue cloth, with stripes as on trousers: knee boots and steel spurs, as described at page 1, except that there is a V cut in front of the boots at the top, and that a gold gimp oval boss, 2 inches long, and $1\frac{1}{4}$ inch wide is introduced at the bottom of the V cut. The boss to be prepared so that it may be put on and off at discretion.

In the 11th Hussars, the trousers and pantaloons are of crimson cloth.

G.O. 81, 1884.

For Levées and in the evening when in full dress.

Pantaloons—Blue cloth (scarlet Berlin diagonal cloth in the 10th Hussars), with one stripe of $\frac{3}{4}$ inch gold lace down each side seam, traced with gold Russia braid, showing a blue light of $\frac{1}{8}$ inch.

Hessian Boots and Spurs—The boots have a V cut at the top in front, and round the top gold gimp lace $\frac{5}{8}$ of an inch wide terminating in an oval boss in front, 2 inches long, and $1\frac{1}{4}$ inch wide. The height of the boots at the back to reach just above the centre of the calf of the leg, the slope behind to be $1\frac{1}{2}$ inches lower than the top of the peak which forms the V cut in front; patent boxes worked into the heels. The boss to be prepared so that it may be put on and off at discretion. Straight neck spurs are to be worn with Hessian boots. Length of neck $1\frac{5}{8}$ inches, exclusive of the rowel.

A.O. 33, 1888. *Busby*—Black sable fur; outside measurement, $6\frac{1}{4}$ inches high in front, and $7\frac{3}{4}$ inches at the back; $\frac{1}{2}$ inch smaller round the top than the bottom; back shaped to fit the head. A gold gimp oval cockade, 2 inches deep and $1\frac{1}{2}$ inches wide, in the centre in front, the top on a level with the top of the cap. A spring socket behind the cockade. A cloth bag, covering the top of the cap, and falling down the right side to within an inch of the bottom; a line of gold braid along the seam of the bag, and down the centre, with a gold gimp button at the bottom. For colour, see page 50. A gilt hook at the top on the right, to hook up the chain.

Plume—Egret feathers, 13 inches high from the top of the cap; encircled by a gilt ring, a gilt corded ball socket, with 4 upright leaves. Colour of plume is stated on the next page. A.O, 33, 1888.

Cap-Chain—Dead and bright gilt corded chain; lined with black Morocco leather.

Cap-Line—Gold purl cord, with sliders and olive ends; encircling the cap diagonally three times, passing through a gilt ring under the bag, then round the body, and looped on the breast. In the 11th Hussars the line is plaited.

Helmet, White—See pages 8 to 10.

Sword—Half basket steel hilt, with two fluted bars on the outside; black fish-skin grip, bound with silver wire; slightly curved blade, 35½ inches long and 1¼ inch wide at the shoulder, grooved and spear-pointed.

Scabbard—Steel, with a large shoe at the bottom, and a trumpet-shaped mouth.

Sword-Knot—Gold and crimson cord, with gold acorn.

Sword-Belt—Gold lace, 1¼ inch wide, with sword-slings of the same width; Morocco leather lining and edging, of the colour of the sabretache; gilt snake fastening. See Pouch-Belt.

Sabretache—Cloth face, crimson in the 11th and 20th Hussars, buff, in the 13th, French grey in the 21st Hussars, and scarlet in the other regiments; with lace of authorized regimental pattern. Embroidered regimental device in the centre, dimensions not to exceed 7¾ inches at the top, 10½ inches at the bottom, nor 12 inches in length. Morocco leather pocket, of the same colour as the cloth face. Three slings ¾ inch wide. In the 11th Hussars the crest and motto of H.R.H. the late Prince Consort is worn over the regimental device. The sabretache is not to hang below the calf of the leg. See Pouch-Belt. G.O. 81, 1884.

Pouch-Belt—In the 10th Hussars, black patent leather, with gilt metal chain ornament; in the other regiments, gold lace, the width not to exceed 2 inches; Morocco leather lining and edging of the same colour as the sabretache. Gilt ornamented buckle, tip and slide in the 7th, 8th, 10th, 15th, and 18th Hussars; in the other regiments the buckle, tip, and slide are of silver, and silver engraved plates with chain and pickers are worn.

The undermentioned regiments have a silk stripe ¼-inch *full* in the centre of the pouch-belt and a stripe ⅛-inch *full*, in the centre of the lace round the sabretache; and ⅛-inch stripe in the centre of the sword-belt, of the colours specified for each—3rd and 4th Hussars, scarlet; 13th, buff; 14th, gold; 19th white; 20th, crimson; and 21st, French grey.

61002/3685 In the 13th Hussars only, honours are worn on the pouch-belt. In the 15th Hussars, $\frac{1}{8}$-inch scarlet stripe in sword-belt.

Pouch—As described below, for each regiment, with embroidery, or metal ornaments of regimental patterns.

Regiment.	Busby-Bag.	Plume.	Description of Pouch.
3rd	Garter Blue	White	Black leather, silver flap, and gilt ornaments.
4th	Yellow	Scarlet	Black leather, silver flap, and gilt ornaments.
7th	Scarlet	White	Scarlet cloth, embroidered in gold.
8th	Scarlet	Red and White	Scarlet cloth, embroidered in gold.
10th	Scarlet	Black and White	Black patent leather of special pattern.
11th	Crimson	Crimson and White	Black leather, gilt metal flap, and silver ornaments.
13th	Buff	White	Black leather, silver flap, and gilt ornaments.
14th	Yellow	White	Black leather, silver flap, and gilt ornaments.
15th	Scarlet	Scarlet	Scarlet cloth, embroidered in gold.
18th	Blue	Scarlet and White	Scarlet leather, embroidered in gold.
19th	White	White	Black leather, silver flap, and gilt ornaments.
20th	Crimson	Crimson	Black leather, silver flap, and gilt ornaments.
21st	French Grey	White	Black leather, silver flap, and gilt ornaments.

UNDRESS.

Frock—As described for officers of Dragoons.

Trousers and Pantaloons and Knee Boots for Mounted Duties.—The same as in full dress, except that in the 13th Hussars the double stripes on the trousers and pantaloons are of white cloth, instead of gold lace.

Patrol-Jacket instead of Blue Frock Coat—3rd, 7th, 10th, 11th, 14th, 15th, 19th, and 21st Hussars. As for Dragoon Guards and Dragoons, with the following exceptions—The jacket is trimmed with Astrachan fur all round including the collar and cuffs. Braid as for Dragoon Guards and Dragoons, except on the collar, which has no braid other than the figured braiding in the centre of the back.

Serge Patrol-Jacket—Blue; in other respects as for Dragoon Guards and Dragoons. See page 45.

Forage Cap—Crimson cloth in the 11th Hussars, scarlet in the 15th, and blue in the other regiments; with band of 1¾ inch gold lace; gold purl button and braided figure on the crown, and a line of gold braid round the crown-seam.

Forage Cap for Active Service and Peace Manœuvres—As for Dragoon Guards and Dragoons, except that the cloth will be crimson in the 11th, and scarlet in the 15th Hussars.

Stable-Jacket—Blue cloth, with olivets and lace, or cord, according to regimental patterns. Shoulder-straps and badges of rank as for tunic. The 3rd Hussars wear scarlet collars, and the 13th, buff.

Mess-Waistcoat—According to regimental patterns.

Kamarband—See pages 6 and 7.

Sword-Belt—10th Hussars *only*. Crimson Morocco leather, edged with gold wire, with scroll of the same material down the centre. Slings to match.

Sabretache—Black patent leather; dimensions not to exceed 7 inches at the top, 9¾ inches at the bottom, nor 11 inches in length. In the 10th Hussars the Prince of Wales's plume, in silver, is worn on the sabretache.

The other articles as in full dress.

Cloak and Cape—Blue cloth, of the same pattern as for officers of Dragoon Guards and Dragoons, with crimson lining in the 11th Hussars, and scarlet in the other regiments.

Regimental Staff Officers

The Adjutant and Riding-Master wear the same uniform as the other officers of their rank.

The Quartermaster wears the uniform of his honorary rank.

Horse Furniture.

*Shabracque**—Of authorized regimental pattern in regiments in which the shabracque is retained as an article of equipment. The shabracque must not be re-introduced in regiments which have discontinued or may discontinue its use. The shabracque is not worn by officers in India.

Throat Ornament—Horsehair, 18 inches long, of the colours as described below, viz. :—

3rd Hussars	....	White.
4th „	....	Scarlet.
7th „	....	White.
8th „	....	Red and White.
10th „	....	Black and White.
11th „	....	Crimson and White.
13th „	....	White.
14th „	....	White.
15th „	....	Scarlet.
18th „	....	Scarlet and White.
19th „	....	White.
20th „	....	Crimson.
21st „	....	White.

Brass ball and socket.

Lambskin, for the 14th and 19th Hussars—Black Ukraine lambskin, 3 feet 6 inches long, and 13 inches deep, edged with yellow cloth in the 14th, and with white cloth in the 19th Hussars; moleskin lining; black leather seat, and large flap to open for wallets. Not worn in India.

A.O. 116, 1886.

61002/3881 *Leopard-Skin*—A leopard-skin, instead of lambskin, is worn in India and elsewhere by the 3rd, 4th, 7th, 8th, 10th, 11th, 13th, 15th, 18th, 19th, 20th, and 21st Hussars.

The* other articles of horse furniture as described for officers of Dragoon Guards and Dragoons.

IV. LANCERS.

Full Dress.

Tunic—Blue cloth [scarlet in the 16th Lancers], double-breasted, with front, collar and cuffs of the regimental facings; the front to be worn buttoned back, except on the march or in bad weather; the cuffs pointed, the collar and cuffs ornamented with inch lace round the top. Two rows of buttons in front, 7 in each row, the rows 8 inches apart at the top, and 4 inches at the waist, where the buttons are flat to go under the girdle;

G.O. 81, 1884. * The 10th Hussars are permitted to wear, in review order only, a scarlet shabracque, and a bridle, breast-plate, and crupper, ornamented with shells.

2 buttons at the waist behind. A flap on back of each skirt, edged with square gold cord, 3 buttons on each flap. A welt of the regimental facings in the sleeve and back seams, down the front, and round the skirts, which are lined with white in the 16th, with black in the other regiments. Shoulder-straps of gold wire cord, lined with scarlet, in the 16th Lancers ; blue in other regiments. Small button at the top ; badges of rank in silver.

The Field Officers are further distinguished by lace round the bottom of the collar, and by a second line of lace round the top of the cuff.

Lace and Buttons—Of regimental patterns.

Trousers, &c.—Blue cloth, with 2 stripes of $\frac{3}{4}$ inch lace, $\frac{1}{4}$ inch apart, down each side seam ; Wellington boots, steel spurs, except at Levées and in the evening in mess or full dress, when brass spurs will be worn. Steel spurs are worn at all times in the 17th Lancers. 61002/4144

Pantaloons, &c., for Mounted Duties—Blue cloth, with stripes as on trousers ; knee boots and steel spurs, as described at page 1, except that there is a V cut at the top in front of the knee boots.

Girdle—Gold lace, $2\frac{1}{2}$ inches wide, with 2 crimson silk stripes.

Cap [except for 9th Lancers]—Lancer pattern ; $6\frac{1}{2}$ inches high in front, 7 inches at the sides, and $8\frac{1}{2}$ inches at the back ; 7 inches square at the top. Skull covered with black patent leather, the upper part and top with cloth of the same colour as the facings. Gold gimp and orris cord across the top and down the angles. On the left side, in front, a gold bullion rosette, with Royal Cypher, embroidered on blue velvet in the 12th and 17th Lancers, on green in the 5th, and on scarlet in the 16th ; at the back of the rosette, a spring socket for the plume stem. A band of inch lace round the waist, with two bands of gold braid below, the upper $\frac{1}{2}$ inch wide ; the lower $\frac{1}{4}$ inch ; and a similar double band of braid round the bottom of the cap, the $\frac{1}{2}$-inch braid being the lower ; the lace and the several bands of braid to be $\frac{1}{8}$ inch apart. A gilt plate in front, with silver badge of regimental pattern. Black patent leather peak, embroidered with three stripes of gold purl. Plain gilt burnished chain, $\frac{5}{8}$ inch wide, attached to gilt lions' heads at the sides. Gilt rings and hook at the back of the waist, for the cap line and chain.

Cap, for 9th Lancers—Of the size and shape described above. The skull and top covered with black patent leather ; the upper part only with blue cloth. Strips of gilt metal covering the angles, with gilt metal ornaments at the corners of the top.

On the left side, in front, a gilt metal rosette, with a button in the centre, and a spring socket for the plume stem behind the rosette. A band of gilt metal, an inch wide, round the waist. A ring and hook at the back for the cap-line and chain. A gilt plate in front with double A.R. cypher, gilt arms and badges of regimental pattern. Black patent leather peak, with a binding of gilt metal, ¼ inch wide. Gilted cord chain ⅝ inch wide, attached to lions' heads at the sides.

Cap-Line—Gold gimp and orris cord, with slide and olive ends, encircling the cap once, passing round the body, and looped on the left breast.

Plume—Horse-hair, of the colour stated below, 12 inches long, and rising 4½ inches above the top of the cap; plume socket, a gilt corded ball, with 4 upright leaves.

For 5th Lancers	...	Green.
„ 9th „	...	Black and White.
„ 12th „	...	Scarlet.
„ 16th „	...	Black.
„ 17th „	...	White.

Plumes for Levées, and in Review Order—Drooping plumes of cock's feathers, length 14 inches in front, and 7 inches behind, of the colours authorized for the horse-hair plumes.

Helmet, White—See pages 4 and 5.

Sword, Sword-knot, and Scabbard—As described for officers of Hussars.

Sword-Belt—Gold lace, 1¼ inch wide, with ⅛ inch silk stripe in the centre, fastening with a gilt snake clasp; Morocco leather lining and edging; slings of the same width and materials as the belt, fastened to gilt rings, gilt buckles and leather straps. The silk stripes, lining, and edging of the colour of the regimental facings.

Sabretache—See pages 4 and 5.

Pouch-Belt—Gold lace, 2 inches wide, with ¼ inch *full* silk stripe, Morocco leather lining and edging as for sword-belt; silver breast-plate, of regimental pattern, with pickers and chains, buckle, tip, and slide.

There are no silk stripes in the belts of the 9th Lancers, and the ornaments on the pouch-belt are of gilt metal.

Pouch—Scarlet leather in the 5th, 9th, 12th, and 16th Lancers, blue leather in the 17th, with gold embroidery round the top. Solid metal flap, 7½ inches long and 2¾ inches deep; in the 9th Lancers, gilt with double cypher A.R.; in the other regiments, silver, with the Royal Cypher and Crown in gilt metal.

Gloves—White leather gauntlets.

Undress.

Frock—As described for officers of Dragoon Guards and Dragoons.

Patrol Jacket, instead of Blue Frock Coat—12th Lancers—As for Dragoon Guards and Dragoons.

Serge Patrol-Jacket—Blue; scarlet in the 16th Lancers. In other respects as for Dragoon Guards and Dragoons. See page 45.

Trousers—As in full dress, with Wellington boots, and steel spurs.

Pantaloons, &c.—As in full dress.

The 17th Lancers wear white cloth stripes, instead of lace, on the trousers and pantaloons.

Forage Cap—Blue cloth (scarlet in the 12th Lancers), with band of 1¾ inch lace, gold purl button on the top, and gold braid crossing the crown at right angles, and ending under the band.

Forage Cap for Active Service and Peace Manœuvres—As for Dragoon Guards and Dragoons, except that in the 12th Lancers the cloth will be scarlet.

Stable-Jacket—Blue cloth [scarlet in the 16th Lancers] edged with inch lace (1½ inches for Field Officers) all round, including the collar, and forming dummies at the back seams. Gold chain gimp at the bottom of the collar. Collar, pointed cuffs, and welts in the sleeve and back seams, of the regimental facings. Hooks and eyes in front. Shoulder-straps and badges of rank as for tunic. G.O. 81, 1884.

Mess-Waistcoat—Of regimental patterns.

The other articles, except the gauntlets, as in full dress.

Kumarband—See pages 6 and 7.

Cloak and Cape—Blue cloth, of the same pattern as for officers of Dragoon Guards and Dragoons, lined with white in the 17th Lancers, with scarlet in the other regiments.

Regimental Staff Officers.

The Adjutant and Riding-master wear the same uniform as the other officers of their rank.

The Quartermaster wears the uniform of his honorary rank.

Horse Furniture.

Shabracque—Of authorized regimental pattern in regiments in which the shabracque is retained as an article of equipment. The shabracque will not be re-introduced in regiments which have discontinued or may discontinue its use. The shabracque is not worn by officers in India.

Lambskin—The edging is of white cloth in the 17th Lancers: red in other regiments. The lambskin is not worn in India.

The other articles of horse furniture as described for officers of Dragoon Guards and Dragoons.

IV.—ARTILLERY.

I. ROYAL ARTILLERY.

1. GENERAL AND STAFF OFFICERS.

GENERAL OFFICERS.—The uniform and horse furniture prescribed for their rank.

OFFICERS ON THE GENERAL STAFF, OR ON THE PERSONAL STAFF OF GENERAL OFFICERS, AND GENERAL OFFICERS COMMANDING ROYAL ARTILLERY IN DISTRICTS:—The uniform and horse furniture pre-
61002/4143 scribed for their respective appointments, in every particular.

OFFICERS ON THE STAFF OF THE ROYAL ARTILLERY BOTH AT HEADQUARTERS AND ELSEWHERE.—Uniform, dress and undress, and horse furniture, in every respect as for officers holding similar appointments on the General Staff, except that the tunic and jacket are blue with scarlet cloth collar and cuffs, the mess waistcoat is scarlet, the sword-knot, cloak and cape of regimental pattern, the shoulder-straps, the lace on the tunic, and that of the dress trousers, the forage cap, and the belts, and the scarlet stripes of the undress pantaloons and trousers, are of Artillery pattern and width. The full dress Royal Artillery pouch-belt and pouch will be worn in both dress and undress uniform. The peak to forage cap will be the same as that for the General Staff, both as regards shape and embroidery. The sabretache for mounted duties will be that described for Staff Officers at page 4, but with slings of Artillery pattern.

Officers appointed to the Staff for 3 years only, will provide themselves with uniform as directed in N.B. page 29.

COLONELS ON THE STAFF OF THE ROYAL ARTILLERY, COLONELS COMMANDING ROYAL ARTILLERY DISTRICTS, REGIMENTAL COLONELS,
61002/4203 AND CHIEF INSTRUCTORS OF GUNNERY.—In full dress wear, regimental uniform with cocked hat and plume; when mounted in Review Order, gold laced pantaloons and steel spurs. In undress, as detailed above for Staff of the Royal Artillery. In mess dress, Regimental uniform. Horse furniture as prescribed for Colonels on the Staff at page 22. The regimental sword and scabbard are worn in all orders of dress.

Colonels on the Staff of the Royal Artillery, Colonels commanding Royal Artillery Districts, and Regimental Colonels who may belong to the Royal Horse Artillery, wear, in full dress, regimental uniform and horse furniture, and in undress as laid down in preceding paragraph.

Officers Commanding Auxiliary Artillery.—In full dress wear regimental dress with cocked-hat and plume. In undress as detailed above for regimental Colonels, except that they will wear the regimental undress belts instead of full dress belts. Horse furniture of regimental pattern. In Review Order, when mounted, they will wear pantaloons with scarlet stripes. G.O. 16, 1885.

2. HORSE ARTILLERY AND RIDING ESTABLISHMENT.

Full Dress.

Jacket—Blue cloth, edged all round with gold cord forming a figure 8 at the bottom of each back seam. Scarlet cloth collar, square in front, but slightly rounded at the corners; hook and eye at the bottom, black silk tab. The collar edged all round with gold cord; laced as described below, according to rank; and with a grenade embroidered in frosted silver 2⅜ inches long at each end. On each side in front, loops of gold cord, 1⅜ inches apart from centre to centre, fastening with ball buttons, and a crow's foot at the top of the loops. Gold cord along the back seams, forming a crow's foot at the top of each seam, and an Austrian knot at each side of the waist. Shoulder-straps of plaited gold wire cord, lined with blue. A small button of regimental pattern at the top. Badges of rank embroidered in silver. 61002/3577

Field Officers have ⅝ inch lace all round the collar, within the cord: and a chevron of 1½ inch lace on each cuff, with figured braiding above and below the lace, extending to 11 inches from the bottom of the cuff.

Captains and Lieutenants have lace round the top only of the collar; and an Austrian knot of gold cord on each sleeve, 7 inches deep, traced round with gold braid 8 inches deep and figured, for Captains; 7½ inches deep and plain, for Lieutenants.

Lace—Gold, of regimental pattern.

Buttons—Gilt, burnished, with a gun and crown.

Trousers, &c.—Blue cloth, with 1¾-inch lace down the side seams; Wellington boots, and brass spurs.

Pantaloons and spurs for Mounted Duties—Blue cloth, with scarlet stripes 1¾ inches wide down side seams; knee boots and steel spurs, as described at page 1, except that there is a V cut at the top in front of the knee boots.

A.O. 33, 1888. *Busby*—Black sable skin, 6¼ inches high in front, 7¾ inches at the back, and ½ inch smaller round the top than the bottom. A scarlet cloth bag, covering the top of the cap, and falling down the right side to within an inch of the bottom. A spring socket at the top in front. Black leather chin-strap and brass buckle.

Helmet, White—See pages 8 to 10.

Cap-Line—Gold cord, with an acorn at each end, passing round the cap diagonally 3 times, then round the neck, and looped on the left breast.

A.O. 33, 1888. *Plume*—White egret feathers, 13 inches high, with gilt ring and socket.

Sword—Half-basket steel hilt, with 2 fluted bars on the outside; black fish-skin grip, bound with silver wire; slightly curved blade 35½ inches long, and 1¼ inches wide, grooved and spear-pointed.

Scabbard—Steel, with a large shoe at the bottom and a trumpet-shaped mouth.

Sword-Knot—Gold cord, with a gold acorn.

Sword-Belt—Gold lace, an inch wide, lined with blue Morocco leather, sword slings of the same width without swivels, and tache-slings ¾ inch wide; gilt S hook fastening, with "Ubique" on the hook, and 2 oval gilt plates bearing the Royal Crest.

Sabretache—Blue Morocco leather, faced with blue cloth; 1½ inch lace round the face, ¼ inch from the edge. An embroidered device within the lace of the Royal Arms above, and a gun below, with an oak and laurel wreath, and the motto "Ubique" above the gun, and "Quo fas et gloria ducunt" below it.

Pouch—Blue Morocco leather collapsing pouch with 2 pockets; the leaf 5¾ inches long and 2¾ inches deep, covered with blue cloth, and edged with ¾ inch lace. An embroidered device within the lace, similar to that on the sabretache.

Pouch-Belt—Gold lace, 2 inches wide, lined with blue Morocco leather; gilt ornamented buckle and slide, and a grenade encircled with a wreath, at the end.

Undress.

Patrol Jacket for Officers under the Rank of Regimental Colonel—Blue cloth, rounded in front, and edged with inch black mohair braid all round and up the openings at the sides; 5 loops of flat plait on each side in front, fastening with netted olivets, and with crow's feet and olivets at the ends. Stand-and-fall collar. The sleeves ornamented with flat plait, forming crow's feet, 6 inches from the bottom of the cuffs. Double flat plait on each back-seam, with crow's foot at top and bottom, and 2 eyes at equal distances. Pockets edged with flat plait, forming a crow's foot at each end and an eye top and bottom in the centre. Shoulder straps, of the same material as the garment, edged with half-inch black mohair braid, except at the base; black netted button at the top. Badges of rank in gilt metal.

The jacket to be long enough to reach the saddle, when the officer is mounted, and loose enough to be worn over the stable jacket.

The patrol jacket is to be worn over, or with a false collar of the same pattern as, the stable jacket. The silver embroidered grenade, authorized to be worn on the collar of the stable jacket, will not be worn on the false collar. G.O. 81, 1884.

Serge Patrol-jacket—Blue serge: welted seams; stand-up collar, square in front, fastened with one hook and eye, a grenade, 2¼ inches long, in gold embroidery, at each end; shoulder-straps of the same material as the garment, fastened at the top with a small black netted button, ½-inch in diameter, badges of rank embroidered in gold; five gilt ball-buttons down the front; a slit on each side, sleeves ornamented with flat plait, forming crow's feet, 6 inches from bottom of the cuffs; two inside breast-pockets, and watch-pocket. G.O. 81, 1884.

Trousers—Blue cloth, with scarlet stripes, 1¾ inches wide, down the side seams; Wellington boots, and steel spurs.

Pantaloons, &c., for Mounted Duties—As for full dress.

Forage Cap—Blue cloth, with band of 1⅝ inch gold lace, gold button and braided figure, of special pattern, on the crown. The cap to be 2⅝ inches high.

Forage Cap for Active Service and Peace Manœuvres—Blue cloth folding cap, 4½ inches high, with blue side flaps, 4 inches deep, to turn down when required. Gold French braid welts on cap and flaps, and at front and back seams. A grenade embroidered in gold in front.

Stable-Jacket—Blue cloth, with scarlet collar (square in front with top corners slightly rounded, 2 hooks and eyes, black silk tab) and pointed scarlet cuffs, laced all round, including top of collar, with ¾ inch gold lace, regimental pattern, forming a bull's eye at the bottom of each back seam; small gold tracing on collar seam; hooks and eyes down the front, a row of small gilt studs on the left side, scarlet lining. Shoulder-straps with badges of rank as for tunic.

Field Officers have a flat chevron of inch lace, extending to six inches from the bottom of the cuff, with braided eyes above and below the lace, the bottom of the braiding to reach just over the top of the scarlet cuff.

Captains have on each sleeve an Austrian knot of ¼ inch gold Russia braid, traced with ⅛ inch braid. A further tracing of eyes above and below the knot. The Austrian knot extends to 7½ inches from the bottom of the sleeve; the figured braiding to 8 inches.

Lieutenants—As for Captains, but without the tracing of eyes.

A silver embroidered grenade to be worn on the collar, as laid down for the dress jacket, but only 1¾ inches long.

Mess-Waistcoat—Scarlet cloth with collar, ½ inch gold lace, regimental pattern, all round—including collar,—row of gold Russia braid to form eyes, down the front, inside the lace, with figures according to pattern. Pockets edged with gold Russia tracing braid forming a crow's foot and eye at each end, and crow's feet in centre. To fasten with hooks and eyes, small gilt studs up front.

Kamarband—See pages 6 and 7.

Sword-Belt—Black patent leather, 1⅛ inch wide, with mountings similar to those of the dress belt.

Sword-Knot—As for full dress.

Sabretache—Black patent leather, with regimental badge, in gilt metal.

54 / Gen. No. / 2970 *Binocular-Case*—Black patent leather, to hold a binocular field glass, solid leather flap. A gun in gilt metal on the flap.

Pouch-Belt and other Articles—As in full dress.

Cloak—Blue cloth, with sleeves. Stand-and-fall collar, with 3 black hooks and eyes in front, and 3 small flat silk buttons at the bottom to fasten the cape. Round loose cuffs, 6 inches deep. A pocket in each side-seam outside, and one in the left breast inside. 4 buttons down the front. A cloth back-strap, to fasten with a large flat silk button at the top of each pocket; a similar button in front on the right to hold the end of the back-strap when it is not buttoned across behind. White shalloon lining. The cloak to reach within eight inches of the ground. Shoulder straps of the same material as the garment; a small button of regimental pattern at the top. Badges of rank in gilt metal.

Cape—Blue cloth, 32 inches deep, lined with white shalloon. A cloth band round the top, to fasten with a cloth strap and black buckle; and a fly inside the band, with 3 button holes for attaching cape to cloak. 3 buttons down the front.

Regimental Staff Officers.

The same uniform as for the other officers of their respect honorary rank.

Horse Furniture.

Shabracque—Blue cloth, 47 inches long at the bottom and 30 inches deep, rounded before and behind, with 2 inch gold lace and a vandyked border of scarlet cloth round the edges. A gun, with the Royal Cypher and Crown above, and the motto "Ubique" below it, embroidered in gold, at each hind corner.

The other articles as described for Cavalry Regiments.

Shabracques and dress and undress lambskins are not worn in India.

3. FIELD AND GARRISON ARTILLERY, AND COAST BRIGADE.

Full Dress.

Tunic—Blue cloth, with scarlet cloth collar, square in front, but slightly rounded at the corners; hook and eye at the bottom, black silk tab. The collar and sleeves laced and braided according to rank, with a grenade at each end of the collar, as detailed for Horse Brigades. The skirt square in front, open behind, with a blue cloth flap on back of each skirt. Flaps edged with round gold cord, traced inside with gold Russia braid. Skirt lined with black. Scarlet cloth edging down the front, and at the opening behind, 9 buttons down the front, 3 buttons on each flap behind and 2 at the waist behind. Shoulder-straps with badges of rank as laid down for Horse Artillery. 61002/409

Helmet, Home Pattern—See pages 3 and 4.

Helmet-Plate—Gilt, device—the Royal Arms with gun below. "Ubique" above the gun and "Quo fas et gloria ducunt" below. Dimensions—

From top of crest to bottom of plate, back measurement, 3⅞ inches.
Extreme horizontal width, back measurement, 3 inches.

Helmet, White—See pages 8 to 10.

Sword-Belt—Gold lace, 1½ inches wide, lined with blue Morocco leather, and with mountings as for Horse Brigades. Sword slings (and tache slings for Mounted Officers) fastened to a flat steel bar covered with blue Morocco leather, and attached to the inside of the belt by 4 flat steel hooks.

Sabretache, Knee-boots, Spurs, and Pantaloons (for Mounted Officers only); *Pouch, Pouch-Belt, Trousers, Sword, Scabbard, and Sword Knot*—As described for Horse Brigades. G.O. 16, 1884.

Undress.

Mess Waistcoat—Scarlet cloth, edged all round, including collar with ½-inch gold lace, regimental pattern; pockets edged with gold Russia tracing braid, forming a crow's foot and eye at each end, with crow's feet in centre—to fasten with hooks and eyes, small gilt studs up front.

61002/017 *Sword-Belt*—White buff* leather, $1\frac{7}{10}$ inches wide, with sword slings (and tache slings for Mounted Officers), gilt, frosted plate, with regimental device.

Sword-Knot—Buff leather, ½ inch wide, with runner and gold acorn.

Pouch-Belt—White buff† leather, 2 inches wide.

Patrol-Jackets, Trousers, Spurs, Pantaloons (for mounted duties), *Forage Cap, Forage Cap for active service and peace manœuvres, Stable-Jacket, Kamarband, Sabretache* (for Mounted Officers), *Binocular Case, Cloak and Cape*—As described for Horse Brigades.

Regimental Staff Officers.

The same uniform as the other officers of their respective honorary rank.

Horse Furniture.

For Mounted Officers as described for Horse Artillery, except that the shabracque and dress lambskin are not worn.

Undress lambskins are not worn in India.

II.—ROYAL MALTA ARTILLERY.

A.O. 184, 1889. Uniform, &c., as for Royal Artillery, except the pouch ornament, waist-plate, and helmet-plate, which are of special patterns.

---

* White patent leather Sword-Belts in possession may continue to be worn until they require to be replaced.

† White patent leather Pouch-Belts in possession may continue to be worn until they require to be replaced.

III.—ARTILLERY MILITIA.

[Including the Channel Islands Artillery.]

Uniform, &c., as for Garrison Artillery, with the following exceptions. The letter **M** in embroidered silver will be worn below the badges of rank on garments for which gold shoulder straps are authorized, and in gilt metal on garments for which cloth straps are authorized.

Candidates for the Line between the ages of 17 and 22 need not provide themselves with full dress uniform, but may wear the undress of the Royal Artillery on regimental duty and under no other circumstances, such as Levées and public ceremonies. A. Militia. 2515

Dress Pouch,
Dress Sabretache,
Helmet Plate,
Plate for Undress Sabretache.
} "Ubique" omitted, and the designation of the county to which the regiment belongs substituted for "Quo fas et gloria ducunt," or in the case of the Channel Islands Artillery Militia, the name of the regiment as "Royal Jersey Artillery."

Dress Waist-Belt,—"Ubique" omitted from snake fastening.
Undress Waist-Belt—"Ubique" omitted from ornament on plate.

Adjutant and Quartermaster.

An Officer selected from the full pay of the Royal Artillery for the appointment of adjutant or quartermaster to the Militia will wear the uniform of the corps of the Regular Army to which he belongs; in the case of a quartermaster, he will wear it so long as he is borne on the seconded list of that corps. 38407 Dress. 75

V.—ENGINEERS.

I.—ROYAL ENGINEERS.

1. GENERAL AND STAFF OFFICERS.

General Officers.—The uniform and horse furniture prescribed for their rank.

Officers on the General Staff of the Army, or on the Personal Staff of General Officers—The uniform and horse furniture prescribed for their respective appointments, in every particular.

Deputy Adjutant-General, Assistant Adjutant-General, or Deputy Assistant Adjutant-General, and Brigade Major of Engineers—Uniform and horse furniture as for General Staff of their respective grades, but with sword, waist-belt, and sabretache of regimental patterns.

The uniform of *Commanding Royal Engineers, when Colonels on the Staff*, will be regimental, except that the plume and forage cap will be that of Colonel on the Staff. (See also page 22.)

2. REGIMENTAL OFFICERS.

Tunic—Scarlet cloth, with collar and cuffs of Garter blue velvet. The collar edged all round with round-back gold cord; ¾ inch lace all round within the cord for Field Officers, round the top only for Captains and Lieutenants; at each end a grenade embroidered in silver. The cuffs pointed and ornamented as described below, according to rank. 9 buttons in front and 2 at the waist behind. The skirt rounded off in front, closed behind, with a plait at each side, and lined with white. The front, skirt, and plaits edged with Garter blue velvet. Shoulder knots of treble twisted round-back gold cord, lined with scarlet. A small button of regimental pattern at the top. Badges of rank in silver.

Field Officers have 1½ inch lace round the top of the cuff; and figured ⅛ inch Russia braiding above and below the lace, extending to 11 inches from the bottom of the cuff.

Captains have an Austrian knot of round-back gold cord on each sleeve, traced all round with braided eyes, the braid extending to 8 inches from the bottom of the cuff.

Lieutenants have a similar knot, but without the figured braiding.

Lace and Buttons—Of regimental patterns.

Dress Trousers—Blue cloth, with 1¾ inch lace down the side seams; Wellington boots and brass spurs.

**Dress Pantaloons, &c., for Mounted Duties*—Blue cloth with gold lace stripes as for trousers; knee boots and brass spurs, as described at page 1.

Cocked-Hat—As described at page 2, with loop of inch lace, button, and black watered silk cockade; gold bullion tassels.

Plume—White cock's feathers, drooping outwards, 5 inches long.

Helmet, Home Pattern—See pages 3 and 4.

†All officers performing Regimental duty or Garrison duty (other than Staff) will wear the Helmet with the Tunic; other officers will wear the Cocked-Hat.

Helmet-Plate—Gilt; device—Royal Arms with scrolls and mottoes "Quo fas et gloria ducunt" and "Ubique."—Dimensions:—From top of crest to bottom of plate, back measurement, 3⅞ inches. Extreme horizontal width, back measurement, 3 inches.

Helmet, White—See pages 8 to 10.

Sword—As described at page 5, with hilt of gilt metal, pierced and engraved according to special pattern.

Scabbard—For Field Officers, brass, except those attached to Royal Engineer Troops and Field Companies, who will wear steel when not attending Court or Levées; other officers, steel.

Sword-Knot—Gold cord, with gold acorn; for all duties.

‡*Sword-Belt*—Russia leather, 1½ inches wide, with removable flap. Removable slings an inch wide, the front sling lined with Russia leather; and a double swivel on the eye of dee of front sling for hooking up sword; running carriage for back sling; 2 stripes of gold embroidery on belt and slings. Round billets for sword slings, and flat billets for sabretache slings. 3 dees on inside of belt, with Russia leather protecting flap, to attach sabretache slings. G.O. 35, 1886.

---

* Dress Pantaloons will be worn in Review Order by Colonels on the Staff, Commanding Royal Engineers of Districts and Sub-Districts, and by officers of Royal Engineers on the Staff, but not by officers acting temporarily in any of these capacities.

† All Officers attending Court or Levées will wear the full dress of their rank (including Cocked Hat, but without Sabretache). In India the white helmet with the plume as for cocked hat, but 7 inches long will be worn instead of the latter head-dress. G.O. 60, 1885

‡ Belts of plain bridle leather, with the mountings described above, may be worn on active service.

Square gilt wire buckles for sword and sabretache slings. Gilt burnished plate, with regimental device in silver.

Sabretache—As described at page 4.

**Shoulder-Belt*—Russia leather, 2 inches wide, with 3 stripes of gold embroidery, the centre one wavy, the others straight; gilt engraved buckle, tip, and slide.

Binocular Case—Black patent leather, to hold a binocular field glass; solid leather flap, with gilt regimental badge.

Frock for Regimental Field Officers—Blue cloth, single-breasted, with rolling collar; ornaments on sleeve as on the tunic, but in black mohair braid, traced. 8 loops of ¾ inch black braid down the front, with barrel buttons placed according to regimental pattern. The front edges, collar, back and sleeve seams, and back-skirts trimmed with ⅞ inch black braid traced. 61002/3508 Hooks and eyes in front. Two olivets at the back, to support the waistbelt. The skirt lined with black. Shoulder straps of the same material as the garment edged with ½ inch black mohair braid, except at the base; black netted button at the top. Badges of rank in gold.

†*Patrol Jacket*—As described at page 4, with the following exceptions:—

G.O. 81, 1884. Stand-and-fall collar and cuffs of blue velvet. 5 loops of flat plait on each side in front, with crow's feet at the ends, and 3 rows of olivets, pockets edged with flat plaits, forming an eye at each end. Crow's foot on each sleeve (instead of the Austrian knot), 6½ inches deep from the bottom of the cuff. Shoulder-straps with badges of rank as for frock.

G.O. 16, 1885. *Serge Patrol-Jacket*—Scarlet serge, rounded in front; blue cloth facings, stand-up collar, edged all round with gold Russia braid, ⅛ of an inch wide; a black silk tab with loop on the left side, a small black silk button inside 2½ inches from the right end of the collar, and another 3¼ inches from the left. Cuffs pointed and edged with Russia braid, ⅛ of an inch wide, forming a crow's foot at the top and extending to 6 inches from the bottom. 5 buttons down the front, with hook and eye at the top. A slit on the left side 3¾ inches long, for the sword to pass through, with a flap inside. 2 pockets on the left side, and one on the right, with flaps 6¼ inches long and 2½ inches deep. Welted seams in the sleeves and centre of back. The front, bottom, side slits, and pocket-flaps edged with blue cloth. Scarlet Italian cloth lining. A pocket inside each breast. Shoulder straps of the same material as the garment, with small regimental button at the top; badges of rank in gold.

* Belts of plain bridle leather, with the mountings described above, may be worn on active service.

† The Patrol Jacket may be worn by Regimental Field Officers, but on no occasion when the Cocked Hat is worn.

Undress Trousers, &c.—Blue cloth, with scarlet stripes, 2 inches wide, down the side seams; brass spurs for Field Officers, except those attached to Royal Engineer Troops and Field Companies, who will wear steel; steel spurs for other Mounted Officers.

Pantaloons, &c., for Mounted Duties—Blue cloth, with stripes as on the trousers; knee boots, and brass, or steel spurs, as described in preceding Article.

Forage Cap—Blue cloth, straight up, 3 inches high, with band of 1¾ inch gold lace. Black patent leather drooping peak and chin straps. The peak ornamented with ½ inch, *full*, gold embroidery. A gold netted button on the crown. Field Officers will have a gold French braid welt round the crown; Officers under the rank of Field Officer, a blue cloth welt.

Forage Cap for Active Service and Peace Manœuvres, or when officers are actually employed in boat work, or when proceeding on duty direct to or from boats.—Blue cloth folding cap, 5 inches high, with blue cloth side flaps, 4 inches deep, to turn down when required. Gold French braid welts on cap and flaps, and at front and back seams. Embroidered badge on the left side,—a grenade in gold, with scroll under with motto "Ubique" in silver on a light blue ground. G.O. 3, 1887.

Mess-Jacket—Scarlet cloth, with Garter blue velvet collar and cuffs. Gold Russia braid, ⅛ inch wide, all round the jacket and along the bottom of the collar, with small eyes at the ends of the collar and bottom of the front, and a crow's foot at the centre of collar seam and of waist. At each end of the collar, a grenade embroidered in gold. Hooks and eyes and gilt studs down the front. Pointed cuffs, 5 inches deep, edged—for Field Officers, with 1 inch lace, traced above with Russia braid ⅛ inch, forming a crow's foot at the top; for Captains, with ⅛ inch Russia braid forming a crow's foot at the top; a row of small eyes above and below the braid, terminating in plain braid round the crow's foot; for Lieutenants, with plain Russia braid, ⅛ inch, forming a crow's foot at the top; scarlet silk serge lining. Shoulder-knots with badges of rank as for tunic.

**Mess Waistcoat*—Scarlet cloth, with hooks and eyes and gilt studs down the front, and edging of gold braid all round and on collar seam. Pockets edged with gold braid forming crow's feet at ends and centre.

Kamarband—See pages 6 and 7.

---

* In hot climates an open white washing waistcoat without lappels, and fastened by four gilt buttons of regimental pattern, may be worn with the shell jacket in Mess Dress. Collars and black ties.

Great-Coat and Cape—Blue cloth, of the pattern described at page 2, lined with scarlet shalloon, the collar lined with Garter blue velvet. Shoulder-straps of the same material as the garment; a small button of regimental pattern at the top. Badges of rank in gold

WORKING DRESS.

61002/3975 For officers when actually employed on Submarine Mining duties.

The jacket described below may be worn also by officers of Royal Engineers on Annual Practices.

Pea-Jacket—As supplied to non-commissioned officers and men of Submarine Mining Companies.

Jacket—Plain blue serge, of special quality, short, with standing collar, five small buttons (R.E.), shoulder-straps and badges of rank, one plain pocket outside on left breast, one pocket inside right breast, two flap pockets in skirt.

Cap—As for active service.

Trousers—Blue serge of quality as for jacket, with red stripes 2 inches wide, down the side seams. Two cross pockets.

Coat, Waterproof—Naval pattern, without badges of rank, cashmere, best quality.

Boots, Knee—Canada pattern.

HORSE FURNITURE.

Officers attached to R.E. Troops, same as Cavalry, but without shabracque; other Mounted Officers as follows:—

G.O. 116, 1886. *Saddle*—Hunting,* or the saddle described at page 5, with plain stirrups, and blue girths.

Bridle and Wallets—As for General Staff, but with regimental bosses.

Saddle-Cloth—For Colonels on the Staff, Commanding Royal Engineers of Districts and Sub-Districts, and Officers of Royal Engineers on the Staff only—As for General Staff, but with regimental lace.

REGIMENTAL STAFF OFFICERS.

Uniform, &c., as for other officers of their respective honorary rank.

---

* Breast-plates used with hunting saddles for parades will be provided with bosses of the General Staff pattern.

II.—ENGINEER MILITIA.

Uniform, &c., as for officers of Royal Engineers with the following exceptions:—

Buttons—"Engineer Militia" on the garter.

Helmets and Accoutrements—The regimental mottoes are omitted on the waist-plate; the words "Engineer Militia" are substituted for "Royal Engineers," on the garter; and on the tip of the shoulder-belt the letters **E.M.** for **R.E.**

Shoulder-Knots—The letter **M** is placed below the badges of rank.

Adjutant and Quartermaster.

An officer selected from the full pay of the Royal Engineers for the appointment of adjutant or quartermaster to the Militia will wear the uniform of the corps of the Regular Army to which he belongs; in the case of a quartermaster he will wear it so long as he is borne on the seconded list of that corps. 38407 / Dress. / 75

VI.—INFANTRY.

I.—FOOT GUARDS.

Tunic—Scarlet cloth; blue cloth collar and cuffs; the collar embroidered in front and round the top; at each end, the badge of the regiment embroidered in silver; the cuffs round, 2¾ inches deep, embroidered round the top. Blue flap on each sleeve, 5½ inches long and 2¼ inches wide; scarlet flap on each skirt behind, reaching within ½ inch of the bottom of the skirt; 2 buttons at the waist behind, about 3 inches apart. The front, collar, cuffs, and flaps edged with white cloth, ¼ inch wide; and the skirts lined with white. Blue cloth shoulder-straps, embroidered with two rows of purl embroidery, except at the base. Small button at the top. Badges of rank in silver.

The Grenadier Guards have a grenade at each end of the collar; 9 buttons in front, at equal distances; and 4 bars of embroidery, at equal distances, on each skirt and sleeve flap.

The Coldstream Guards have a Star of the Garter at each end of the collar; 10 buttons in front, 2 and 2; and 4 bars of embroidery, 2 and 2, on each skirt and sleeve flap.

The Scots Guards have a thistle at each end of the collar; 9 buttons in front, 3 and 3; and 3 bars of embroidery, at equal distances, on each skirt and sleeve flap.

The Field Officers and Captains are in addition to the badges of rank on the shoulder-straps further distinguished by embroidery round the bottom of the collar and round the skirt and sleeve flaps, and by a second bar of embroidery round the cuff.

Embroidery—Gold, of special pattern; that round the collar, cuffs, and flaps to be ½ inch wide.

Lace—Gold, of regimental pattern.

Buttons—Gilt, of regimental pattern.

Trousers—At Levées, Drawing-Rooms, and in the evening, blue cloth, with 1½ inch gold lace down the side seams; on other occasions, blue cloth, with scarlet stripes 1½ inch wide.

Pantaloons, &c., for mounted duties—Blue cloth, with scarlet stripes, 1¾ inch wide; knee boots and spurs as described at page 1.

Cap—Black bearskin, 8 inches high, fastened under the chin by a plain gilt taper chain.

Plume—Grenadier Guards—White goat's hair, 6 inches long, on the left side. Coldstream Guards—Scarlet cut feather, 6 inches long, on the right side. The Scots Guards wear no plume

Sword—As described at page 5, steel hilt, with regimental device pierced and chased in the guard; black fish-skin grip, bound with gilt wire; the blade embossed with battles and devices according to regimental patterns.

Scabbard—Steel, lined with wood, with German silver mouthpiece.

Sword-Knot—Gold cord, with gold acorn, in full dress; on other occasions, buff leather with gold acorn.

Sword-Belt—In full dress, gold lace, lined with crimson Morocco leather, 1½ inches wide, with slings an inch wide; for ordinary use, buff leather of the same dimensions.

Waist Plate—Round gilt clasp, with regimental badge on the centre-piece, and the title of the regiment on the outer circle.

Sabretache—See page 6.

Sash—On State occasions, crimson and gold; at other times, crimson silk net.

Spurs—Brass.

Frock—Blue cloth, braided according to regimental pattern. Shoulder-straps of the same material as the garment, edged with ½-inch black mohair braid, except at the base; black netted button at the top. Badges of rank in gold.

Forage Cap—Blue cloth, of special pattern, with embroidered peak and plain chin strap, band 1½ inches wide, and regimental badge in front. The Grenadier Guards wear a black braid band, and gold embroidered grenade; the Coldstream Guards a similar band, and the Star of the Garter; the Scots Guards a regimental check band, the Star of St. Andrew in front, and a gold cord round the edge of the crown.

Serge Patrol-Jacket—Scarlet; full in chest; stand-up collar of the same colour and material as the rest of the jacket, with red
tab. Blue cloth shoulder-straps with small regimental button 61002/4138
at top. Badges of rank of small pattern. Six large regimental buttons down the front, arranged thus:—

Grenadier Guards—At equal distances apart.

Coldstream Guards—By pairs.

Scots Guards—By threes. A band round the waist to button in front. A patch pocket with flap and small button on each breast, and below the band. Two gathers above and below the band behind the pockets, and two in front.

Forage Cap for Active Service and Peace Manœuvres—Blue cloth folding cap, 5 inches high, with blue side flaps, 4 inches deep, to turn down when required. Gold French braid welts on cap and flaps, and at front and back seams. Regimental badge on the left side.

Mess-Jacket—Scarlet cloth, with Garter blue collar and cuffs. The collar rolled; regimental badge on collar, 5 inches from seam of shoulder. Cuffs pointed; Field Officers have on each sleeve three rows of small gimp cord forming an eye at the top, Captains two rows, and Subalterns one row.

Waistcoat—Garter blue cloth, with rolled collar; 3 mounted regimental buttons for Grenadier Guards and Scots Guards, 4 for the Coldstream Guards.

Whistle—See page 6.

Great-Coat—Grey cloth, of regimental pattern. Shoulder-straps of the same material as the garment; a small button of regimental pattern at the top. Badges of rank in gold.

Regimental Staff.

The Adjutants wear the uniform of their rank.

The Medical Officers wear the regimental uniform of their rank, except the bearskin cap, sash, and sword-belt, instead of which the following are worn:—

Cocked-Hat—As described at page 2; bound with black silk lace, 2 inches wide; gold lace loop; tassels of gold crape fringe, with crimson crape fringe underneath; plume of black cock's tail feathers, drooping from a feathered stem 3 inches long.

Sword-Belt, *Pouch-Belt*, *Pouch—Dress*, *Pouch—Field*— } As for the Army Medical Department, but with waist-plates and devices on pouches of regimental patterns.

Quartermasters wear regimental uniform of their honorary rank with the following exceptions:—

Cocked-Hat—As for the Medical Officers, but with upright feather, 5 inches long. The feather is white in the Grenadier Guards and Scots Guards; red in the Coldstream Guards.

Sash—Crimson silk net.

Sword Belt—Black leather.

The Solicitors wear blue coats of special pattern, with scarlet collars and cuffs and regimental buttons; cocked-hats, with black loops and regimental buttons; blue cloth trousers, with scarlet stripes 1½ inches wide; no swords or belts.

Horse Furniture.

Saddle—Hunting, or the saddle described at page 6; plain stirrups and blue girths.

Wallets—Brown leather, with black bearskin covers, except abroad, where brown leather covers are to be worn. G.O. 63, 1885.

Saddle Cloth—Blue cloth, edged with gold lace an inch wide; 3 feet long and 2 feet deep in the Grenadier and Coldstream Guards; 3 feet long at the bottom and 2 feet 2 inches at the top, and 1 foot 9 inches deep, in the Scots Guards. The Field Officers are distinguished by a second stripe of lace and the badges of rank, embroidered in silver, at each hind corner.

Bridle—Brown leather, cavalry pattern, with gilt bosses bearing regimental device, brown leather breast-plate, and steel chain reins.

II.—INFANTRY OF THE LINE.

(*Exclusive of Highland Regiments and Scottish Regiments wearing trews.*)

Tunic—Scarlet cloth, with cloth collar and cuffs of the colour of the regimental facings; in the Queen's Own (Royal West Kent Regiment) the facings are of velvet. The collar ornamented with ⅝-inch lace along the top, and gold Russia braid at the bottom; the cuffs pointed, with ½-inch lace round the top, and a tracing in gold Russia braid, ¼ inch above and below the lace, the lower braid having a crow's foot and eye, and the upper an Austrian knot at the top. 8 buttons in front, and 2 at the waist behind. The skirt closed behind, with a plait at each side, and lined with white. The front, collar, and skirt-plaits edged with white cloth ¼-inch wide, a hook and eye inside the bottom of the collar. Shoulder-straps of twisted round gold cord, universal pattern, lined with scarlet. A small button of regimental pattern at the top. Badges of rank in silver. G.O. 16, 1885.

Field Officers have a row of braided eyes below the lace on the collar; 2 bars of lace along the top of the cuff, showing ¼-inch of the facings between the bars; and the braiding on the sleeve is in the form of eyes, above and below the lace for Colonels and Lieutenant-Colonels, and above the lace only for Majors. The lace on the sleeve extends to 8, and the Austrian knot to 10 inches, from the bottom of the cuff.

(D.R.)

Captains have no braided eyes on the collar. The lace and braiding on the sleeves are the same as those of Field Officers, except that the tracing is plain, without eyes.

Lieutenants have one bar of lace only on the cuff, the lace extending to $7\frac{1}{2}$, and the Austrian knot to $9\frac{1}{2}$ inches, from the bottom of the cuff. In other particulars the lace and braiding are the same as those of Captains.

Facings—Blue cloth for Royal regiments, white cloth for English (and Welsh) regiments, green cloth for Irish Regiments.

Lace for Tunics—Gold, $\frac{5}{8}$-inch wide. Rose pattern for English (and Welsh) regiments; shamrock pattern for Irish regiments. In the following regiments, a black line is introduced at the top and bottom of the lace :—

The Norfolk, Somersetshire, East Yorkshire, Leicestershire, East Surrey, Loyal North Lancashire, the York and Lancaster, and the Connaught Rangers.

Lace for Full Dress Trousers and Sword-Belt—Gold lace, special pattern.

Special Badges—See "*Badges of Territorial Regiments.*"

Buttons—Gilt, of regimental patterns. See "*Badges of Territorial Regiments.*"

Trousers—Blue cloth, with a scarlet welt $\frac{1}{4}$-inch wide down each side seam; in summer, blue tartan, with similar stripes. On State occasions and at balls, blue cloth, with gold lace $1\frac{1}{8}$ inch wide, and with $\frac{1}{8}$-inch crimson silk stripe in the centre, down the side seams.

Pantaloons, &c., for Mounted Duties—Blue cloth, with stripes as on the trousers; knee boots and spurs as described at page 1.

Spurs—For Field Officers, brass; for Adjutants, steel.

Helmet—See article "*Helmet, Home Pattern*" (*a*), pages 3 and 4.

Helmet-Plate—In gilt metal, a star surmounted by the Crown; on the star a laurel wreath; within the wreath, a garter inscribed, *Honi soit qui mal y pense*; within the garter, the badge approved for the territorial regiments (see "*Badges of Territorial Regiments*"). On the bottom of the wreath a silver scroll with the designation of the regiment. The dimensions of the plate are—from top of the Crown to bottom of plate, back measurement, 5 inches; extreme horizontal width of star, back measurement, $4\frac{1}{4}$ inches; the bottom central ray of the plate comes half-way over the cloth band of the helmet. Deviations from this pattern are noted in "*Badges of Territorial Regiments.*"

Helmet, White—See pages 8 to 10.

Sword—As described at page 5; the hilt of gilt metal, with device of Royal Cypher and Crown, and lined with black patent leather.

Scabbard—For Field Officers, brass; for other officers, steel.

Sword-Knot—Gold and crimson strap, with gold acorn.

Undress Sword-Knot—White buff leather.

Sword-Belt—White buff* leather, $1\frac{1}{2}$ inches wide, with slings an inch wide, flap, and gilt hook. 61002/4017

Waist-Plate—Round gilt clasp, badge on centre piece, universal ends. For badges and any deviations from this pattern see "*Badges of Territorial Regiments.*"

Sabretache—See pages 4 and 5.

Sword-Belt to be worn on State occasions and at Balls—Gold-lace $1\frac{1}{8}$ inch wide, of the same pattern as that for the full dress trousers, lined with crimson Morocco leather; slings of similar lace $\frac{3}{4}$ inch wide. Waist-plate—Round gilt clasp; and, in silver, on a frosted gilt centre, the Royal Crest; a wreath of laurel forms the outer circle. Ends of special pattern.

Sash—Crimson silk net, on ordinary occasions. On State occasions and at balls, gold and crimson net, $2\frac{1}{2}$ inches wide, in $\frac{1}{2}$-inch stripes of gold and crimson silk alternately; gold and crimson runner and tassels.

Blue Patrol Jacket—As described at page 4.

Scarlet serge Patrol Jacket†—Full in the chest. Collar, cuffs, and shoulder straps of cloth of the colour of the regimental facings. A small regimental button at the top of the shoulder strap. Badges of rank in gold. Collar rounded in front, with black enamelled leather tab and hook and eye. Two pleats on each side; on the left side an opening for the support of the sword-belt. Five small regimental buttons down the front. A patch pocket with pointed flap and small button on each breast. Cuffs pointed, 5 inches deep in front, and 2 inches behind. Scarlet lining. No collar badge. 61002/4091

Forage Cap—Blue cloth, straight up, 3 inches high, with black patent leather drooping peak and chin strap. The peak ornamented with $\frac{1}{2}$-inch *full* gold embroidery. Band $1\frac{3}{4}$ inches wide, of black oak-leaf lace. In regiments styled "Royal" and in the King's (Liverpool Regiment) the band is of scarlet cloth, $1\frac{1}{2}$ inches wide. Field Officers have a gold French braid welt instead of blue cloth round the top of the cap. For badges, see "*Badges of Territorial Regiments.*"

Forage Cap for Active Service and Peace Manœuvres—Blue glengarry, pattern similar to that worn by non-commissioned officers and men, but not so deep, bound an inch wide with black silk riband, with riband ends $1\frac{3}{8}$ inches wide. Black silk

---

* Enamelled leather sword-belts in possession may continue to be worn until they require to be replaced.

† The Scarlet Serge Patrol Jackets of the India pattern may continue to be worn until required to be replaced.

cockade on the left side. Badges worn on the cockade with a scarlet edging. Royal regiments will wear a scarlet tuft; other regiments, blue. For badges, see article "*Badges of Territorial Regiments.*"

Mess-Jacket—Scarlet cloth, with collar and pointed cuffs of the regimental facings. Gold braid edging all round, including the top and bottom of the collar. A loop of gold braid at bottom of collar to fasten across the neck. A row of gilt studs and hooks and eyes down the front. Scarlet lining. Shoulder-straps with badges of rank as for tunic.

Field Officers have a row of braided eyes on the collar below the upper line of braid. Colonels and Lieutenant-Colonels have 2 chevrons of braid on each sleeve, ¾ inch apart, the upper forming an Austrian knot extending to 10 inches from the bottom of the cuff, and the lower braid a crow's foot and eye; a row of braided eyes above and below the chevrons as on the tunic. Majors have the same braiding on the sleeve, omitting the lower row of braided eyes.

Captains have similar braiding, but without the braided eyes; the Austrian knot extends to 9 inches only.

Lieutenants have a single chevron of braid forming an Austrian knot 8 inches high, and a crow's foot and eye below it.

Second Tunic—Of light cloth or serge; in all other respects the same as the dress tunic. It is at the option of officers to provide themselves with this article or not.

Mess-Waistcoat—Cloth of the colour of the regimental facings; gold braid edging round the top, down the front, and along the bottom to the side seams. The pockets edged with braid, forming crow's feet and eyes at top and bottom and at the ends. A row of gilt studs and hooks and eyes down the front. In regiments with white facings the waistcoat may be of white or scarlet cloth, or a white washing waistcoat, without lappels, and fastened with four gilt buttons of regimental pattern. In the Connaught Rangers a mess-waistcoat of special pattern is authorized.

G.O. 128, 1885.

Kamarband—See pages 6 and 7.

Whistle—See page 6.

Great-Coat and Cape—Grey cloth, of the pattern described at page 2. Shoulder-straps of the same material as the garment; a small button of regimental pattern at the top. Badges of rank in gold.

Leggings—Black leather, 9 inches high for an officer 5 feet 8 inches in height; a variation not exceeding 1 inch for officers above 5 feet 10 inches or under 5 feet 6 inches. A leather strap, ¾-inch wide, is sewn all round the top, terminating with brass buckle and thong. Three leather buttons with corresponding button-holes.

REGIMENTAL STAFF OFFICERS.

ADJUTANTS wear the uniform of their rank.

QUARTERMASTERS wear regimental uniform of their honorary rank with the following exceptions :

Sword-Belt—Black.

Pouch—Black patent leather (to hold writing materials), the flap 7 inches long and 3½ inches deep. No device.

Pouch-Belt—Plain black Morocco leather, without lace or stripe ; gilt buckle, tip and slide.

Sashes—Are not worn.

HORSE FURNITURE.

Saddle—Hunting ; or the saddle described at page 5 ; plain stirrups and blue girths.

Bridle and Breast-Plate—Brown leather, with gilt bosses. On the bosses and within the words "Infantry Mounted Officers," the Rose, Thistle, and Shamrock, with a crown above. Front and rosettes of the colour of the regimental facings. Steel chain reins.

Wallets—Brown leather, with black bearskin covers, except abroad, where the covers are to be brown leather. G.O. 93, 1885.

III.—LIGHT INFANTRY.

(Exclusive of the Highland Light Infantry.)

The uniform and horse furniture are the same as for Infantry of the Line, with the following exceptions :—

Helmet—See article "*Helmets, Home pattern,*" (*a*) and (*c*), pages 3 and 4.

Special Badges—See "*Badges of Territorial Regiments.*"

Forage Cap—Dark green cloth.

Forage Cap for Active Service and Peace Manœuvres—Dark green, with dark green tuft.

NOTE.—In undress, the officers of the Oxfordshire Light Infantry are allowed to wear shirt collars. For regulations as to India, see page 10.

IV.—FUSILIERS.

(*Exclusive of the Royal Scots Fusiliers.*)

The uniform and horse furniture are the same as for Infantry of the Line, with the following exceptions :—

Tunic—The Royal Welsh Fusiliers wear "the flash."

Cap—Black racoon skin, 9 inches high in front. A gilt grenade in front with a badge on the ball ; gilt burnished chain, lined with black velvet.

Plume, for Northumberland Fusiliers only—Red and white hackle feather, 4½ inches high, the red above ; worn on the left side.

Special Badges—See "*Badges of Territorial Regiments.*"

Helmet, White—Grenades, as approved for racoon-skin caps, are substituted for helmet-plates.

V.—HIGHLAND REGIMENTS.

(Royal Highlanders, Seaforth Highlanders, Gordon Highlanders, Cameron Highlanders, Argyll and Sutherland Highlanders.)

Doublet—Scarlet cloth, with collar and cuffs of the regimental facings. The collar laced and braided according to rank, as described for Infantry of the Line. Gauntlet cuffs, 4 inches deep in front and 6 inches at the back, edged with ⅝-inch lace round the top and down the back seam ; 3 loops of gold braid, with buttons on each cuff. 8 buttons in front, and 2 at the
G.O. 16, 1884. waist behind. Inverness skirts, 6½ inches deep, with skirt-flaps 6 inches deep ; 3 loops of gold braid with buttons on each skirt-flap. The front, collar, skirts and flaps edged with white cloth, ¼-inch wide, and the skirts and flaps, lined with white. Shoulder-straps of twisted round gold cord, universal pattern, lined with scarlet ; a small button of regimental pattern at the top. Badges of rank in silver.

Field Officers have a second bar of lace round the top of the cuff, and ½-inch lace round the skirts and skirt-flaps. Colonels have 2 lines of braid, and Lieutenant-Colonels, 1 line within the lace on the cuffs.

Captains have a line of braid within the lace on the cuffs.

Lieutenants have the same lace on the cuffs as Captains, but without the line of braid.

The several bars of lace and lines of braid on the cuffs are to be ¼ inch apart.

Facings—Blue cloth in the Royal Highlanders and Queen's Own Cameron Highlanders ; yellow cloth in the other regiments.

Lace—Gold, thistle pattern, ⅝-inch wide. In the Gordon Highlanders a black line is introduced at top and bottom.

Special Badges—See "*Badges of Territorial Regiments.*"

Buttons—Gilt, of regimental patterns. See "*Badges of Territorial Regiments.*"

Pantaloons and Knee Boots for mounted duties—Tartan of authorized pattern ; knee boots, as described at page 1.

Spurs—Steel ; brass for Field Officers when in Mess or Levée dress. Pattern as described at page 1.

Belted Plaid, Shoulder Plaid, Kilt, Trews, Hose, Garters, Skean Dhu, Gaiters, Shoes, and Buckles—Of authorized regimental patterns.

Brooch—Of authorized regimental pattern. The diameter not to exceed 3⅞ inches. Undress brooches are not to be worn.

Sporrans—Of authorized regimental patterns. The sporran top is not to exceed 6 inches in width. The breadth of the sporran leather is not to exceed 8½ inches. The length of the top and leather together will not exceed 11 inches, or for badger-skin sporrans, 13 inches. Officers may wear undress sporrans resembling those of the men. The bullion tassels on the dress sporrans will not exceed six. They are only to be worn in "Review Order," and must be removable in regiments that do not adopt the undress sporran.

Head-Dress—Feather bonnets of authorized pattern.

Helmet, White—See pages 8 to 10. G.O. 128, 1896.

Claymore—Steel, basket hilt, lined with scarlet cloth ; straight cut-and-thrust blade, 1⅓ inches wide at the shoulder, and 32 inches long.

Scabbard—Steel, for all ranks.

Waist-Belt—White leather, 1½ inches wide, with slings 1 inch wide, hanging from two gilt rings.

Sabretache—See page 4 and 5.

Shoulder Belt, for Company Officers—White leather 3 inches wide, with slings hanging from gilt rings.

Waist-Plate, *Breast-Plate,* *Dirk,* **Dirk-Belt and Plate, Dress* *Dirk-Belt, Undress*—	Of authorized regimental patterns. The Dirk is not to exceed in length 17¼ inches over all, from extreme end of Dirk-handle to the point of the sheath. The blade should not be more than 1⅝ inches in breadth at the broadest part. The Undress Dirk-Belt is to be of plain white or black leather.

Sash—Crimson silk, Highland pattern. Dimensions, unstretched—15 inches wide in the middle and 7 inches at the commencement of the fringe.

Mess Jacket—Scarlet cloth, of the same pattern as for Infantry of the Line. In the Gordon Highlanders, double narrow braid with a black centre.

Mess-Waistcoat—Cloth of the colour of the facings, scarlet cloth or regimental tartan ; in other respects, the pattern will be as for the cloth mess-waistcoats of Infantry of the Line. In the Gordon Highlanders, double narrow braid with a black centre.

Kamarband—See pages 6 and 7.

Forage Cap for undress, with trews—For the Seaforth Highlanders and Gordon Highlanders only. As for Infantry of the Line, with diced bands of authorized regimental patterns. For badges, see "*Badges of Territorial Regiments.*"

Glengarry—Blue, of pattern similar to that worn by the men. Plain in the Royal Highlanders, and Cameron Highlanders ; diced
G.O. 128, 1885. in the Seaforth Highlanders, Gordon Highlanders, and Argyll and Sutherland Highlanders. Bottom of cap bound with black silk. Badges to be worn on the left side.

Great-Coat and Cape, Blue Patrol Jacket, Scarlet Serge Patrol Jacket, and Whistle—	As for Infantry of the Line.

REGIMENTAL STAFF OFFICERS.

The ADJUTANTS wear the uniform of their rank, with steel spurs.

QUARTERMASTERS wear regimental uniform of their honorary rank, with the following exceptions :—

Waist-Belt—Black Morocco leather.

G.O. 81, 1884. *Pouch and Pouch-Belt*—As for Infantry of the Line.

Sash—Not worn.

HORSE FURNITURE.

As described for Infantry of the Line.

* To be worn with slings on full dress occasions by Field Officers.

VI.—SCOTTISH REGIMENTS (WEARING TREWS).

1. THE ROYAL SCOTS, AND THE KING'S OWN SCOTTISH BORDERERS.

The uniform and horse furniture are the same as for Infantry of the Line, with the following exceptions :—

Lace for Doublet—Gold, thistle pattern.

Doublet—As for Highland regiments ; blue facings.

Special Badges—See "*Badges of Territorial Regiments.*"

Claymore and Scabbard—As for Highland Regiments, but with a removable basket hilt for Levées, &c., on other occasions a cross-bar hilt. G.O. 128, 1885.

Sword-Belt.—Buff leather, 2 inches wide, with slings an inch wide, flap, and gilt hook.

Sword-Belt, to be worn on State occasions and at Balls.—Gold lace, thistle pattern, 2 inches wide, with slings 1 inch wide. G.O. 116, 1886.

Sash (instead of the sashes described at page 75).—Crimson silk, Highland pattern. G.O. 128, 1885.

Trews—Tartan of authorized pattern

Pantaloons for mounted duties—Tartan, pattern as for trews.

Forage Cap—Diced band of regimental pattern.

Forage Cap for Active Service and Peace Manœuvres— } Ditto, 1¼ inches wide.

2. THE HIGHLAND LIGHT INFANTRY.

The uniform and horse furniture are the same as for kilted regiments, with the following exceptions :—

Chaco—Blue cloth, 4 inches high in front and 6½ inches at the back, the crown 6 inches long and 5½ inches across. Diced band, black corded boss with device in front, green tuft, plate of special pattern, cap lines. At back, for ventilation, a bronze ornament ; a bronze ornament with hook on each side at the top, to hook up the lines. Horizontal peak ; black leather chin strap.

Colonels and Lieutenant-Colonels have two rows of ⅝-inch lace, thistle pattern, round the top of the chaco ; Majors have one row. G.O. 81, 1884.

Special Badges—See "*Badges of Territorial Regiments.*"

Trews and Pantaloons—Tartan of authorized regimental pattern.

Claymore—Removable basket hilt for Levées, &c. On other occasions a cross-bar hilt.

Mess-Waistcoat—Special pattern.

Forage Cap—As for Infantry of the Line, but of green cloth, with diced band; a crimson cloth welt for officers under the rank of Field Officer.

Forage Cap for Active Service and Peace Manœuvres— As for Infantry of the Line, but of dark green cloth, with diced band $1\frac{1}{4}$ inch wide, and dark green tuft.

The Belted Plaid, Kilt, Sporran, Hose, Gaiters, Skean Dhu, Garters, Shoes, and Buckles, are not worn

3. The Royal Scots Fusiliers.

The uniform and horse furniture are the same as for Fusiliers (see page 78), with the following exceptions :—

Lace for Doublet—Gold, thistle pattern.

Doublet—As for Highland regiments; blue facings.

Special Badges—See "*Badges of Territorial Regiments.*"

G.O. 128, 1885. *Claymore and Scabbard*—As for Highland regiments; but with a removable basket hilt for Levées, &c., on other occasions a cross-bar hilt.

Sword-Belt.—Buff leather, 2 inches wide, with slings an inch wide, flap and gilt hook.

G.O. 116, 1886. *Sword-Belt, to be worn on State Occasions, and at Balls.*—Gold lace, thistle pattern, 2 inches wide, with slings 1 inch wide.

Sash (*instead of sashes described at page* 75).—Crimson silk, Highland pattern.

Trews—Tartan, of authorized pattern.

Pantaloons for mounted duties—Tartan, as for trews.

Forage Cap—Diced band of regimental pattern.

Forage Cap for Active Service and Peace Manœuvres— Ditto, $1\frac{1}{4}$ inches wide.

4. The Scottish Rifles.

Doublet—Rifle green cloth, collar and cuffs of Rifle green cloth, the collar square in front. The front edged with $\frac{1}{2}$ inch black mohair braid: down the front on each side, at equal distances, six bars, each $1\frac{1}{4}$ inches wide, of black mohair braid; hooks and eyes down the front; two black netted buttons at the waist behind; pocket inside the left breast; black silk lining; gauntlet cuffs: three loops of black Russia braid, with a black netted button at the top of each loop. Skirts of special pattern, 7½ inches deep, with skirt flaps of special pattern, 7 inches deep; three loops of Russia braid on each flap, with a black netted button at the bottom of each loop; shoulder-straps of black chain gimp; badges of rank in bronze. For Colonel and Lieutenant-Colonel, the collar is edged all round with ½-inch mohair braid; within the mohair braid a rich tracing in double Russia braid. The cuffs are 5½ inches deep in front, and 8½ inches at the back; two bars of ½-inch mohair braid round the top, ⅜-inch apart, and ½-inch mohair braid down the back seam. The second bar and the mohair braid on the back seam richly traced with Russia braid; the skirts and flaps edged with ½-inch black braid.

For Major—Collar as for a Colonel. The cuffs are 4 inches deep in the front, and 6½ inches at the back; ½-inch mohair braid round the top and down the back seam, traced inside as on collar. Skirts and flaps as for a Colonel.

For Captain—Collar edged at the top with ½-inch black mohair braid, traced with small eyes of double Russia braid. Cuffs as for a Major, except that the mohair braid is traced in double Russia braid, with large eyes forming a figure 8 at the top corner in front. Skirts and flaps edged with ¼-inch black mohair braid.

For Lieutenant—Collar edged round the top with ½-inch black mohair braid, traced with Russia braid, forming an eye at the top corners in the front. Cuffs as for a Captain, except that the mohair braid has a plain tracing of black Russia braid, forming an eye at each of the top corners. Skirts and flaps as for a Captain.

Braid—Black mohair, except on band of forage cap.

Special Badges—See "*Badges of Territorial Regiments.*"

Buttons—Black netted; for great-coat, bronze. See "*Badges of Territorial Regiments.*"

Trews—Tartan of authorized pattern.

Pantaloons, &c. for mounted duties—Tartan as for trews; knee boots as described at page 1, with steel spurs.

Helmet, Home Pattern—See article "*Helmet, Home Pattern,*" (*a*) and (*d*), page 4.

Helmet-Plate—Bronze. See "*Badges of Territorial Regiments.*"

Helmet, White—See pages 8 to 10.

Sword—As described at page 5; steel hilt, with device of bugle and crown.

Scabbard—Steel for all ranks.

Sword-Knot—Black leather strap and acorn.

Sword-Belt—Black patent leather, 1½ inches wide, with slings an inch wide. (To be worn over the doublet.)

Waist-Plate—See "*Badges of Territorial Regiments.*"

Pouch-Belt—Black patent leather, 3 inches wide, with silver breast ornament, whistle and chain of regimental patterns.

Pouch—Black patent leather with the Thistle in silver on the flap.

Sabretache—As laid down at pages 4 and 5; the Thistle, in silver, on the flap.

Gloves—Black leather.

Patrol Jacket—Rifle green cloth, of the size and shape prescribed at page 6, with collar and cuffs of Rifle green cloth. Inch black mohair braid down the front, at the bottom of the skirts, and on the slits. The mohair braid traced inside with Russia braid, forming eyes at each angle of the slits. The back seams trimmed with inch mohair braid, traced on both sides with Russia braid, forming 3 eyes at the top, and 2 eyes at the bottom. On each side in front, five loops of black square cord, fastening with olivets; each loop forms an eye above and below in the centre, and a drop at the end; a cap on each drop. Cuffs pointed with inch mohair braid, with a *plain* tracing of black Russia braid above and below. Collar cut square and edged with inch mohair braid: a tracing below the braid and on the collar seam, forming an eye in the corners; at the back, below the centre of the collar, the tracing forms a plume 6 inches deep. Black lining, hooks and eyes. A pocket on either side below the fourth loop, and one inside the left breast. Shoulder-straps with badges of rank as for tunic.

G.O. 35, 1886. *Serge Patrol Jacket.*—Rifle green, slightly rounded in front, stand-up collar, square in front, with two hooks and eyes, and black silk tab, the collar seam piped with the same material as the garment. Gauntlet cuffs, piped at the top, 4 inches deep in front, and 5½ inches at the back, with flap and five regimental horn buttons at back seam. A body seam at each side with a slit 4½ inches deep. All seams welted except the side body seams. Back strap, diamond shaped, sewn down the centre, and fastened on each side to a regimental horn button. Five regimental horn buttons down the front. A pocket on each side with pointed flap, and an outside pocket on either breast with pointed flap. An inside pocket in lining of left breast. The jacket lined with alpaca. Shoulder straps of the same material as the garment, a small button at the top. Badges of rank in bronze.

Forage Cap—Rifle green cloth, with band of 1½ inch black lace, thistle pattern, black purl button and braided figure on the crown; black leather chin strap; no peak.

Forage Cap for Active Service and Peace Manœuvres—Rifle green cloth, special pattern, ornamented in front with a Thistle in silver, on a Rifle green corded boss.

Mess Jacket—Rifle green cloth: collar and cuffs of Rifle green cloth. The collar square in front. Inch mohair braid all round the body, forming barrels or dummies at bottom of the back seams; a tracing of black Russia braid terminating in an eye at the bottom corners in front. Back seams, trimmed with black chain gimp, forming a crow's foot at the top, and an Austrian knot and curl at the bottom. A tracing of black Russia braid on either side of the gimp on each back seam; on the outside only of the crow's foot an Austrian knot with curl. Pockets trimmed with black chain gimp, forming a double crow's foot and eye; the gimp traced with black Russia braid, with eyes at intervals. Five plaited olivets down the front on the left side; hooks and eyes. Cuffs pointed with black chain gimp forming an Austrian knot in front, and continued to the bottom of the cuff at either side of the back seam. The gimp traced on the outside with black Russia braid. The Austrian knot extends to 7½ inches from the bottom of the cuff. Collar edged all round with ½-inch mohair braid; pockets inside the left breast; black silk lining; a loop at bottom of collar to fasten across the neck; shoulder-straps with badges of rank, as for tunic.

Mess-Waistcoat—Rifle green cloth, single breasted; no collar; open half-way down; edged with ½-inch mohair braid; hooks and eyes; pockets edged with black Russia braid, forming three eyes in the centre at the top, three eyes in the centre at the bottom, and a crow's foot at each end.

Kamarband—See pages 6 and 7.

Great-Coat and Cape—Grey cloth, of the pattern described at page 2, with bronze buttons; shoulder-straps of the same material as the garment; a small button of regimental pattern at the top; badges of rank in bronze.

REGIMENTAL STAFF OFFICERS.

Uniform as for the other officers of their rank.

HORSE FURNITURE.

As prescribed for Infantry of the Line, with the following exceptions:—

Shabracque—Black lambskin, 3 feet 4 inches long, 21 inches deep in front, and 12 inches behind, covering the saddle and wallets; cloth edging of the colour of the regimental facings; moleskin lining.

Wallet Covers (with undress)—Black patent leather, with silver studs.

Bridle, Breast-Plate, &c.—Black leather, with silver whole buckles and silver bit bosses; green front and rosettes; black and green horse-hair throat ornament, 18 inches long, with silver ball socket.

Pattern of Bit-Boss—Within a garter, surmounted by a crown, a bugle with strings; on the garter, "The Cameronians."

VII.—RIFLE REGIMENTS.

(*Exclusive of The Scottish Rifles.*)

1. The King's Royal Rifle Corps.

Tunic—Rifle green cloth, edged all round, except the collar, with black square cord. Scarlet cloth collar and cuffs. The collar edged with ½-inch black braid: the cuffs pointed, and ornamented as described below, according to rank. The skirt rounded off in front, closed behind, and lined with black. On each side of the breast, 5 loops of black square cord, with netted caps and drops, fastening with black olivets. On each back-seam, a line of the same cord, forming three eyes at the top, passing under a netted cap at the waist, below which it is doubled, and ending in an Austrian knot reaching to the bottom of the skirt. Shoulder-straps of black chain gimp, with small button of regimental pattern at the top. Badges of rank in bronze.

Field Officers have figured braiding below the lace on the collar; and 1½-inch black lace round the top of the cuff, with figured braiding above and below the lace, extending to 11 inches from the bottom of the cuff.

Captains have a row of braided eyes, below the lace on the collar; and an Austrian knot of black square cord on the sleeve, with a tracing of braided eyes all round it, extending to 8 inches from the bottom of the cuff.

Lieutenants have a tracing of plain braid only, below the lace on the collar; and an Austrian knot on the sleeve, with a tracing of plain braid round it, extending to 7 inches only from the bottom of the cuff.

Braid—Black mohair.

Buttons—Bronze. See "*Badges of Territorial Regiments.*"

Trousers, &c.—Rifle green cloth, with 2-inch black braid down the side seams; in summer, Rifle green tartan, without stripes; Wellington boots and steel spurs, for Mounted Officers.

Pantaloons, &c., for mounted duties—Rifle green cloth, with stripes as on the cloth trousers; knee boots, as described at page 1, with steel spurs.

P.C. Gen. No. 6042

Busby—Black Persian lambskin, height in front 5 inches, rising to 6 inches in the centre of each side of the busby and sloping back to the bottom edge. The crown of Rifle green cloth, with figured ornament of special pattern. Black silk square cord plait in front carried up to a small bronze bugle at the centre of the top of each side with two rows of square silk cord at back, ending in a knot, to which is attached a bronze ring. A black corded oval boss on the top in front with the Crown, bronze relieved, on the centre. Below the boss, a bronze relieved Maltese Cross of special pattern. Chin-strap of black patent leather. Black silk square cord body line with swivel to attach to the ring at the back of the busby, black egg moles and sliders.

Plume—Black egret feathers, with scarlet vulture feathers below. A bronze corded ball socket with four upright leaves. The height of the plume from the top of the ball is 6½ inches.

Helmet, White—See pages 8 to 10.

Helmet-Plate—Bronze. See "*Badges of Territorial Regiments.*"

Sword—As described at page 7; steel hilt, with device of bugle and crown.

Scabbard—Steel for all ranks.

Sword-Knot—Black leather strap and acorn.

Sword-Belt—Black patent leather, 1½ inches wide, with slings an inch wide; silver snake clasp and mountings.

Pouch-Belt—Black patent leather, 2¾ inches wide, with silver breast ornament, of same design as the helmet-plate, except that the Bugle with strings is on a silver frosted ground; whistle and chain, of regimental patterns. P.C. 2 K.R.R.C. 539

Pouch—Black patent leather, with a silver bugle on the flap.

Sabretache—As laid down at pages 4 and 5; device on flap, a bugle with strings, in silver.

Gloves—Black leather.

Patrol-Jacket—Rifle green cloth of the size and shape prescribed at page 6, with collar and pointed cuffs of the regimental facings. Inch black mohair braid down the front, at the bottom of the skirts, and on the slits; the mohair braid traced inside with Russia braid, forming eyes at each angle of the slits. The back seams trimmed with inch mohair braid, traced on both sides with Russia braid, forming three eyes at the top and two at the bottom. On each side in front, five loops of black square cord fastening with olivets. Each loop forms an eye above and below in the centre and a drop at the end. A cap on each drop. Cuffs edged with inch mohair braid, traced with Russia braid, forming a crow's foot and eye at the top and an eye in the angle at the bottom. Collar edged all round with ½-inch mohair braid, traced inside with Russia braid, forming an eye at each end. At the back, below the centre of the collar, the tracing forms a plume, 6 inches deep, and a crow's foot and eye at the bottom. Black lining, hooks and eyes. A pocket on either side below the fourth loop, and one inside the left breast. Shoulder-straps with badges of rank as for tunic. G.O. 80 1886.

Forage-Cap—Rifle green cloth, with band of $1\frac{1}{2}$-inch black mohair braid, black netted button and braided figure on the crown, and black leather chin strap. No peak.

61002/3307 G.O. 35, 1886. *Serge Patrol-Jacket*—Rifle green, rounded in front, stand-up collar with hook and eye and black silk tab, scarlet piping on the seam. Cuffs plain. A body seam on each side. A black strap, diamond shaped, sewn down the centre and fastened on each side to a regimental bronze ball button. Five regimental bronze ball buttons down the front. Two pockets in each side with flaps. Black alpaca fore-part lining. Shoulder-straps of the same material as the garment, with small bronze ball button at the top. Badges of rank in bronze.

Forage-Cap for Active Service and Peace Manœuvres—Green cloth, special pattern, ornamented in front with a silver bugle placed on a scarlet cord boss.

Mess-Jacket—Rifle green cloth, scarlet collar and scarlet cuffs. Black mohair braid all round the body, forming barrels (or dummies) at bottom of back seams. Back seams trimmed with a double row of $\frac{1}{4}$-inch mohair braid, forming a crow's foot at top, and finishing over the barrels (or dummies) at the bottom. Pockets trimmed with $\frac{1}{4}$-inch mohair braid, forming a crow's foot at each end and in centre. Five waved loops of square cord in front, with four rows of knitted olivets, two olivets on each loop. Pointed cuffs of inch mohair braid, with tracing of black Russia braid, forming a row of small eyes on the outside and inside of the cuffs, and extending $6\frac{1}{2}$ inches from the bottom of each cuff. Mohair braid, $\frac{1}{2}$-inch wide, all round the collar, trimmed through the centre with plumes, and row of small eyes along top edge ; a loop at bottom of collar to fasten across the neck ; shoulder-straps with badges of rank as for tunic.

Mess-Waistcoat—Rifle green cloth, single-breasted, no collar, open half-way down. Hooks and eyes. $\frac{1}{2}$-inch mohair braid on edges, with a $\frac{1}{4}$-inch braid down the front, one inch from the edge. Scarlet cloth between the two braids with row of eyes of black Russia braid down front edge on the scarlet cloth. Pockets trimmed with $\frac{1}{4}$-inch mohair braid, forming a crow's foot at each end, edged all round with scarlet cloth.

Kamarband—See pages 6 and 7.

Great-Coat and Cape—Grey cloth, of the pattern described at page 2, with bronze buttons. Shoulder-straps of the same material as the garment: a small button of regimental pattern at the top ; badges of rank in bronze.

Regimental Staff Officers.

Uniform as for the other officers of their rank.

Horse Furniture.

As prescribed for Infantry of the Line, with the following exceptions :—

Shabracque—Black lambskin, 3 feet 4 inches long, 21 inches deep in front and 12 inches behind, covering the saddle and wallets ; cloth edging of the colour of the regimental facings ; moleskin lining.

Wallet Covers (with undress)—Black patent leather, with silver studs.

Bridle, Breast-Plate, &c.—Black leather, the head-stall lined with scarlet cloth, with scalloped edges ; silver whole buckles and silver bit bosses ; green front and rosettes ; black and scarlet horse-hair throat ornament, 18 inches long with silver ball socket.

Pattern of Bit-Boss—Within a garter surmounted by a crown, a bugle with strings. On the garter, "King's Royal Rifle Corps."

2. The Royal Irish Rifles.

The uniform and horse furniture are the same as for the King's Royal Rifle Corps, with the following exceptions :—

Tunic—Dark green cloth collar and cuffs.

Buttons—See "*Badges of Territorial Regiments.*"

Helmet-Plate—See "*Badges of Territorial Regiments.*"

Sabretache—In silver, on the flap, a bugle with strings surmounted by the Sphinx over Egypt.

Pouch-Belt—3 inches wide, breast ornament as for helmet-plate, but in silver; whistle and chain of regimental patterns.

Pouch—Black patent leather ; in silver, on the flap, a bugle with strings, surmounted by the Sphinx over Egypt.

Patrol-Jacket—Dark green cloth collar and cuffs.

Serge Patrol-Jacket—Rifle green, slightly rounded in front, stand-up collar, square in front, with two hooks and eyes, and black silk tab. Dark green Russia braid on collar seam. A body seam at each side with a slit $4\frac{1}{2}$ inches deep. Five bronze regimental buttons down the front. Cuffs, dark green cloth, pointed, 5 inches deep in front and $1\frac{3}{4}$ inches at the back. A pocket on each side, and a patch pocket on the left breast. Black alpaca lining. Shoulder-straps of the same material as the garment ; a small bronze regimental button at the top. Badges of rank in bronze. 61002/3307 G.O. 81, 1886.

Forage Cap—Band of $1\frac{1}{2}$ inch black lace, shamrock pattern.

Forage Cap for Active Service and Peace Manœuvres—Dark green cord boss; in silver, on the boss, the Harp surmounted by a crown; on the Harp, a scroll, inscribed "Royal Irish Rifles."

Mess Jacket—Rifle green cloth; dark green cloth collar, square in front; dark green cloth cuffs; inch black mohair braid all round the body, forming barrels (or dummies) at bottom of back seams. The mohair braid traced inside with Russia braid, forming an eye at each bottom corner in front. The back seams trimmed with double ¼-inch Russia braid, forming in single braid at the top a crow's foot and eye, and terminating in single braid in an eye at the bottom, above the dummies. On each side, in front, four waved loops of ¼-inch Russia braid, each loop forming a drooping crow's foot at the end; two double-stitched olivets on each loop. Cuffs pointed with ¼-inch black Russia braid, forming a crow's foot in front, and continued to the bottom of the cuff at either side of the back seam. The crow's foot extends to 6 inches from the bottom of the cuff. The ¼-inch braid traced inside and outside with small Russia braid. A further tracing of small eyes above and below the ¼-inch braid, terminating in a figured braiding below in the front. The collar edged top and bottom with ½-inch mohair braid, with a double row of eyes within the braid, terminating in an eye at each corner of the collar. A loop at bottom of collar to fasten across the neck. Pocket inside the left breast; black silk lining; hooks and eyes down the front. Shoulder-straps with badges of rank as for tunic.

Mess-Waistcoat—Green, instead of scarlet cloth, between the two braids down the front; the mohair braid on the pockets edged with green.

Kamarband—See pages 6 and 7.

Horse Furniture.

Shabracque—Green cloth edging.

Bridle, Breast-Plate, &c.—The head-stall is not lined. The garter of the bit-bosses inscribed "Royal Irish Rifles;" dark green horse-hair throat ornament.

3. The Rifle Brigade.

The uniform and horse furniture are the same as for the King's Royal Rifle Corps, with the following exceptions:—

Tunic—Black velvet collar and cuffs.

Buttons—See "*Badges of Territorial Regiments.*

Busby—A bronze relieved bugle is below the corded boss. P.C. Gen. No. 6042

Plume—Black vulture feathers below the black egret feathers.

Helmet-Plate—See "*Badges of Territorial Regiments.*"

Pouch-Belt—3 inches wide; silver breast ornament, whistle and chain, of regimental patterns.

Patrol-Jacket—Rifle green cloth, of the size and shape prescribed at page 6, with collar and cuffs of black velvet. Inch black mohair braid down the front, at the bottom of the skirts, and on the slits. The mohair braid traced inside with Russia braid, forming eyes at each angle of the slits. The back seams trimmed with inch mohair braid traced on both sides with Russia braid, forming three eyes at the top and two eyes at the bottom. On each side, in front, five loops of black square cord, fastening with olivets. Each loop forms an eye above and below in the centre, and a drop at the end. A cap on each drop, cuffs pointed with inch mohair braid, traced at the bottom with Russia braid, forming an eye in the angle. Collar edged with inch mohair braid; a tracing below the braid, and on the collar seam, forming an eye in the corners. At the back, below the centre of the collar, the tracing forms a plume 6 inches deep; black lining, hooks and eyes. A pocket on either side below the fourth loop, and one inside the left breast. Shoulder-straps with badges of rank as for tunic.

Serge Patrol Jacket—Rifle green, square in front, stand-up collar with hook and eye and black silk tab. Cuffs plain. A body seam on each side, seven regimental horn buttons down the front. Two pockets on each side with pointed flaps. A small button with tab under each flap. A drawing string inside, at the waist. Shoulder straps of the same material as the garment, a small button at the top. Badges of rank in bronze. 61002/3307 G.O. 35, 1886.

Forage Cap for Active Service and Peace Manœuvres—Black cord boss.

Mess Jacket—Rifle green cloth; black velvet collar, square in front. Inch mohair braid all round the body, forming barrels (or dummies) at bottom of back seams. The mohair braid traced inside with Russia braid, forming an eye at each bottom corner in front. The back seams trimmed with double ¼-inch black Russia braid, forming in a single braid an Austrian knot at the top. Five plaited olivets on the left side; hooks and eyes down the front. Cuffs, black velvet, pointed with inch mohair braid, traced at the bottom with Russia braid, forming an eye in the angle. The mohair braid extends to 6 inches from the bottom of the cuff. Collar edged with inch mohair braid; a tracing of black Russia braid below the mohair braid, and on the collar seam, forming an eye in the corners. Pockets edged with ¾-inch G.O. 16, 1884.

Russia braid, forming a crow's foot at each end. Black lining; shoulder-straps with badges of rank as for tunic.

Mess-Waistcoat—Rifle green cloth, single-breasted, without collar, open to the second olivet of the shell-jacket; edged with $\frac{1}{8}$-inch black mohair braid, traced inside with black Russia braid, forming an eye at each bottom corner in front. The pockets edged with black Russia braid, forming plumes at the top and bottom, in the centre, and at each end.

Kamarband—See pages 6 and 7.

Horse Furniture.

Shabracque—Black cloth edging.

Bridle, Breast-Plate, &c.—The head-stall is not lined; the garter of the bit-bosses inscribed, "Rifle Brigade;" black horse-hair throat ornament.

VIII.—MOUNTED INFANTRY.

Officers of Mounted Infantry will wear the same dress as that
61002/4012 prescribed for officers of Infantry on active service, with following exceptions :—

Hunting Breeches—Bedford cord, strapped, with continuations, and horn buttons.

*Boots**—Brown Russia leather, "butcher" pattern, laced at the instep, with spur straps and guard to match.

Walking Boots—Black, laced, stout.

Puttees—Dark blue (black for rifle regiments), with strings.

Cap—Field service.

Sword Belt—Brown leather, "Sam Brown" pattern.

*Cross Belt**—Brown leather with binocular case to match.

IX.—WEST INDIA REGIMENT.

Uniform and horse furniture as for Infantry of the Line, with the following exceptions :—

Lace for Tunic—Bias and Stand pattern.

Special Badges—See "*Badges of Territorial Regiments.*"

White Trousers—Are worn on ordinary occasions.

* For Field Service only.

X.—LIEUTENANT-COLONEL COMMANDING REGIMENTAL DISTRICT.

1. Districts Exclusive of the 83rd Regimental District and the Rifle Depôt.

Tunic—As for Infantry; facings blue.
Lace—As for Staff.
Buttons—As for General Staff.
Dress Trousers—As for Infantry.
Undress Trousers—Ditto, but with scarlet stripe, 1½ inches wide.
Pantaloons—Scarlet stripe, 1½ inches wide.
Boots—As for mounted services.
Spurs—Brass.
Cocked-Hat and Plume—As for an Assistant Adjutant-General. 61002
*Forage-Cap**—Staff pattern (see page 27). 4194
Frock-Coat—Blue cloth, single-breasted, with rolling collar; the collar, front and back, and the skirts edged with ¾ inch mohair braid; 5 loops of the same braid on each side in front, with two olivets on each loop; 2 olivets at waist behind, encircled with braided crow's foot; the cuffs pointed with 1-inch mohair braid; the braid extends to 5 inches from the bottom of the cuff. The skirt lined with black. Shoulder-straps of the same material as the garment, edged with ½-inch mohair braid, except at the base; black netted button at the top. Badges of rank in gold.
Sashes—As for Infantry. Not to be worn with the frock coat. 61002
Horse Appointments—As for an Assistant Adjutant-General. 4166
Saddle Cloth—Blue cloth, 3 feet long at the bottom, and 2 feet deep, with gold lace of Staff pattern an inch wide, the badges of rank embroidered in silver on the hind corners.
Sabretache—As for Mounted Officers of Infantry.
Sword-
Scabbard,
Waist-Plate, } As for Field Officers of Infantry of the Line.
Sword-Knot
Sword-Belt— } Gold lace both for dress and undress.
Shell-Jacket,
Mess-Waistcoat— } As for Infantry.
Waistcoat—(to be worn with frock-coat). As for Staff.
Great-Coat and Cape—As for Infantry.
Whistle— Ditto.

* Caps in possession may continue to be worn until they require to be replaced.

2. Eighty-third Regimental District.

Uniform and horse furniture as for other Officers Commanding Regimental Districts, except that the badge on the forage-cap will be a bugle with strings surmounted by the Sphinx over Egypt, in gold embroidery; but should the Regiment in which the Commanding Officer last served have been a Rifle Regiment, the uniform and horse furniture will be as for the Royal Irish Rifles.

3. Rifle Depôt.

Uniform of the Rifle Brigade, without facings.

XI.—MILITIA BATTALIONS

Uniform and horse furniture as for the Line battalions of the Territorial Regiments of which they form part, with the following exceptions:—

Shoulder-straps—The letter **M** in silver, or in silver embroidery, is worn below the badges of rank on garments for which gold shoulder-straps are authorized, and in gilt metal or in gold embroidery on garments for which cloth straps are authorized. Officers of Militia Rifles wear an **M** in bronze on all shoulder-straps.

Special Badges—Battles are omitted.

In the Militia Battalions of the Royal Highlanders, Seaforth Highlanders, and Argyll and Sutherland Highlanders, the Belted Plaid, Kilt, Sporran, Hose, Garters, Skean Dhu, Shoes, and Buckles are not worn. Boots will be worn as laid down at page 1.

In the Militia Battalions of the Royal Irish Rifles, the device on the flap of the pouch is a bugle with strings, in silver.

38107 / Dress. / 75 In Militia Battalions of Rifle Regiments, the breast-plates are of special pattern. On the helmet a Maltese cross on a red cloth ground will be worn. The cross will be of bronze, surmounted by a crown, and having a lion at each of its four divisions. In the centre of the cross there will be a bugle, within a circle, bearing the designation of the regiment or battalion. The cross, measured at the back, will be 2½ inches long, and 2½ inches wide.

Assistant and Quartermaster.

An officer selected from full pay for the appointment of adjutant or quartermaster of Infantry Militia, will wear the uniform of the battalion of Militia to which he is appointed.

XII.—CHANNEL ISLANDS LIGHT INFANTRY MILITIA.

As for Militia Battalions of Light Infantry of the Line, with the following distinctions :—

1. Royal Jersey Light Infantry.

Lace—Gold, special pattern.

Buttons—The Royal Crest.

Collar Badge—In gilt metal, the Cross of St. Andrew ; on the Cross, a shield charged with three lions-leopardés, in silver. The shield surmounted by the Crown in gilt metal.

Helmet-plate—In gilt metal, within a circle inscribed "Royal Jersey Light Infantry," a bugle with strings on a black velvet ground. The number of the regiment within the strings of the bugle.

Waist-plate—In silver, on a frosted gilt centre, a bugle with strings, surmounted by the Crown. The number of the regiment within the strings of the bugle. On the circle, "Royal Jersey Light Infantry."

Forage Cap Badge—In gold embroidery, on a blue cloth ground, a bugle with strings, surmounted by the Royal Crest. The number of the regiment within the strings of the bugle. A sprig of laurel on each side of the bugle ; below, a crimson velvet scroll, inscribed "Royal Jersey." The bugle is of special pattern.

2. Royal Guernsey Light Infantry.

Lace—Gold, special pattern.

Buttons—Bugle with strings, surmounted by a sprig of laurel. Within the strings of the bugle, the number of the regiment.

Collar Badge—A lion-leopardé, in gold embroidery.

Helmet-plate—In gilt metal, a garter inscribed "*Pro aris, rege et focis.*" In silver, within the garter, on a black velvet ground, a shield surmounted by a sprig of laurel. The shield charged with three lions-leopardés. In silver, above the garter, a scroll inscribed "DIEX AÏE." In silver, below the shield, a bugle with strings. Within the strings, the number of the regiment. On universal wreath at the bottom, a scroll inscribed, "Royal Guernsey Militia."

Waist-plate—In silver, on a frosted gilt centre, a bugle with strings, surmounted by a sprig of laurel. The number of the regiment within the strings of the bugle. On the circle, "Royal Guernsey Militia." The bugle is of special pattern.

Forage Cap Badge—In gold embroidery, on a blue cloth ground, a bugle, with strings, surmounted by a sprig of laurel. The number of the regiment within the strings of the bugle ; below, a crimson velvet scroll, inscribed "Royal Guernsey." The bugle is of special pattern.

XIII.—ROYAL MALTA REGIMENT OF MILITIA.

As for Militia Battalions of Infantry of the Line, with the following distinctions:—

On Buttons—Within a garter, inscribed "Royal Malta Militia," and surmounted by the Crown, a Maltese Cross.

On Collar of Tunic—A Maltese Cross in burnished silver: on the centre of the Cross, the Crown in gilt metal.

On Helmet-plate—A Maltese Cross in gilt metal, surmounted by the Crown. On the Cross, a scroll in silver, inscribed "Royal Malta Militia, MDCCC."

On the Waist-plate.—In silver, on a frosted gilt centre, a laurel wreath with the Crown above; a Maltese Cross in silver within the wreath. On the circle "Royal Malta Militia, MDCCC."

On the Round Forage-Cap.—In gold embroidery on a scarlet ground, a wreath. Within the wreath, a garter inscribed "Royal Malta Militia" on a blue silk ground. Within the garter, a Maltese Cross in burnished silver on a ground of which one half is in white lined silk and the other in scarlet lined silk. The garter is surmounted by the Crown on a blue cloth ground. Below the garter, a scroll, inscribed "MDCCC."

VII.—ARMY SERVICE CORPS.

FULL DRESS.

Tunic—Blue cloth, with collar and cuffs of white cloth. The collar rounded in front and ornamented with ¾-inch lace round the top, and a gold cord similar to that in the shoulder-straps round the bottom; eight buttons in front and two at the waist behind. The skirt rounded off in front, and closed behind with a plait at each side, and lined with black silk; white cloth edging, ⅛ inch wide, all round (except the collar) and up the skirt plaits; shoulder-straps of twisted round gold cord, universal pattern, lined with blue; a small button, of regimental pattern, at the top. Badges of rank in silver. 61002/3705 *

Field Officers have a row of braided eyes below the lace on the collar; a chevron of 1½-inch lace on each cuff, with figured ⅛-inch Russia braiding above and below the lace, extending to 11 inches from the bottom of the cuff.

Captains have an Austrian knot of round-back gold cord on each sleeve, traced all round with braided eyes; no braided eyes on the collar.

Lieutenants have a similar knot, but without the figured braiding.

Lace—Gold, Staff pattern for tunic, jacket, and mess waistcoat, and regimental pattern (with ⅛-inch dark blue stripe in the centre) for cap and dress trousers.

Buttons—Of regimental pattern.

Trousers, Boots, and Spurs—Blue cloth, with 1½-inch lace down the side seams; Wellington boots. Steel spurs for Mounted Officers, except at levées and in the evening in mess or full dress when brass spurs will be worn.

Pantaloons, &c., for Mounted Duties—Blue cloth with two stripes of white cloth, each ¾ inch wide and ⅛ inch apart, down each side seam. Knee boots and steel spurs, as described in page 1.

Helmet—See page 4; plate with "A.S.C." in centre on a black enamelled ground.

Helmet, White—See pages 8 to 10.

Sword—Half-basket, steel hilt, with two fluted bars on the outside; black fish-skin grip, bound with silver wire; slightly curved blade, $35\frac{1}{2}$ inches long and $1\frac{1}{4}$ inches wide, grooved and spear pointed.

Scabbard—Steel, with a large shoe at the bottom and a trumpet-shaped mouth.

Sword-Knot—Gold and blue cord, with gold and blue acorn.

Sword-Belt—Pale Russia leather, $1\frac{1}{2}$ inches wide; with removable slings an inch wide, the front sling lined with Russia leather; a swivel-hook on the eye of dee of front sling for hooking up sword, running carriage for back sling; two stripes of gold embroidery on belt and slings; flat billets for sword and sabretache slings with square gilt-wire buckles; three dees on inside of belt, with Russia leather protecting flap to attach sabretache slings. Gilt burnished plate with device in silver, the Royal Cypher and Crown.

Sabretache (for Mounted Officers)—Black patent leather. Device on flap, the Royal Cypher and Crown in gilt metal.

Shoulder-Belt—Pale Russia leather, 2 inches wide, with three stripes of gold embroidery, each $\frac{1}{4}$ inch wide; gilt chased buckle, tip, and slide.

Binocular Case—Black patent leather, to hold a binocular field glass, solid leather flap, reaching to the lower edge of the case, ornamented with Royal Cypher and Crown in gilt metal.

Undress.

Patrol-Jacket—Blue cloth, rounded in front, and edged with inch black mohair braid all round and up the openings at the side; five loops of flat plait on each side in front, fastening with olivets, and with crows' feet and olivets at the ends. Stand-and-fall collar, and a false upright collar of white cloth, with one row of $\frac{5}{8}$-inch gold lace round the top to button on inside collar of jacket. The sleeves ornamented with flat plait, forming crows' feet, 6 inches from the bottom of the cuffs. Double flat plait on each back seam, with crow's foot at top and bottom, and two eyes at equal distances. Pockets edged with flat plait forming a crow's foot at each end and an eye in the centre, top and bottom. Shoulder-straps of the same material as the garment, edged with $\frac{1}{2}$-inch black mohair braid, except at the base. Black netted button at the top. Badges of rank in gold. The jacket to be long enough to reach the saddle, when the officer is mounted.

Serge Patrol-Jacket—Blue, full in the chest; collars and cuffs of the same colour and material as the rest of the jacket. Shoulder-straps of white cloth with dark blue stripe $\frac{1}{8}$ inch wide running down the centre, with small regimental button at the top.

61002
4161

Badges of rank in gold. Stand-up collar, slightly rounded in front with black enamelled leather tab and hook and eye. Three small regimental buttons down the front. Four pleats at the waist behind and two pleats at each side in front. A band round the waist to button in front. A patch pocket with flap and small button on each breast; a patch pocket with flap on each side below the band. Cuffs 1½ inch deep with an opening at the back extending to 3 inches. The cuff fastened with small regimental button. A box pleat in front at the top of the band.

Trousers, Boots, and Spurs—Blue cloth with stripes, pattern as for pantaloons; Wellington boots, steel spurs for Mounted Officers.

Pantaloons, &c., for Mounted Duties—As for full dress.

Forage-Cap—Blue cloth, with gold embroidery ¾ inch wide on peak, and band of 1½-inch lace of regimental pattern. Gold purl button and braided figure on crown.

Forage-Cap for Active Service, &c.—Blue cloth folding cap, 5 inches high, with white cloth top, and blue side flaps 4 inches deep, to turn down when required, Black mohair welts on cap and flaps, and at front and back seams. Badge on the left side, the Royal Crest.

Mess-Jacket—Blue cloth, edged all round with ¾-inch gold lace, forming a bull's eye or ring at the bottom of each back seam; white collar and cuffs; a line of ⅛-inch gold braid along the collar seam; cuffs pointed and edged with ¾-inch lace, a loop of gold braid at bottom of collar to fasten across the neck; a row of gilt studs down the front on the left side, fastened with hooks and eyes, white silk lining. Shoulder-straps with badges of rank as for tunic.

*Mess-Waistcoat**—White cloth with collar, edged with ½-inch gold lace all round, including collar; to fasten with hooks and eyes; gilt studs down the front on the left side. The pockets edged with Russia braid, with crows' feet at ends and centre.

Sword-Belt—White buff† leather, 1½ inches wide, with sword slings 1 inch wide, sewn into gilt rings—(tache slings for Mounted Officers)—three dees on belt for sabretache slings. Flat billets for sword and tache slings, with square gilt wire buckles. Gilt burnished plate with device in silver, the Royal Cypher and Crown.

Shoulder-Belt†—White buff leather, 2 inches wide; no buckle, tip, or slide.

* In hot climates an open white washing waistcoat, without lappels, and fastened by four gilt buttons of regimental pattern may be worn with the shell-jacket in mess dress; collars and black ties.

† White patent leather Sword-Belts and white patent leather Shoulder-Belts in possession may continue to be worn until they require to be replaced.

Sword-Knot—Buff leather, ½-inch wide, with runner and acorn.

Cloak—Blue cloth, with sleeves. Stand-and-fall collar, with three black hooks and eyes in front, and three small flat silk buttons at the bottom to fasten the cape. Round loose cuffs, 6 inches deep. A pocket in each side seam outside, and one in the left breast inside. Four buttons down the front. A cloth back-strap, to fasten with a large flat silk button at the top of each pocket; a similar button in front on the right to hold the end of the back-strap when it is not buttoned across behind. Blue ratinett lining. The cloak to reach within 8 inches of the ground. Shoulder-straps of the same material as the garment; a small button of regimental pattern at the top. Badges of rank in gilt metal.

Cape—Blue cloth, long enough to cover the knuckles, lined with blue ratinett; a cloth band round the top to fasten with a cloth strap and black buckle, and a fly inside the band, with three button holes for attaching cape to cloak. Three buttons down the front.

Horse Furniture.

Officers attached to Transport Companies, Army Service Corps, same as Cavalry—no shabracque.

Other Mounted Officers, as for General Staff—no saddle-cloth.

QUARTERMASTERS AND RIDING-MASTERS.

Uniform, &c., as for other officers of their respective honorary rank.

VIII.—DEPARTMENTS.

I.—CHAPLAINS' DEPARTMENT.

Frock—Black cloth, single-breasted, with stand-up collar, square in front, with an opening $2\frac{1}{2}$ inches in width; 6 buttons down the front, and 6 loops of small round braid on each side; the top loops 6 inches long, and those at the waist 3 inches; 2 buttons at the waist behind; the skirt lined with black, and to reach to 2 inches below the knee. A Maltese Cross worked in black and gold at each end of the collar. Shoulder-straps of twisted round black cord, universal pattern, lined with black, with black netted button on the top. Badges of rank in black and gold. A.O 261, 1889.

The several classes are distinguished as follows:

The 1st Class have the collar edged round the top and bottom with $\frac{1}{2}$-inch black braid, and a crown and two stars, embroidered in black and gold on the shoulder-straps, and 3 braid loops and buttons on each cuff.

2nd Class, as for 1st Class, but with a crown and one star on the shoulder-straps.

3rd Class, as for 1st Class, but with a crown on the shoulder-straps.

4th Class, as for 1st Class, but with two stars on shoulder-straps, and without braid on collar and cuffs.

Buttons—Plain black silk.

Trousers—Black cloth, with black braid $1\frac{3}{4}$ inches wide down the side seams.

Forage-Cap—Black cloth, with black patent leather drooping peak, ornamented with $\frac{3}{8}$-inch black embroidery. Band $1\frac{3}{4}$ inches wide, of black lace, Staff pattern; black netted button and braided figure on crown. A Maltese Cross worked in black and gold on the band in front.

Forage-Cap for Active Service and Peace Manœuvres—Black cloth folding cap 5 inches high, with side flaps 4 inches deep, to turn down when required. Black mohair braid welts on cap and flaps, and on front and back seams. Badge as on round forage cap on the left side.

Gloves—Black leather.

Patrol-Jacket for Service in the Field—Black cloth or serge, according to climate, stand-up collar, height not to exceed 2 inches, square in front, with an opening $2\frac{1}{2}$ inches in width; $\frac{1}{2}$-inch mohair braid all round the collar, a Maltese Cross worked in black and gold at each end. Inch mohair braid traced with Russia braid down the front, along the bottom, up the slits, and on the back seams. The tracing forms an eye at each angle of the braid. Five bars, each 2 inches wide, of mohair braid, at equal distances down the front on each side; the top bar extends to the shoulder seams, and the bottom to 4 inches. Cuffs pointed, with inch mohair braid, traced with black Russia braid, forming an eye above and below the mohair braid. The mohair braid reaches to $5\frac{1}{2}$ inches from bottom of cuff. Pockets in front, edged top and bottom, with inch mohair braid; black lining. Pocket inside left breast. Hooks and eyes down the front. Shoulder-straps of the same material as the garment, edged with $\frac{1}{4}$-inch black mohair braid, except at the base; black netted button at the top. Badges of rank in gold.

Great-Coat and Cape—Black cloth, of the pattern described at page 2, but with badges of rank in black and gold.

II.—MEDICAL STAFF.

1. DIRECTOR-GENERAL AND SURGEON-GENERAL.

Tunic—Blue cloth ; the skirt rounded off in front and closed behind. Black velvet collar and cuffs ; the collar laced round the top and bottom with inch lace ; the cuffs pointed, with 2 bars of inch lace round the top showing ¼ inch of black velvet between the bars ; a figured braiding of alternate large and small eyes above and below the lace, according to special pattern, the top of the braided figure is 10 inches from the bottom of the cuff. 8 buttons down the front, and 2 at the waist behind. Scarlet cloth edging all round (except the collar) and up the skirt-plaits ; and the skirts lined with black silk. A plaited strap on each shoulder of round gold cord $\frac{3}{16}$-inch in diameter, intertwined with a small dead gold cord, and small button at the top ; on each strap, crossed sword and baton with star above, in silver. G.O. 4. 1885.

Lace—Gold, Staff pattern, for tunic and shell-jackets, and special pattern (with 2 lines of black silk) for cap, dress trousers, dress pantaloons, and saddle cloth.

Buttons—Gilt, with burnished edge. On the button a star ; on the star, a garter surmounted by the Crown. The garter inscribed "Medical Staff." Within the garter, the Royal Cypher.

Dress Trousers and Pantaloons—Blue cloth, with 2½-inch lace down the side seams.

Boots—As described at page 1.

Spurs—Brass.

Cocked-Hat—As described at page 2, with loop of double gold bullion, gold purl netted button ; tassels, flat gold-worked head ; 6 gold bullions, with 5 crimson bullions under them.

Plume—Black cock's-tail feathers, drooping outwards, 10 inches long from the top of a feathered stem 3 inches long

Helmet, White—As described at pages 4 and 5.

Sword—Mameluke, gilt hilt, with device of sword and baton crossed, encircled with oak-leaves ; ivory grip ; scimitar blade

Scabbard—Brass, ridged, with crossed lockets and rings.

Sword-Knot—Gold and black cord, with gold and black acorn.

Sword-Belt—Black Morocco leather, 1½ inches wide, with slings 1 inch wide ; 3 stripes of gold embroidery ⅜ inch wide on belt, and $\frac{3}{16}$ inch wide on slings ; a gilt hook to hook up the sword.

Waist-Plate—Round gilt, chased clasp; with the Royal Crest in silver, on the centre-piece

Pouch-Belt—Black Morocco leather, 2 inches wide, with 4 stripes of gold embroidery, each $\frac{3}{8}$ inch wide; gilt chased buckle, tip, and slide.

Pouch (for Note Book and Pencil)—Black Morocco leather; the flap 6 inches long and $3\frac{1}{2}$ inches deep, with 3 stripes of gold embroidery $\frac{3}{8}$ inch wide, round the bottom and sides; in the centre, a gilt chased Royal Cypher and Crown.

Frock—Blue cloth, single breasted. Black velvet rolling collar and pointed cuffs; the cuffs ornamented with black braid of the same pattern as the cuffs of the tunic. The collar, front, and back skirts edged with $\frac{3}{4}$-inch black mohair braid; 5 loops of the same braid on each side in front, with 2 olivets on each loop; 2 olivets at the waist behind, encircled with braided crow's foot; the skirts lined with black. Shoulder-straps with badges of rank as for tunic.

Patrol-Jacket for Active Service and Peace Manœuvres—Blue cloth, with stand-and-fall collar of black velvet, edged with inch black mohair braid, and a false upright collar of black cloth, with $\frac{3}{4}$-inch gold lace round the top, to button on inside collar of jacket. Inch mohair braid traced with Russia braid all round, up the slits, and along the back seams. The tracing forms an eye at each angle of the braid, except at the top of the slits and back seams, where it forms a crow's foot, 1 inch in length, and at the bottom in the centre, where it forms a long crow's foot, $1\frac{1}{2}$ inches in length. Five loops of inch mohair braid at equal distances down the front on each side, with two olivets on each loop, the top loops extend to the shoulder seams, and the bottom to 4 inches. Black velvet cuffs, pointed with inch mohair braid traced with black Russia braid forming an Austrian knot above and below the mohair braid. The mohair braid reaches to 7 inches from bottom of cuff, and the Austrian knot at the top to 9 inches. Pockets in front edged at the bottom with inch mohair braid; black silk lining; pocket inside left breast. Hooks and eyes in front. Shoulder-straps of the same material as the garment, edged with $\frac{1}{2}$-inch black mohair braid, except at the base; black netted button, at the top. Badges of rank in gold.

Mess-Jacket—Blue cloth, edged all round with inch gold lace, forming a bull's-eye or ring at the bottom of each back seam; black velvet collar and cuffs; $\frac{3}{8}$-inch gimp lace on the collar seam; cuffs pointed and edged with inch lace; a loop of gold braid at bottom of collar to fasten across the neck; a row of gilt studs down the front on the left side, fastened with hooks and eyes. Scarlet silk lining. Shoulder-straps with badges of rank as for tunic.

61002
4063

Mess-Waistcoat--Scarlet cloth, edged with $\frac{3}{16}$-inch gold Russia braid all round and on collar seam. Pockets edged with similar braid, forming a crow's foot at each end. A row of gilt studs and hooks and eyes down the front.

Waistcoat to be worn with blue Frock Coat—The same as for the mess-waistcoat, except that the gilt studs down the front and the edging of braid round the pockets will be omitted.

Kamarband—See page 7.

Undress Trousers and Pantaloons—Blue cloth, with scarlet stripes 2½ inches wide, and welted at the edges, down the side seams.

Forage-Cap—Blue cloth, with gold embroidered Staff peak, and band of 2-inch lace; gold and black purl button and gold-braided figure on the crown.

Forage-Cap for Active Service and Peace Manœuvres—Blue cloth folding cap, 5 inches high, with black cloth top, blue side flaps, 4 inches deep, to turn down when required; black mohair braid welts on cap and flaps and at front and back seams. Badge on the left side, the Royal Crest with sword and baton crossed.

Great-Coat and Cape—Blue milled cloth, of pattern described for mounted officers at page 3, lined with scarlet ratinett; the collar lined with black velvet. Shoulder-straps of the same material as the garment; a small button at the top. Badges of rank in gold.

HORSE FURNITURE.

Saddle—Hunting; or the saddle described at page 6; plain stirrups, and blue girths.

Wallets—Brown leather, with black bearskin covers, except abroad, where the covers will be of brown leather. G.O. 93, 1885.

Saddle-Cloth—Blue cloth, 3 feet 2 inches long and 2 feet 2 inches deep, with 2 stripes of 1½-inch lace ¼-inch apart all round; at each hind corner crossed sword and baton with star above, in silver.

Bridle—Brown leather, Cavalry pattern; with brown leather front and rosettes; steel chain reins; gilt bosses on bit and breast-plate, having the Royal Cypher within a garter, and a Crown above.

---

2. DEPUTY SURGEON-GENERAL.

Uniform and horse furniture as for Surgeon-General, with the following exceptions :—

Badges of Rank—Crown and two stars below.

Tunic—The collar ornamented with $\frac{3}{4}$-inch lace round the top, gold Russia braid along the bottom, and a figured braiding of alternate large and small eyes below the lace ; the lace on the cuffs to be $\frac{3}{4}$-inch, and the braiding below the lace of small eyes only. Shoulder-straps of twisted round gold cord, universal pattern, lined with blue ; small button at the top. Badges of rank in silver.

Dress Trousers, Pantaloons, and Forage-Cap—The lace $1\frac{3}{4}$ inches wide.

Undress Trousers and Pantaloons—The scarlet stripes $1\frac{3}{4}$ inches wide.

Cocked-Hat—The loop of $\frac{3}{4}$-inch Staff lace ; flat tassels, netted gold purl head, 8 small gold bullions, with 7 crimson bullions under them.

Plume—Black cock's-tail feathers, drooping outwards, 8 inches long from the top of a feathered stem 3 inches long.

Frock—The collar and cuffs of blue cloth ; shoulder-straps of blue cloth edged with $\frac{1}{2}$-inch black mohair braid, except at the base ; a black netted button at the top. Badges of rank in gold.

Patrol-Jacket for Active Service and Peace Manœuvres.—The collar and cuffs are of blue cloth.

Mess-Jacket—The lace $\frac{3}{4}$ inch wide ; a line of gold Russia braid along the bottom of the collar. Shoulder-straps with badges of rank as for tunic.

Sword—As described at page 5 , the hilt of gilt metal, with device of Royal Cypher and Crown, and lined with black patent leather.

Scabbard—Brass.

Sword-Knot—Gold and black lace strap, with gold and black acorn.

Sabretache—As described at pages 4 and 5. Device on flap, gilt chased Royal Cypher and Crown.

Forage-Cap for Active Service and Peace Manœuvres—Badge on left side, the Royal Crest.

Horse Furniture.

Saddle-Cloth—Blue cloth, 3 feet long and 2 feet deep, edged with inch lace ; at each hind corner a crown and two stars below, in silver.

3. BRIGADE SURGEON.

Uniform and horse furniture as for Deputy Surgeon-General, with the following exceptions:

Badges of Rank—Crown and one star below.

Tunic—The figured braiding on the collar, and above and below the lace on the sleeve, to be small eyes.

Sword-Belt—As for Deputy Surgeon-General, but with only 2 stripes of embroidery.

Pouch-Belt—As for Dputy Surgeon-General, but with only 3 stripes of embroidery on belt.

Pouch (for Instruments)—Black Morocco leather of special pattern to contain the Regulation instrument case; the flap $6\frac{1}{2}$ inches long and 4 inches deep, with two stripes of gold embroidery $\frac{3}{8}$ inch wide, round the bottom and sides; in the centre, a gilt chased Royal Cypher and Crown.

Plume—Black cock's-tail feathers, 6 inches long, without feathered stem.

Patrol-Jacket and Helmet—When on parade with the Medical Staff Corps, a patrol-jacket and helmet, as laid down for Surgeons-Major over 20 years' service, will be worn instead of the frock and cocked-hat. 38407 / Q.R. / 278

Serge-Jacket.—Plain; blue serge; five large buttons of the pattern described on page 107 down the front; black velvet standing collar; black velvet shoulder-straps with badges of rank; cuffs, round, 3 inches deep, of the same material as the garment; one pocket inside right breast, two flap pockets in skirt. 61002 / 4102

4. SURGEON-MAJOR OVER TWENTY YEARS' SERVICE.

Uniform and horse furniture as for Brigade Surgeon, with the following exceptions:—

Patrol-Jacket instead of Frock—As ordered for other officers under the rank of Surgeon-General *for Active Service and Peace Manœuvres.*

Cocked-Hat—Will not be worn, except by officers employed at Army Headquarters or on the Staff of a Governor or General Officer.

Helmet—Home pattern; as described at page 4.

Helmet-Plate—The Royal Arms in gilt metal. The dimensions of the plate are as follows:—

From top of crest to end of scroll, back measurement .... $3\frac{1}{2}$ inches.

Extreme horizontal width, back measurement .... $3\frac{1}{8}$ „

5. SURGEON-MAJOR OF LESS THAN TWENTY YEARS SERVICE.

Uniform and horse furniture as for Surgeon-Major of over 20 years' service, except :—

Badge of Rank—Crown.

Tunic—The braid below the lace on the sleeve is plain without eyes.

6. SURGEON.

Uniform, &c. (*including Pantaloons, Knee Boots, and Horse-Furniture when required to be mounted*), as for Surgeon-Major, with the following exceptions :—

Badges of Rank—Two stars.

Tunic—The braided eyes on the collar are omitted ; the braid above as well as below the lace on the sleeve is plain, without eyes.

Scabbard—Steel.

Forage-Cap—Lace 1½ inches wide.
Spurs for Mounted Officers—Dress, brass ; undress, steel.

HORSE FURNITURE.

Saddle-Cloth—No badges of rank.

7. QUARTERMASTER.

Uniform, &c., as for an officer with whom his honorary rank corresponds, with the following exceptions :—

Tunic—One bar of lace on cuffs for Quartermasters with the honorary rank of Lieutenant.

Pouch—Black patent leather pouch, of special pattern, to hold writing materials. The Royal Cypher and Crown in gilt metal, on the centre of the flap.

Pouch-Belt—Two stripes only of gold embroidery on the outer edges.

8. SURGEON ON PROBATION.

The mess and undress uniform of Surgeon, including the Serge Jacket, with the following exceptions:

Badge of Rank—One star.

Sword, *Sword-Belt*, *Dress Trousers* — Will not be worn.

9. APOTHECARIES.

Apothecaries to the Forces will continue to wear their present uniform.

10. MEDICAL OFFICERS OF HOUSEHOLD TROOPS.

Medical Officers of the Household Cavalry and Foot Guards wear the dress laid down at pages 40 and 72.

11. MILITIA MEDICAL STAFF.

Medical Officers of Militia on the departmental list will wear uniform and horse furniture as for Officers of the Medical Staff of corresponding rank, with the exception that the letter **M** will be worn below the badges of rank as authorized for Officers of Militia Battalions at page 94.

Medical Officers of Militia Battalions who have not elected to serve on the Departmental List will continue to wear the uniform of their regiments, but with cocked hats (with lace of loop and button of regimental patterns), plumes, belts, and pouches as for officers of corresponding rank in the Medical Staff.

Medical officers of Militia who join the Army Medical Reserve of officers will continue to wear the uniform of their respective corps, but with the badges of rank indicative of their rank in the Army Medical Reserve of officers, when the latter is higher than their regimental rank. 38407 / Dress. / 75

12. RETIRED MEDICAL OFFICER APPOINTED TO A MEDICAL CHARGE.

Retired Medical Officers appointed to medical charges under the provisions of Article 352 of the Royal Warrant for Pay, &c., will, while so employed, wear the uniform described for retired Departmental Officers at page 139.

III.—ORDNANCE STORE DEPARTMENT.

1. COMMISSARY-GENERAL OF ORDNANCE.

Tunic—Blue cloth; the skirt rounded off in front and closed behind. Scarlet cloth collar and cuffs; the collar laced round the top and bottom with inch lace; the cuffs pointed, with 2 bars of inch lace round the top, showing $\frac{1}{2}$ inch of scarlet cloth between the bars; a figured braiding of alternate large and small eyes above and below the lace, according to special pattern, the top of the braided figure is 10 inches from the bottom of the cuff. 8 buttons down the front, and 2 at the waist behind. The front and skirt plaits edged with scarlet cloth, $\frac{1}{4}$ inch wide; and the skirts lined with black silk. A plaited strap on each shoulder of round gold cord, $\frac{3}{16}$ inch in diameter, intertwined with a small dead gold cord, and small gilt button at the top; on each strap, crossed sword and baton with star above in silver.

Lace—On tunic, gold, Staff pattern; on trousers, belts, cap, &c., gold, special pattern, with a scarlet stripe in the centre, $\frac{1}{8}$ inch wide.

Buttons—Gilt, with Royal Crest in the centre, and the word "Ordnance" round the edge.

Dress Trousers and Pantaloons —Blue cloth, with 2-inch lace down the side seams.

Cocked-Hat—As described at page 2, with loop of double gold bullion; tassels, flat gold-worked head, 6 gold bullions with 5 red bullions under them.

Plume—White swan feathers, drooping outwards, 8 inches long, with black feathers under them long enough to reach to 2 inches below the ends of the white ones; feathered stem 3 inches long.

Helmet, White—See pages 8 to 10.

Spurs—Brass.

Sword—Mameluke gilt hilt, with device of sword and baton crossed, encircled with oak leaves; ivory grip; scimitar blade.

Scabbard—Brass, ridged, with cross lockets and rings.

Sword-Knot—Gold and red cord, with gold acorn.

Sword-Belt—Gold lace, 2 inches wide, with slings 1 inch wide, lined with red Morocco leather, a gilt hook to hook up the sword.

Waist-Plate—Round gilt clasp, with the Royal Crest on the centre-piece, and the words "Ordnance Store Department" on the outer circle.

Shoulder-Belt—Gold lace, 2½ inches wide, with ½-inch red light in the centre, lined with red Morocco leather; gilt buckle, tip, and slide.

Binocular Case—Black patent leather, to hold a binocular field glass, solid leather flap, reaching to the lower edge of the case, ornamented with Royal Cypher and Crown in gilt metal.

Frock—Blue cloth, single breasted. Blue velvet rolling collar and pointed cuffs; the cuffs ornamented with black braid of the same pattern as the cuffs of the tunic. The collar, front, and back skirts edged with ¾-inch black mohair braid; 5 loops of the same braid on each side in front, with 2 olivets on each loop; 2 olivets at the waist behind, encircled with a braided crow's foot; the skirts lined with black. Shoulder-straps with badges of rank as for tunic.

Patrol-Jacket for Active Service and Peace Manœuvres—As describe at page 6, with blue velvet collar and cuffs. Shoulder-straps of the same material as the garment, edged with ½-inch black mohair braid, except at the base; black netted button at the top. Badges of rank in gold.

Undress Trousers and Pantaloons—Blue cloth; 2 stripes of scarlet cloth with welted edges, $\frac{11}{16}$ inch wide and ⅛ inch apart, down each side seam.

Forage-Cap—Blue cloth, with gold embroidered Staff peak and band of 2-inch gold lace with scarlet stripe in centre ⅛ inch wide; gold purl netted button, and braided figure on the crown. G.O. 26, 1887.

Forage-Cap for Active Service and Peace Manœuvres—Blue cloth folding cap, 5 inches high, with scarlet cloth top, and blue side flaps, 4 inches deep, to turn down when required. Black mohair braid welts on cap and flaps, and at front and back seams. Badge on the left side, the Royal Crest with sword and baton crossed.

Great-Coat and Cape—Blue milled cloth, lined with red, of pattern described at page 2; the collar lined with red velvet. Shoulder-straps of the same material as the garment; a small button of departmental pattern at the top. Badges of rank in gold.

Boots and Spurs—As described at page 1.

Mess-Jacket—Blue cloth, edged all round with 1-inch gold lace, forming a bull's-eye or ring at the bottom of each back seam; scarlet cloth cuffs and collar, ⅜-inch gimp lace on the collar seam, cuffs pointed and edged with 1-inch lace ; a loop of gold braid at bottom of collar, to fasten across the neck ; a row of gilt studs down the front, on the left side; fastened with hooks and eyes ; red silk lining. Shoulder-straps, with badges of rank as for tunic.

Mess-Waistcoat—Blue cloth, edged all round and at the bottom of the collar with gold Russia braid. The pockets edged with Russia braid, with crow's foot at ends and centre. A row of gilt studs, and hooks and eyes down the front.

Kamarband—See pages 6 and 7.

Horse Furniture.

Saddle—Hunting; or the saddle described at page 6; plain stirrups and blue girths.

Saddle-Cloth—Blue cloth, 3 feet 2 inches long at the bottom, and 2 feet 2 inches deep, with 2 stripes of 1½-inch lace all round, ¼ inch apart; at each hind corner, badge of crossed sword and baton, with star above in silver.

G.O. 93 1885. *Wallets*—Brown leather, with black bearskin covers, except abroad, where the covers will be brown leather.

Bridle—Brown leather, Cavalry pattern, with blue front and rosettes; gilt bosses on bit and breast-plate, having the Royal Cypher within a garter, and Crown above.

2. DEPUTY COMMISSARY-GENERAL OF ORDNANCE.

Uniform and horse furniture as for Commissary-General of Ordnance, with the following exceptions :—

Tunic—The collar ornamented with ¾-inch lace round the top, gold Russia braid along the bottom, and a figured braiding of alternate large and small eyes below the lace ; the lace on the cuffs to be ¾-inch, and the braiding below the lace to be of small eyes only. Shoulder-straps of twisted round gold cord, universal pattern, lined with blue ; small button of departmental pattern at the top. Badges of rank, a crown and two stars, in silver.

Dress Trousers, Pantaloons, and Forage-Cap—The lace to be 1½ inches wide.

Cocked Hat—The loop of ¾-inch lace; flat tassels, netted gold purl head; 8 small gold bullions, with 7 red bullions under them.

Plume—Mushroom-shaped, of white cock's-tail feathers, 4 inches long, with black feathers under them long enough to reach 2 inches below the ends of the white ones.

Frock—The collar and cuffs of blue cloth; shoulder-straps of blue cloth edged with ½-inch black mohair braid, except at the base; a black netted button at the top. Badges of rank in gold.

Patrol-Jacket for Active Service and Peace Manœuvres—Blue velvet collar and cuffs are not worn.

Shell Jacket—The lace ¾ inch wide; a line of gold Russia braid along the bottom of the collar, with an eye in the centre. Shoulder-straps with badges of rank as for tunic.

Sword—As described at page 5; the hilt of gilt metal, with device of Royal Cypher and Crown, and lined with black patent leather.

Scabbard—Brass.

Sword-Knot—Red and gold lace strap, with gold acorn.

Sword-Belt—The lace 1½ inches wide.

Sabretache—As described at page 6. Device on flap, the Royal Cypher and Crown in gilt metal.

Pouch-Belt—Gold lace, 2 inches wide.

Pouch—Black patent leather, of special pattern, to hold writing materials; the Royal Cypher and Crown in gilt metal, on the centre of the leaf.

Forage-Cap for Active Service and Peace Manœuvres—Badge on left side, the Royal Crest.

Horse Furniture.

Saddle Cloth—Blue cloth, 3 feet long at the bottom, and 2 feet deep, with a stripe of inch lace all round, edged with scarlet cloth; at each hind corner, a crown and two stars below in silver.

3. ASSISTANT COMMISSARY-GENERAL OF ORDNANCE.

Uniform and horse furniture as for Deputy Commissary-General of Ordnance, with the following exceptions:—

Tunic—The figured braiding on the collar, and above and below the lace on the sleeve, to be small eyes.

Badges of Rank—Crown and one star, or a crown only, according to rank

Patrol-Jacket—This jacket will be worn instead of the frock by all officers not employed at Army Head-Quarters, or on the Staff of Army Corps, Divisions, Districts, or Brigades.

Forage-Cap—The embroidery on the peak has a red-line, ⅛ inch wide, along the centre.

Undress Belts—White buff* leather with gilt mountings, as in dress, to be worn by officers of the rank of Major when not performing administrative duties.

4. DEPUTY-ASSISTANT COMMISSARY-GENERAL OF ORDNANCE.

Uniform, &c., as for Assistant Commissary-General of Ordnance, with the following exceptions :—

Badges of Rank—Two stars.

Tunic—The braided eyes on the collar are omitted ; the braid above and below the lace on the sleeve is plain, without eyes.

Belts—Gold lace belts will be worn on State occasions and at balls ; at other times white buff* leather belts with gilt mountings as in dress.

Scabbard—Steel.

Spurs for Mounted Officers—Dress, brass ; undress, steel.

5. PROBATIONERS.

The uniform of their regiments, with the addition of pantaloons and boots, as worn by Mounted Officers of their regiments, if required to be mounted, or the uniform prescribed for a Deputy-Assistant Commissary-General of Ordnance.

6. QUARTERMASTERS.

Uniform, &c.—As for other officers of their respective honorary rank.

---

* White patent leather belts in possession may continue to be worn until they require to be replaced.

7. ORDNANCE STORE CORPS.

Officers of the Ordnance Store Department attached to the Corps will wear the uniform of their rank, with the following exceptions;—

Helmet, instead of Cocked-Hat—As for Infantry; plate with O.S.C. in centre, on a black ground.

Spurs—Steel or brass, according to rank—for Mounted Officers.

IV.—ARMY PAY DEPARTMENT.

1. CHIEF PAYMASTER.

Tunic—Blue cloth, the skirt rounded off in front and closed behind. Yellow cloth collar and cuffs; the collar laced round the top with ¾-inch lace, with a tracing of small braided eyes below the lace; gold Russia braid at the bottom; the cuffs pointed with two bars of ¾-inch lace, showing ¼-inch blue cloth between the bars; a tracing of small eyes in gold Russia braid above and below the lace, forming an Austrian knot at the top, and a crow's foot and eye at the bottom. The lace extends to 8 and the Austrian knot to 10 inches from the bottom of the cuff. [G.O. 16] 1884.] Eight buttons down the front, and two at the waist behind. The front, collar, and skirt plaits edged with yellow cloth, ¼ inch wide, the skirts lined with black silk. Shoulder-straps of twisted round gold cord, universal pattern, lined with blue. A small button of departmental pattern at the top; badges of rank, a crown and two stars below in silver.

Lace—On tunic, gold Staff pattern; on trousers, belts, cap, &c. gold, special pattern, with a yellow stripe in the centre.

Buttons—Gilt, with Royal Crest in the centre, and the words "Army Pay Department" round the edge.

Dress Trousers—Blue cloth, with 1½-inch lace down the side seams with ¼-inch yellow stripe in centre.

Cocked-Hat—As described at page 2, with loop of ¾-inch lace; tassels, flat gold worked head, 6 gold bullions with 5 blue bullions under them.

Plume—Mushroom-shaped, of white cock's-tail feathers 4 inches long, with yellow feathers under them long enough to reach 2 inches below the white.

Helmet, White—See pages 4 and 5.

Spurs—Brass.

Sword—As described at page 5; the hilt of gilt metal, with device of Royal Cypher and Crown, and lined with black patent leather.

G.O. 16, 1884. *Scabbard*—Brass.

Sword-Knot—Yellow and gold cord, with gold acorn.

Sword-Belt—Gold lace, 1½ inches wide, with slings ¾ inch wide, lined with yellow Morocco leather.

G.O. 471, *Sabretache* (*for Mounted Officers*)—As described at page 6. Device on flap, the Royal Cypher and Crown in gilt metal.

Waist-Plate—Round gilt clasp, with the Royal Crest on the centre-piece, and the words "Army Pay Department" on the outer circle.

Pouch-Belt—Gold lace, 2 inches wide, with ⅜-inch yellow stripe in the centre, lined with yellow Morocco leather; gilt buckle, tip, and slide.

Pouch—Black patent leather, of special pattern, to hold writing materials; Royal Cypher and Crown in gilt metal, on the centre of the leaf.

Frock—Blue cloth, single-breasted; blue cloth rolling collar; the cuffs of blue cloth, pointed with two bars of ¾-inch mohair braid round the top, showing ¼ inch blue cloth between the bars, a black Russia braiding of small eyes above and below the lace terminating at the top in an Austrian knot, and at the bottom in a double crow's foot and eye. The collar, front, and back skirts edged with ¾-inch black mohair braid, five loops of same braid on each side in front, with two olivets on each loop. Two olivets at the waist behind, encircled with crow's foot. Skirts lined with black. Shoulder-straps of the same material as the garment, edged with ½-inch black mohair braid, except at the base; black netted button at the top. Badges of rank in gold.

G.O. 471, 1889. *Patrol-Jacket to be worn on Service in the Field or at Peace Manœuvres*—Blue cloth, with stand-and-fall collar edged with inch black mohair braid, and a false upright collar of yellow cloth with ¾-inch gold lace round the top, to button on inside collar of jacket. 1-inch mohair braid traced with Russia braid all round, up the slits, and along the back seams. The tracing forms an eye at each angle of the braid, except at the top of the slits and back seams, where it forms a crow's foot 1 inch in length, and at the bottom in the centre where it forms a long crow's foot 1½ inches in length. Five loops of inch mohair braid at equal distances down the front on each side, with two olivets on each loop, the top loops extend to the shoulder seams, and the bottom to 4 inches. Cuffs of same cloth as the jacket, pointed with inch mohair braid traced with black Russia braid forming an Austrian knot above and below the mohair braid. The mohair braid reaches to 7 inches from bottom of cuff, and the Austrian knot at the top to 9 inches. Pockets in front edged at the bottom with inch mohair braid, black silk lining; pocket inside left breast; hooks and eyes in front. Shoulder-straps of the same material as the garment, edged with ½-inch mohair braid, except at the base; black netted button at the top. Badges of rank in gold.

Mess-Jacket—Blue cloth, with yellow cloth collar and cuffs; the collar edged with ¾-inch Staff pattern lace round the top, and gold Russia braid at the bottom; the cuffs pointed and edged with ¾-inch lace. The jacket edged all round with gold lace, ¾ inch wide, forming a ring or bull's-eye at bottom of each back seam. Gilt studs down the front, on the left side; hooks and eyes in front. Blue silk lining; shoulder-straps with badges of rank as for tunic. G.O. 471, 1889.

Mess-Waistcoat—Blue cloth, edged all round, and at the bottom of the collar with gold Russia braid. The pockets edged with Russia braid, with crow's foot at ends and centre. A row of gilt studs and hooks and eyes down the front.

Kamarband—See pages 6 and 7.

Undress Trousers (and Pantaloons when required)—Blue cloth, with two stripes of yellow cloth, each ⅝ inch wide, with a blue light ⅛ inch wide down each side seam.

Knee Boots and Spurs, when required—As described at page 1. Spurs, brass.

Forage-Cap—Blue cloth, with gold embroidered drooping peak, having a yellow silk line ⅛ of an inch wide along the centre; band of 1½-inch lace with ⅛-inch yellow stripe in the centre; gold purl button, and braided figure on the crown.

Forage-Cap for Active Service and Peace Manœuvres—Blue cloth folding cap, 5 inches high, with yellow cloth top, and blue side flaps, 4 inches deep, to turn down when required. Black mohair braid welts on cap and flaps, and at front and back seams. Badge on the left side, the Royal Crest.

Great-Coat and Cape—Blue milled cloth, as described at page 2. White lining; shoulder-straps of the same material as the garment; a small button of departmental pattern at the top. Badges of rank in gold.

HORSE FURNITURE.

Saddle—Hunting; or the saddle described at page 5; plain stirrups, and blue girths.

Saddle-Cloth—Blue cloth, 3 feet long at the bottom, and 2 feet deep, with a stripe of 1-inch lace all round, edged with yellow cloth; at each hind corner, badges of rank in silver.

Wallets—Brown leather, with black bear skin covers, except abroad, where the covers will be of brown leather. G.O. 93, 1880.

Bridle—Brown leather, Cavalry pattern, with blue front and rosettes; gilt bosses on bit and breast-plate, having the Royal Cypher within a garter, and Crown above.

NOTE.—Officers may, at their option, alter their uniform so as at once to conform to the above instructions, or they may wait until articles in possession require to be renewed.

STAFF PAYMASTER.

Uniform and horse furniture (when forage allowance is specially authorized) as laid down for a Chief Paymaster, with the following exceptions:—

Tunic—The braid below the lace on the cuffs plain, without eyes.
Badge of Rank—A crown. After seven years' service as Staff Paymaster, a crown and one star below.
Undress Sword and Pouch Belts—White enamelled leather, with gilt mountings, as in dress.
G.O. 471 1889. *Frock*—Will not be worn, except by officers in financial charge of districts.
Patrol Jacket—As laid down for Chief Paymaster for Active Service and Peace Manœuvres.

3. *PAYMASTER.

As for a Staff Paymaster, with the following exceptions:—

Tunic—The braided eyes on the collar are omitted; the braid above and below the lace on the sleeve is plain, without eyes.
Badges of Rank—Two stars.*
Dress Belts will be worn only on State occasions and at balls.
G.O. 471, 1889. *Scabbard*—Steel.

HORSE FURNITURE.

(*When forage allowance is specially authorized.*)

As for a Staff Paymaster, except that badges of rank on the saddle-cloth are not worn. Spurs, steel.

---

* Paymasters with the honorary rank of Major, and Brevet-Majors appointed from regiments, wear the uniform laid down for Staff Paymasters who have less than seven years' service in that rank.

4. PROBATIONERS.

Officers whilst on probation for the Army Pay Department will, if on full pay, continue to wear the uniform of the corps to which they belong. Officers appointed on probation, from half-pay, who may not be in possession of the uniform of their late corps, will provide themselves with the undress uniform laid down for a Paymaster of the Army Pay Department]

5. OFFICERS APPOINTED ON TEMPORARY AUGMENTATION.

These officers are not required to provide the departmental uniform.

6. PAYMASTERS NOW SERVING WHO MAY NOT BE APPOINTED TO THE ARMY PAY DEPARTMENT BUT WHO ARE LIABLE TO BE COMMISSIONED "AS PAYMASTERS FOR ARMY SERVICES."

The above officers are to wear their present regimental uniform.

V.—VETERINARY DEPARTMENT.

1. PRINCIPAL VETERINARY SURGEON.

Tunic—Blue cloth, the skirt rounded off in front and open behind. Maroon velvet collar and cuffs, ¾-inch lace all round the collar. The cuffs pointed and edged with round-back gold cord, forming a triple Austrian knot, traced with gold Russia braid inside and out, and extending to 11 inches from the bottom of the cuffs; 8 buttons down the front and two at the waist behind; a blue flap on each skirt behind, edged with round-back gold cord, 3 buttons on each flap. The front, collar, and skirts edged with maroon velvet, the skirts lined with black silk Shoulder-straps of twisted round gold cord, universal pattern lined with blue; a small button of departmental pattern at the top. Badges of rank: a Crown and two stars below, in silver.

Lace—Gold, Staff pattern.

Buttons—Gilt burnished. On the button a star; on the star a circle with the words "Army Veterinary Department" and surmounted by a Crown; within the circle the Royal Cypher on a burnished ground.

Dress Trousers, &c.—Blue cloth, $1\frac{3}{4}$-inch gold lace, with $\frac{1}{4}$-inch maroon silk stripe in centre, down the side seams. Wellington boots. Brass spurs.

Pantaloons, &c., for Mounted Duties—Blue cloth, with stripes as on trousers. Knee boots and brass spurs as described at page 1.

Cocked-Hat—As described at page 2, with loop of four-fold gold chain gimp; gold bullion tassels.

Plume—Red cock's feathers, drooping outwards, 8 inches long.

61002/4076 *Sword*—Staff pattern, as described on page 5.

Scabbard—Brass.

Sword-Knot—Gold and crimson cord, with gold acorn.

Sword-Belt—Gold lace, $1\frac{1}{2}$-inches wide, with slings an inch wide; maroon stripe, $\frac{1}{4}$-inch wide, in centre of lace; maroon Morocco leather lining.

Waist-Plate—Gilt rectangular plate, frosted, with burnished rim; on the centre, the Royal Cypher and Crown, encircled with oak-leaves, in silver.

Sabretache—See page 6

Pouch-Belt ~~to be worn at Levées, Balls, and State Occasions~~—Gold lace, 2 inches wide, with a maroon silk stripe in centre, $\frac{1}{2}$ inch wide; gilt chased buckle, tip, and slide. The Royal Cypher with Crown above the tip. Lining similar to that on sword-belt.

Pouch—Maroon velvet collapsing pouch; the flap 6 inches long and $3\frac{1}{2}$ inches deep. The flap ornamented with $\frac{3}{4}$-inch gold lace with $\frac{1}{8}$-inch maroon silk stripe in centre; in the middle of flap, embroidered in gold, an oak-leaf wreath enclosing the Royal Cypher and Crown.

to be worn at Balls &c.

UNDRESS.

61002/4076 *Frock-Coat*—Blue cloth, single breasted. Blue cloth rolling collar and pointed cuffs; the cuffs ornamented with black braid of the same pattern as the cuffs of the tunic, but with a single Austrian knot. The collar, front, and back skirts edged with $\frac{3}{4}$-inch black mohair braid; 5 loops of the same braid on each side in front, with 2 olivets on each loop; 2 olivets at the waist behind, encircled with braided crow's foot; the skirts lined with black. Shoulder-straps with badges of rank as for tunic.

Waistcoat (to be worn with frock coat)—Blue cloth, without collar, edged with gold Russia braid, and fastening with hooks and eyes. A pocket on each side. 61002 4076

Undress Trousers and Pantaloons—Blue cloth, with scarlet cloth stripes, 1¾ inches wide, down each side seam.

Boots and Spurs—As laid down at page 1. Spurs, brass.

Mess-Jacket—Blue cloth, edged all round, including the collar, with ¾-inch gold lace, forming two bull's-eyes at bottom of back seams. Gold Russia braid at bottom of collar. The collar and cuffs of maroon velvet; the cuffs pointed, with ¾-inch lace round the top. Gilt studs down the front on the left side. Hooks and eyes in front, scarlet lining. Shoulder-straps with badges of rank as for tunic.

Mess-Waistcoat—Blue cloth, edged with ¾-inch gold lace, to fasten with hooks and eyes. A row of gilt studs down the front, on the left side. The pockets edged with gold Russia braid, forming a crow's foot at each end.

Instrument Case—Black Morocco leather, of special pattern.

Forage-Cap—Blue cloth, with band of 1¾-inch gold lace, with ¼-inch maroon stripe in centre, gold purl button, and gold braided figure on the crown; the peak, Staff pattern.

Forage-Cap for Active Service and Peace Manœuvres—Blue cloth folding cap, 5 inches high, with maroon velvet top; blue side flaps, 4 inches deep, to turn down when required. Gold French braid welts on cap and flaps, and at front and back seams. Badge on the left side, the Royal Crest.

Cloak and Cape—Blue cloth, lined with scarlet shalloon. Pattern as for Cavalry.

Horse Furniture.

As for the General Staff of the Army.

Veterinary Lieut. Colonel

2. ~~INSPECTING VETERINARY SURGEON.~~

Uniform and horse furniture as for the Principal Veterinary Surgeon, with the following exceptions:—

Badges of Rank—A crown and one star below.
Plume—6 inches long.
Helmet, White—See pages 8 to 10.
Kamarband—See pages 6 and 7.

3. VETERINARY SURGEON (1*st Class*).

Uniform, &c., as for an Inspecting Veterinary Surgeon, with the following exceptions:—

Tunic—½-inch lace at the top and gold Russia braid at the bottom of the collar; a double Austrian knot on sleeves, traced as for an Inspecting Veterinary Surgeon, 9 inches deep.

Badges of Rank—A crown or two stars according to rank.

Patrol-Jacket instead of Frock-Coat—Blue cloth, stand-up collar, rounded in front, ½-inch mohair braid at top and bottom of collar. Inch mohair braid traced with Russia braid all round, up the slips and along the back seam, the Russia braid forming small eyes at each angle. Five loops of inch mohair braid at equal distances down the front on each side, with 2 olivets on each loop. The cuffs pointed, with inch mohair braid, traced with Russia braid forming an Austrian knot at the top, extending to 9 inches from the bottom of the cuff. Pockets in front edged top and bottom with inch mohair braid. Hooks and eyes in front. Black lining, pocket inside left breast Shoulder-straps of the same material as the garment, edged with ½-inch black mohair braid, except at the base; black netted button at the top. Badges of rank in gold.

Forage-Cap—Blue cloth, with band of 1¾ inch gold lace, with ¼ inch maroon stripe in centre, gold purl button and gold braided figure on the crown. No peak.

Sword-Belt—White patent leather, 1½ inches wide, with slings an inch wide, gilt mountings, gilt snake clasp.

Pouch-Belt—White patent leather, 2 inches wide, with gilt chased buckle, tip, and slide; the Royal Cypher above the tip.

Sword and Scabbard—As for Officers of Hussars.

Helmet—As described at pages 3 and 4.

Helmet-Plate—As for Infantry, with A.V.D. on a black ground.

Spurs—Steel.

4. VETERINARY SURGEON.

Uniform, &c., as for a Veterinary Surgeon, 1st Class, with the following exceptions:—

Tunic—A single Austrian knot on sleeves, 7 inches deep.

Badge of Rank—A star.

Instrument Case—Black Morocco leather, of special pattern.

NOTE.—Veterinary Surgeons gazetted to the Household Cavalry wea[r] uniform as laid down at page 49.

5. PROBATIONERS.

Probationers will wear the undress of the Veterinary Depar[t]ment.

IX.—RESERVE OF OFFICERS.

Officers, as officers of the "Reserve of Officers," are not required to provide themselves with any uniform until their services are actually required. They are, however, authorized to wear uniform in accordance with the following regulations :—

(*a*.) OFFICERS RETIRED FROM THE REGULAR FORCES WITH LIABILITY TO SERVE IN CASE OF NATIONAL EMERGENCY.

The uniform of the Regiments in which they last served, but with the letter **R** on the shoulder-straps below the badges of rank

(*b*.) OFFICERS RETIRED FROM THE REGULAR FORCES WITHOUT LIABILITY TO FURTHER SERVICE, BUT WHO HAVE BEEN GRANTED COMMISSIONS AS OFFICERS OF THE "RESERVE OF OFFICERS."

As laid down for officers not holding regimental commissions at page 127, with the following exceptions :—

Shoulder-straps—The word "**RESERVE**" in silver or in silver embroidery is worn below the badges of rank on garments for which gold shoulder-straps are authorized, and in gilt metal or in gold embroidery on garments for which cloth straps are authorized.

Waist-plate—On the outer circle "Reserve of Officers."

(*c*.) OFFICERS OF THE AUXILIARY FORCES WHO MAY BE PERMITTED TO HOLD COMMISSIONS AS OFFICERS OF THE "RESERVE OF OFFICERS" IN ADDITION TO THEIR COMMISSIONS IN THE AUXILIARY FORCES.

The uniform of their corps.

(*d*.) OFFICERS RETIRED FROM THE INDIAN MILITARY FORCES WHO MAY BE GRANTED COMMISSIONS AS OFFICERS OF THE "RESERVE OF OFFICERS."

Uniform as at (*b*.).

(*e*.) OFFICERS RETIRED FROM THE AUXILIARY FORCES WHO MAY BE GRANTED COMMISSIONS AS OFFICERS OF THE "RESERVE OF OFFICERS." G.O. 135. 1892.

The uniform of the corps in which they last served, with the word "**RESERVE**" below the badges of rank on the shoulder straps in silver, or in silver embroidery, on garments for which gold shoulder-straps are authorized, and in gilt metal, or gold embroidery, on garments for which cloth straps are authorized

X.—LIEUTENANTS AND DEPUTY LIEUTENANTS OF COUNTIES.

1. LIEUTENANTS OF COUNTIES.

Tunic—Scarlet cloth, single breasted, 9 buttons in front, 2 behind,
edged with white cloth, body and skirts lined white, collar
123375/3752 cuffs, and slashes, of blue cloth embroidered in silver, slashes
on sleeve 6 inches long, embroidered scarlet slash on skirts,
silver plaited shoulder knot on each shoulder.

Buttons—Plated-sword and baton crossed.

Trousers—Blue cloth, with silver lace $2\frac{1}{2}$ inches wide down the side seams.

Cocked Hat—Black beaver or silk, silver double bullion loop flat gold tassels, 6 gold bullions with crimson bullions under them.

Plume—White swan feathers, drooping outwards 10 inches long, with red feathers under.

Sword—Mameluke, gilt hilt, with device of crossed batons encircled with oak leaves, ivory grip, scimitar blade, brass scabbard with rings.

Sword Knot—Crimson and gold.

Sword Belt—Russia leather $1\frac{1}{2}$ inches wide, with slings and inch wide square plate with wreath encircling V. R. and Crown.

Sash—Gold and crimson net, 6 inches wide, worn diagonally over left shoulder, ends crossed through a runner at the waist; gold fringe tassels, 9 inches long.

Spurs—Gilt.

Embroidery and Lace—For English and Welsh counties oak leaf and acorn pattern.

Scotch, thistle pattern.

Irish, shamrock pattern.

2. DEPUTY LIEUTENANTS OF COUNTIES.

Tunic—Scarlet cloth, single breasted, 9 buttons in front, 2 behind, edged with white cloth, body and skirts lined with white, collar and cuffs of blue cloth embroidered in silver, embroidered scarlet slash on back skirt.

Buttons—Plated, crown and wreath pattern.

Trousers—Blue cloth, with lace $1\frac{3}{4}$ inches wide down the side seam.

Cocked-Hat—Black beaver or silk, loop embroidered in silver, gold bullion tassels.

Plume—White swan, drooping outwards 7 inches long.

Lieutenants of Counties.

Sword—Straight, silver grip, and black scabbard with gilt mountings and rings.

Sword Knot—Gold lace with bullion tassel.

Sword Belt—Silver lace, 1¾ inches wide, lined scarlet leather, with slings an inch wide, waist-plate silver, square, with frosted ground.

English counties with wreath and rose.
Welsh „ „ wreath and Prince of Wales's plume.
Scotch „ „ wreath and thistle.
Irish „ „ wreath and shamrock.
No spurs.

Embroidery and Lace—The English and Welsh counties, oak-leaf and acorn pattern.
Scotch, thistle pattern.
Irish, shamrock pattern.

Uniforms of the old pattern in possession may continue to be worn.

The device or badge peculiar to the several counties may continue to be worn on the collar of the tunic

XI.—MISCELLANEOUS.

I.—CAVALRY DEPOT.

Uniform and horse furniture of the regiments from which the officers are appointed, or of the regiments in which they last served.

II.—OFFICER COMMANDING DISCHARGE DEPOT.

G.O. 60 1895. Uniform as for Officers Commanding Regimental Districts, with band of $1\frac{3}{4}$-inch black oak-leaf lace and badge of Royal Cypher and Crown on the forage-cap, with drooping peak.

III.—OFFICERS ON THE ACTIVE LIST ON HALF-PAY.

Officers on the Active List on half-pay may, until retired or brought back to full pay, wear—

General Officers	The uniform of their rank.
61002 3679 Officers late in command of Regimental Districts	The uniform of the Regimental District from which they retired.
Other Officers, including those who have vacated Staff Appointments	The uniform of the regiments in which they last served.

IV.—OFFICERS OF THE ARMY HOLDING ARMY BUT NOT REGIMENTAL COMMISSIONS, AND OFFICERS OF THE INDIAN ARMY HOLDING HONORARY COMMISSIONS.

Tunic—Scarlet cloth, with blue cloth collar and cuffs. The collar ornamented with $\frac{1}{2}$-inch lace along the top, and gold Russia braid at the bottom; the cuffs pointed, with $\frac{1}{2}$-inch lace round the top, and a tracing of gold Russia braid, $\frac{1}{4}$ inch below the lace, terminating in a crow's foot and eye; 8 buttons in front and 2 at the waist, behind; the skirt closed behind with a plait at each side, and lined with white; the front, collar and skirt plaits edged with white cloth, ¼ inch wide; shoulder straps of twisted round gold cord, universal pattern, lined with scarlet; a small gilt button at the top; badges of rank in silver.

Field Officers have a row of braided eyes below the lace on the collar; 3 bars of lace along the top of the cuff, showing ¼ inch of the facings between the bars; and the braiding on the sleeve is in the form of eyes, below the lace, for Colonels and Lieutenant-Colonels only. The lace on the sleeve extends to 10 inches from the bottom of the cuff.

Captains have no braided eyes on the collar, and only two bars of lace along the top of the cuff; the tracing of the braid below the lace on the sleeves is plain without eyes.

Lieutenants have one bar of lace only on the cuff, extending to 9½ inches from the bottom of the cuff. In other particulars the lace and braiding are the same as those of Captains.

Lace—Gold, two-vellum pattern.

Buttons—Gilt, burnished, with Crown and scalloped edge.

Helmet-Plate—The Royal Arms, in gilt metal. The dimensions of the plate are as follows:

From top of crest to end of scroll, back measurement	3½ inches.
Extreme horizontal width, back measurement	3⅛ inches.

Waist-Plate—Round gilt clasp, with Royal Cypher and Crown on the centre-piece, and the word "Unattached" on the outer circle.

Forage-Cap—As for Infantry of the Line, with Royal Cypher and Crown, embroidered in gold, in front.

All the other articles of uniform as for officers of Infantry of the Line.

V.—GARRISON STAFF.

Tunic—Scarlet cloth of the same pattern as for officers of Infantry of the Line, with blue cloth collar and cuffs.

Lace—Gold, Staff pattern.

Buttons—Gilt, frosted, with burnished laurel round the edge.

Trousers and Spurs, *Pantaloons and Knee-boots for Mounted Duties,* *Cocked-Hat, and Plume,* *Sword, Scabbard, and Sword-Belt*—	As described for General Staff.

Waist-Plate—Gilt rectangular burnished plate, with a device in silver of the Royal Cypher and Crown, with an oak branch at each side, and a scroll below bearing the words "Garrison Staff."

Forage-Cap, Great-Coat and Cape—As for General Staff.

The other articles of uniform, as for officers of Infantry.

HORSE FURNITURE, as for General Staff.

GARRISON QUARTERMASTERS wear black waist-belts, and steel scabbards; pouch-belt and pouch as for Infantry of the Line. Sashes are not worn.

When garrison appointments are of a temporary nature, the Officers holding them may wear their regimental uniforms instead of the uniform described above.

VI.—STAFF CAPTAINS FOR RECRUITING DUTIES.

Uniform of the regiments in which they last served, with the letter **R** on shoulder-straps should they be on the Retired List.

VII.—INDIAN ARMY.

1. STAFF CORPS.

Tunic—Scarlet cloth, with blue cloth collar and cuffs. The collar ornamented with ½-inch lace along the top, and gold Russia braid at the bottom; the cuffs pointed with ½-inch lace round the top, and a tracing of gold Russia braid, ¼-inch below the lace, terminating in a crow's foot and eye; 8 buttons in front and 2 at the waist, behind; the skirt closed behind with a plait at each side, and lined with white; the front, collar, and skirt plaits edged with white cloth ¼ inch wide; shoulder-straps of twisted round gold cord, universal pattern, lined with scarlet; a small button of corps pattern at the top; badges of rank in silver.

Field Officers have a row of braided eyes below the lace on the collar; 3 bars of lace along the top of the cuff, showing ¼ inch of the facings between the bars; and the braiding on the sleeve is in the form of eyes, below the lace, for Colonels and Lieutenant-Colonels only. The lace on the sleeve extends to 10 inches from the bottom of the cuff.

Captains have no braided eyes on the collar, and only two bars of lace along the top of the cuff; the tracing of the braid below the lace on the sleeves is plain without eyes.

Lieutenants have one bar of lace only on the cuff, extending to 9½ inches from the bottom of the cuff. In other particulars the lace and braiding are the same as for Captains.

Lace—Gold, Staff pattern.

Buttons—Gilt, frosted, with edge of special pattern; The Royal and Imperial (V.R. and I.) Cypher in a garter bearing the words "Bengal [Madras or Bombay] Staff Corps," with the Crown above.

Waist-Plate—Round gilt clasp, with the Royal and Imperial (V.R. and I.) Cypher and Crown on the centre-piece, and the words "Bengal [Madras or Bombay] Staff Corps," on the outer circle.

Helmet—As for Infantry of the Line.

Puggaree—White muslin.

Forage-Cap—Blue cloth, with black patent leather drooping peak, ornamented with ½-inch *full* gold embroidery; band of 1½-inch gold lace with ¼-inch crimson silk stripe in the centre; gold purl button and braided figure on the crown.

Mess-Jacket—Scarlet cloth or kerseymere, with blue cloth collar and cuffs; the cuffs pointed; gold braid edging all round, including the top and bottom of the collar; a loop of gold braid at bottom of collar, to fasten across the neck; a row of gilt studs and hooks and eyes down the front; scarlet lining; shoulder-straps with badges of rank as for tunic.

Field Officers have a row of braided eyes on the collar below the upper line of braid. Colonels and Lieutenant-Colonels have three chevrons of braid on each sleeve, ¾ inch apart, the upper extending to 10 inches from the bottom of the cuff, and the lower braid forming a crow's foot and eye; a row of braided eyes below the chevrons, as on the tunic.

Majors have three chevrons on the sleeve, with the crow's foot and eye, but without the row of braided eyes.

Captains have two chevrons, the lower forming a crow's foot and eye, the upper extending to 9 inches only.

Lieutenants have a single chevron of braid extending to 8 inches from the bottom of the cuff, and a crows' foot and eye below it.

Mess-Waistcoat—Blue cloth or kerseymere, gold braid edging round the top, down the front, and along the bottom to the side seams. The pockets edged with braid, forming crow's feet and eyes. A row of gilt studs and hooks and eyes down the front.

All the other articles of uniform as for officers of Infantry of the Line.

Horse Furniture.

As for Infantry of the Line.

Officers serving in Departments.

Officers serving in Departments will wear the uniform of their Departments; but with the Staff Corps buttons, sword-belt, and waist-plate described above.

Officers serving with Regiments.

Officers serving with Regiments will wear the regimental uniforms.

2. Officers on the Active List on Half-pay, Indian Army.

Officers on the Active List on half-pay may, until retired, or brought back to full-pay, wear—

General Officers	The uniform of their rank.
Staff Officers on completion of tenure of appointment .... Other officers	The uniform of the Regiments in which they last served, or that for Officers holding honorary commissions. See page 126.

3. Retired Officers, Indian Army.

General Officers wear the uniform of their rank, but with a plain gold sash 2¼ inches wide, without crimson stripes. The sash will be worn round the waist.

Officers who have retired on full-pay, officers who have retired with half-pay or with pensions, officers who have commuted pensions, officers who are Companions of the Bath, and officers who have left the Army, but whose names are allowed to remain in the Army List, may wear the uniform of the Regiments in which they last served, or that for Unattached Officers, with the letter **R** on the shoulder-straps below the badges of rank.

VIII.—PROVOST MARSHAL.

Tunic—Scarlet cloth, of the same pattern as for officers of Infantry of the Line, with blue cloth collar and cuffs; and lace, braiding, and badges, according to Army rank.

Lace—Gold, Staff pattern.

Buttons—Gilt, frosted, with Royal Cypher and Crown.

Dress Trousers,
 Cocked-Hat— } As for General Staff.

Plume—Black swan feathers, drooping outwards, 5 inches long, with white swan feathers under them.

Sword, Sword-Knot, and Scabbard,
 Sword-Belt and Waist-Plate,
 Shoulder-Belt and Binocular Case,
 Spurs, Undress Trousers,
 Pantaloons and Knee Boots— } As for General Staff.

Patrol Jacket—As described at page 4.

Forage-Cap,
 Great-Coat and Cape,
 Horse Furniture— } As for General Staff.

IX.—MILITARY MOUNTED POLICE.

As for a Provost Marshal, with the following exception:—

Tunic—Blue cloth, with scarlet edgings and scarlet collar and cuffs

X.—GOVERNORS OF MILITARY PRISONS.

As for Infantry of the Line, with the following exceptions:—

Tunic—Blue cloth, with scarlet cloth collar and cuffs. Badges of rank according to the rank last held in the Army.
Lace—Gold, Staff pattern.
Buttons—Gilt, frosted, with Royal Cypher and Crown.
Helmet—Blue cloth, with gilt plate representing the Royal Arms, as laid down at page 3 and 4. At stations abroad the white helmet will be worn. See pages 8 to 10.
Waist-Plate—Round gilt clasp, with the Royal Cypher and Crown on the centre-piece.
Scabbard—Brass or steel, according to rank last held in the Army.
Forage-Cap—As for Infantry; black oak-leaf lace; no badge.
Mess-Jacket—Blue cloth, with scarlet collar and cuffs.
Mess-Waistcoat—Scarlet, in other respects as for the cloth mess-waistcoats of Infantry of the Line.
Great-Coat and Cape—Blue cloth.

This uniform will also be worn by the Governor of the Provost prison at Aldershot.

XI.—STAFF OFFICERS OF PENSIONERS.

Tunic—Blue cloth, double-breasted; with scarlet cloth collar, lappels, and cuffs: the collar edged round the top with ½-inch lace; the lappels made to be worn turned back, or buttoned over; the cuffs round, 3 inches deep, with ½-inch lace round the top. A blue flap on each sleeve, 6 inches long and 2¼ inches wide, with 3 loops and buttons; and a similar flap on each skirt-plait, 10 inches long, with 3 loops and buttons, the top loops at the waist; 2 rows of buttons down the front, 9 in each row, the rows 8 inches apart at the top, and 4 inches at the waist; the skirt lined with black. Shoulder-straps of twisted round gold cord, universal pattern, lined with blue, a small button at the top. Badges of rank in silver.

Field Officers are further distinguished by lace round the bottom of the collar, a second bar of lace round the cuff, and an edging of lace to the flaps on the sleeves and skirts and down the back skirts.

Lace—Gold, Staff pattern.
Buttons—Gilt, frosted, with burnished laurel round the edge.

Trousers—Blue cloth, with scarlet stripes, $1\frac{3}{4}$ inches wide, down the side seams.

Cocked-Hat—As for General Staff, with plume of red and white upright swan feathers, 5 inches long.

Sword, Sword-Knot, and Sword-Belt—As for General Staff.

Waist-Plate—As for Aides-de-Camp to General Officers.

Sash—Crimson silk net, as for Infantry.

Scabbard and Spurs—For Field Officers, brass; for Captains, steel.

Patrol-Jacket—As described at page 4. Shoulder-straps of the same material as the garment, edged with $\frac{1}{2}$-inch black mohair braid, except at the base; black netted button at the top Badges of rank in gold.

Forage-Cap,
Great-Coat and Cape, } As for General Staff.
HORSE FURNITURE—

It is optional with Staff Officers of Pensioners to wear, on State occasions and at balls, trousers with gold lace, as for General Staff, sword-knot as for General Staff, and sash of gold and crimson net as for Infantry.

XII.—INSPECTORS AND SUB-INSPECTORS OF ARMY SCHOOLS.

Tunic—Of the same pattern as for Lieutenants of Infantry of the Line, but of blue cloth, with scarlet cloth collar, cuffs, and edging. Shoulder-straps of twisted round gold cord, universal pattern, lined with blue; a small button at the top. Badges of rank in silver.

Lace—Gold, rose pattern.

Buttons—Gilt, burnished, with a crown in the centre.

61002/4188 *Trousers*—Blue cloth with two stripes of scarlet cloth, each $\frac{1}{4}$-inch wide, with light blue cloth between, $\frac{1}{8}$-inch wide.

Helmet—As for Infantry; gilt plate with "V.R." in silver on light blue ground.

Sword, Sword-Knot, and Scabbard—As for Infantry of the Line.

Sword-Belt and Waist-Plate—As for Infantry of the Line, but of black Morocco leather, the plate bearing only a crown in the centre.

Patrol-Jacket—As described at page 4.

Forage-Cap—Blue cloth with gold embroidered staff peak, and band of $1\frac{1}{2}$-inch gold lace with light blue stripe in centre, $\frac{1}{8}$-inch wide.

Mess-Jacket—As for Infantry of the Line, but of blue cloth, with scarlet cloth collar, cuffs and edging.

Great-Coat and Cape—As for Infantry of the Line, only of blue milled cloth with black lining.

Mess-Waistcoat—As for Infantry of the Line.

XIII.—OFFICERS OF THE ROYAL MILITARY COLLEGE, SANDHURST.

Governor.

The uniform and horse furniture of his rank as a General Officer.

Assistant Commandant and Secretary.

Tunic—Scarlet cloth of the same pattern as for an officer of Infantry of the Line of corresponding rank, with blue cloth collar and cuffs.
Lace—Gold, two-vellum pattern.
Buttons—Gilt, frosted, with burnished laurel round the edge.
Cocked-Hat—As described at page 2; with loop of ½-inch lace; tassels of gold and crimson bullions.
Plume—Red and white swan feathers, drooping outwards, 6 inches long.

The other articles as for Infantry of the Line. On the centre-piece of waist-plate, the Royal Cypher and Crown.

Horse Furniture—As for Infantry.

Quartermaster.

Uniform, &c., as for the Commandant and Secretary, with the following exceptions :—
Helmet—As for Infantry of the Line.
Helmet-Plate—In gilt metal a star surmounted by the crown; on the star a laurel wreath; within the wreath a garter pierced "*Nec aspera terrent*," the ground of blue enamel. In the centre of the garter on a ground of red enamel, the Royal Cypher in gilt metal.

Riding-Master.

Uniform and horse furniture of the Regiment from which appointed, or of the Regiment in which he last served.

XIV.—STAFF COLLEGE.

Commandant.—If a General Officer, the uniform and horse furniture of his rank. If under the rank of General Officer, the uniform and horse furniture as for a Colonel on the Staff.

Military Professors and Instructors at the Royal Military College and Military Professors at the Staff College—The uniform they are authorized to wear, irrespective of their appointments as Professors or Instructors.

XV.—ROYAL MILITARY ACADEMY, WOOLWICH.

Commandant and Secretary.

Uniform and horse furniture as for a Regimental Colonel on the Staff of the Royal Artillery or Royal Engineers, according to the corps from which the officer is appointed.

Adjutant and Quartermaster.

The regimental uniform of his rank.

XVI.—OFFICERS OF THE SCHOOL OF MUSKETRY

Commandant.

If a General Officer, the uniform and horse furniture of his rank; if a Field Officer, those of a Deputy Adjutant-General.

Chief Instructor.

Uniform, &c., as for Assistant Adjutant-General.

Deputy Assistant Adjutant-General.

Uniform, &c., as for the same appointment on the General Staff.

Captain Instructor, Lieutenant - Instructor.

61002/3468 Regimental uniform.

Quartermaster and Acting Adjutant.

61002/4210 As laid down for Garrison Quartermasters* at page 128.

* Uniform in possession may be worn until required to be replaced.

XVII.—ROYAL MILITARY SCHOOL OF MUSIC.

Commandant.

The uniform, &c., are the same as those of an Assistant Adjutant-General.

Quartermaster and Adjutant.

As laid down for Garrison Quartermasters at page 128.

Director of Music.

As laid down for Garrison Quartermaster on page 128. 61002/4159

XVIII.—CORPS OF ARMOURERS.

Quartermaster.

As laid down for Garrison Quartermasters with the following exception:— 49/Armourers/1831

Waist-Plate—Gilt burnished rectangular plate; in the centre, the Royal Cypher and Crown encircled with oak-leaves in silver. A scroll on the bottom of the wreath inscribed "*Dieu et mon droit.*"

XIX.—OFFICERS OF THE ROYAL HOSPITALS AT CHELSEA AND KILMAINHAM.

Tunic—Blue cloth; the skirt 12 inches deep for an officer 5 feet 9 inches in height, with a proportionate variation for any difference in height. Plain scarlet cloth collar and cuffs, without badges of rank on the collar. A blue flap on each sleeve, 6 inches long and $2\frac{1}{2}$ inches wide, with 3 small buttons; and a similar flap, 9 inches long, with 2 buttons, on each skirt behind; 8 buttons down the front, and 2 at the waist behind; a gold cord loop, with a small button, on each shoulder. The front, flaps, and back skirts edged with scarlet cloth, $\frac{1}{8}$ inch wide, and the skirts lined with black.

Lace—Gold, two-vellum pattern.

Buttons—Windsor pattern.

Trousers—Blue cloth, with scarlet stripes, $1\frac{3}{4}$-inches wide, down the side seams.

Cocked-Hat—As described at page 2, with loop of ½-inch lace, tassels, gold purl netted head, 7 gold bullions, with 5 crimson bullions under them.

Plume—White swan feathers, drooping outwards, 5 inches long.

Sword, Scabbard, Sword-Knot, Sword-Belt, Crimson Sash - - - - - } As for Infantry.
ON STATE OCCASIONS—*Dress Trousers, Gold and Crimson Sword-Belt, Sword-Knot, and Sash* - - - - - } As for Infantry.

Waist-Plate—Round gilt clasp, with Royal Cypher and Crown on the centre-piece.

Forage-Cap—As for General Staff, but with band of two-vellum pattern.

Great-Coat and Cape—Blue cloth, as described at page 2, lined with scarlet ratinett, the collar lined with black velvet.

GENERAL OFFICERS wear the trousers, cocked-hat and plume, sword and belt, sword-knot, spurs, sash, and forage-cap of their rank.

61002/3752 LIEUTENANT-GOVERNOR AND SECRETARY, when below the rank of a General Officer, will wear the uniform of a Colonel on the Staff.

CAPTAINS WHO ARE BREVET FIELD OFFICERS may, when not on duty, wear brass scabbards and spurs.

The MEDICAL OFFICERS may wear the tunic described above, with the other articles of uniform as for officers of the Medical Staff.

XX.—OFFICERS OF THE ROYAL MILITARY ASYLUM, CHELSEA.

Tunic—Scarlet cloth, of the same pattern as for officers of Infantry of the Line of their respective ranks, with blue cloth collar and cuffs. Shoulder-straps of twisted round gold cord, universal pattern, lined with scarlet; small button at the top. Badges of rank in silver.

Lace—Gold, two-vellum pattern.

Buttons—Gilt, flat, with Royal Cypher and Crown.

Dress Trousers, Cocked-Hat— } As for General Staff.

Plume—Red and white upright swan feathers, 5 inches long.

Sword, Sword-Knot, and Scabbard, Sword-Belt, and Waist-Plate } As for General Staff, but without embroidery on the sword-belt.

Sashes—Of the same patterns as for Infantry officers; on State occasions, gold and crimson; at other times, crimson silk.

Patrol-Jacket—As described at page 4.
Undress Trousers—As for General Staff.
Forage-Cap—As for "Royal" regiments of Infantry, with band of scarlet cloth, and Royal Cypher and Crown, embroidered in gold, in front.
Great-Coat and Cape—As for Infantry officers.

The QUARTERMASTER does not wear the sash.

XXI.—OFFICERS OF THE ROYAL HIBERNIAN MILITARY SCHOOL, DUBLIN.

The uniform, &c., are the same as those of the officers of the Royal Military Asylum, Chelsea.

XXII.—MILITARY KNIGHTS OF WINDSOR.

FULL DRESS.

Dress-Coat—Scarlet cloth, double-breasted; blue cloth Prussian collar; blue cloth cuffs, turnbacks and skirt linings, 10 button-holes up the front at regular distances; 2 rows of large buttons; square end to collar, with 2 cord holes and 2 small buttons on each side; scarlet flap on each skirt, with 4 cord holes and 4 large buttons on each flap, 2 buttons at the waist behind; scarlet flap on each cuff, with 4 small buttons and button-holes, each skirt ornamented at its termination with an embroidered St. George's cross.
Buttons—Gilt half dome, Garter Star, and Crown over.
Epaulettes—Gold bullion, gilt crescents, St. George's shield with badges of rank above.
Sash—Crimson silk net, bullion tassels. Worn round the waist.
Sword—Crossed hilt; gilt mountings.
Scabbard—Black leather.
Sword-Belt—Black enamelled leather, with frog; gilt clasp, with Garter Star and Crown over, the whole encircled by a laurel wreath.
Cocked-Hat—Black silk, gold lace loop and gilt button, 2 bullion tassels.
Plume—Upright feather, 8½ inches long; the bottom scarlet, the top white.
Trousers—Blue cloth (no stripes).

UNDRESS.

Frock-Coat—Blue cloth, single-breasted; 8 buttons up the front at regular intervals; short side edges, 2 buttons on each skirt, 2 small buttons on cuffs; Prussian collar.
Scales—Gilt crescents with embroidered St. George's cross; V.R. and badges of rank above.
Forage-Cap—Blue cloth, scarlet cloth band, scarlet piping round top of crown; plain black patent leather peak drooping; embroidered St. George's cross or band.
Trousers—As for Dress.
Cloak—Blue cloth, lined with scarlet; deep cape, ined with black, black velvet collar, gilt rose clasp, and 5 gilt buttons up the front.

XXIII.—RETIRED OFFICERS.*

Officers on the Retired List,† *i.e.*, the officers included in the classes specified below, whose names are retained in the Army List, may wear the uniform of the regiments in which they last served, or that for officers not holding regimental commissions (see page 127), but with the letter **R** on the shoulder-straps below the badges of rank.

a. Officers retired on retired pay, or with gratuity, and who are liable for service, in case of national emergency, with the "Reserve of Officers."

b. Officers retired after 15 years' service, who are duly recommended to retain their rank.

c. Officers compulsorily retired on account of age or continuous non-employment.

d. Officers retired on full-pay.

e. Field Officers who have commuted pensions.

f. Officers who are Companions of the Bath.

General Officers will wear the uniform of their rank, with a plain gold sash $2\frac{1}{4}$ inches wide, without crimson stripes.

The sash will be worn round the waist.

* For retired officers, Indian Army, see page 130.

† Officers retired from the Household Cavalry with permission to wear uniform, will not wear breeches and jack boots, but will wear overalls.

61002 / 3701

MILITIA.

Officers on retirement after 15 years' commissioned service, including Army service, who are duly recommended to retain their rank, may wear the uniform of the Militia regiments or battalions in which they last served, with the addition of the letters **MR** on the shoulder-straps below the badges of rank.

DEPARTMENTS.

a. Officers who have retired, or who may retire, with the honorary or corresponding rank of Field Officer. *b.* Officers retired after 15 years' service, who are duly recommended to retain their rank. *c.* Officers compulsorily retired on account of age. *d.* Officers retired on full pay. *e.* Officers with the honorary or corresponding rank of Field Officer, who have commuted pensions. *f.* Officers who are Companions of the Bath.	May wear the uniforms of their respective departments, but with the letter **R** or the letters **MR** below the badges of rank.

The above regulations are not retrospective; *i.e.*, they do not apply to officers who retired prior to the 1st July, 1881. These officers can only be allowed to wear uniform if the regulations existing at the time of their retirement permitted it.

Whenever retired officers require to renew their uniforms, the latest approved patterns will be followed.

The letters **R** and **MR** will be in silver on gold shoulder-straps: in gold on cloth shoulder-straps. In the case of officers retired from Rifles, the letters will be in bronze.

XII.—BADGES OF TERRITORIAL REGIMENTS.

I. Deviations from the universal patterns of Helmet-Plate and Waist-Plate are noted in the annexed Table.
II. The badges authorized to be worn on the collars of Tunics may be worn on the collars of Shell-Jackets.

Regiment.	On Buttons.	On Collar of Tunic.	On Helmet-Plates; Ornaments for Racoon-Skin Caps, and Highland Head-dress.	On the Waist-Plate.	On the round Forage Cap.	On Forage Cap for Active Service and Peace Manœuvres.
The Royal Scots (Lothian Regiment).	The badge of the Order of the Thistle: below the badge, "The Royal Scots."	The Thistle, in gold embroidery, on a blue cloth ground.	The Garter and universal wreath are omitted. The Star of the Order of the Thistle, in gilt metal. On the star, a silver circle, pierced *Nemo me impune lacessit*; the ground of green enamel. Within the circle, on a convex ground of green enamel, the Thistle, in silver. On the universal scroll "The Royal Scots."	In silver, on a frosted gilt centre, St. Andrew with Cross. On the circle, "The Royal Scots Regiment."	In silver, the Star of the Order of the Thistle; in gilt metal on the Star, a raised circle inscribed *Nemo me impune lacessit*. Within the circle, on a ground of green enamel, the Thistle in gilt metal.	As for the round forage cap.

The Queen's (Royal West Surrey Regiment).	Within a circle surmounted by the Crown, the Paschal Lamb. On the circle "The Royal West Surrey Regiment." Below the circle, a scroll inscribed "The Queen's."	The Paschal Lamb, in frosted gilt metal	On a scarlet velvet ground, the Paschal Lamb in silver. On the universal scroll "The Royal West Surrey Regiment."	On a frosted gilt centre, the Paschal Lamb in silver. On the circle, *Pristinæ virtutis memor.*	In gold embroidery, on a blue cloth ground, the Paschal Lamb: the flag in silver with crimson cross.	In gilt metal, the Garter, with motto, surmounted by the Crown. Badge and ground as for helmet-plate.
The Buffs (East Kent Regiment).	A circle surmounted by the Crown. On the circle "The East Kent Regt." "The Buffs"; within, the Dragon; below, on a scroll, *Veteri frondescit honore.*	In silver, the White Horse of Kent on a gilt scroll, inscribed "Invicta."	On a black velvet ground, the Dragon, in silver. On the universal scroll, "The East Kent Regiment."	On a frosted gilt centre, the Dragon, in silver. On the circle "The East Kent Regt. The Buffs.'	The Dragon, in gold embroidery.	In gilt metal, the Garter, with motto, surmounted by the Crown. Badge and ground as for helmet-plate.
The King's Own (Royal Lancaster Regiment).	The Lion of England with Crown above and Rose below. On circle "The King's Own Royal Lancaster Regt."	The Lion, in silver.	In silver, on a scarlet velvet ground, the Lion of England. On the universal scroll "Royal Lancaster Regt."	In silver, on a frosted gilt centre, the Lion. Below the Lion, in gilt metal and red enamel, the Rose of Lancaster. On the circle, "The King's Own Royal Lancaster Regt."	In gold embroidery, the Lion; below the Lion, the Rose of Lancaster.	In gilt metal, the Garter, with motto, surmounted by the Crown. Badge and ground as for helmet-plate.
The Northumberland Fusiliers.	St. George and the Dragon within a Garter inscribed *Quo fata vocant.*	A grenade, in gold embroidery, with St. George and the Dragon in silver, on the ball.	A grenade, in gilt metal. On the ball, a Garter inscribed *Quo fata vocant.* Within the Garter—St. George and the Dragon.	In silver, on a frosted gilt centre, St. George and the Dragon, with scroll above inscribed *Quo fata vocant.* On the circle "Northumberland Fusiliers."	A grenade, in gold embroidery, with St. George and the Dragon, in silver, on the ball.	As for Racoon-skin cap, but smaller.

BADGES OF TERRITORIAL REGIMENTS—*continued.*

Regiment.	On Buttons.	On Collar of Tunic.	On Helmet-Plates; Ornaments for Racoon-skin Caps, and Highland Head-dress.	On the Waist-Plate.	On the round Forage Cap.	On Forage Cap for Active Service and Peace Manœuvres.
The Royal Warwickshire Regiment.	An antelope with collar and chain within a circle, inscribed "The Royal Warwickshire Regiment." The circle surmounted by the Crown.	In silver, the Bear and Ragged Staff: the Bear muzzled and chained.	On a black velvet ground, the Antelope, in silver, with gilt collar and chain. On the universal scroll "The Royal Warwickshire Regiment."	The Antelope, in silver, with gilt collar and chain, on a frosted gilt centre. On the circle—"The Royal Warwickshire."	In gilt metal, the Garter, with motto *Honi soit qui mal y pense*, within a wreath of laurel, in gold embroidery. The Garter surmounted by the Crown in gold embroidery. Within the Garter, on a blue enamelled ground, the Antelope in silver, with gilt collar and chain.	In gilt metal, the Garter, with motto, surmounted by the Crown. Badge and ground as for helmet-plate.
The Royal Fusiliers City of London Regiment.)	The Garter inscribed *Honi soit qui mal y pense*; on the Garter at the top, the Crown: within, the Rose.	A grenade, in gold embroidery, with the White Rose, in silver, on the ball.	In gilt metal, a grenade; on the ball, the Garter surmounted by the Crown. The Garter pierced with the motto; the ground of blue enamel. Within the Garter, the Rose; below the Garter, in silver, the White Horse.	In silver, on a frosted gilt centre, the White Rose with Crown above. On the circle "The Royal Fusiliers."	A grenade, in gold embroidery, with a crown on the flame; recessed in the ball, the garter pierced with the motto; the ground of blue enamel. The White Rose, in silver, in the centre of the Garter.	As for Racoon-skin cap, but smaller; the Rose in silver.

The King's (Liverpool Regiment).	A circle surmounted by the Crown within a laurel wreath: the circle inscribed "The Liverpool Regiment:' within the circle, the White Horse, with a scroll above inscribed *Nec aspera terrent*. Scroll on wreath at the bottom inscribed "The King's."	The Rose of Lancaster, in gilt metal and red enamel. A gilt scroll below, detached from the Rose, and inscribed "King's" in old English capitals.	In silver, on a crimson velvet ground, the White Horse with scroll above inscribed in old English capitals, *Nec aspera terrent*. On the universal scroll "The Liverpool Regiment."	In silver, on a frosted gilt centre, the White Horse, with a scroll above, inscribed in old English capitals, *Nec aspera terrent*. On the circle, "The King's—The Liverpool Regt."	In gilt metal, the Garter pierced with the motto *Honi soit qui mal y pense*; the ground of blue velvet. Within the Garter, on a crimson velvet raised ground, the White Horse, in silver, and a gilt scroll below, inscribed "King's" in old English capitals.	In gilt metal, the Garter, with motto, surmounted by the Crown. Badge and ground as for helmet-plate.
The Norfolk Regiment.	On the circle "The Norfolk Regiment"; within the circle the figure of Britannia holding an olive branch in the right hand; the trident rests against the left shoulder.	The figure of Britannia, in gilt metal.	The figure of Britannia, in silver, on a black velvet ground. On the universal scroll "The Norfolk Regiment."	The figure of Britannia, with Castle of Norwich below, in silver, on a frosted gilt centre. On the circle, "The Norfolk Regiment."	The figure of Britannia, in gold embroidery; the shield embroidered in gold and silk.	In gilt metal, the Garter, with motto, surmounted by the Crown. Badge and ground as for helmet-plate.
The Lincolnshire Regiment.	Within a laurel wreath, a circle surmounted by the Crown. On the circle "The Lincolnshire Regt."; within, the Sphinx over Egypt.	On a silver eight-pointed star, a circle in gilt metal, inscribed "Lincolnshire Regiment." Within the circle, on a ground of blue velvet, the Sphinx over Egypt, in silver.	In silver, on a black velvet ground, the Sphinx over Egypt. On the universal scroll "The Lincolnshire Regt."	In silver, on a frosted gilt centre, the Sphinx over Egypt. On the circle "The Lincolnshire Regiment."	In gilt metal, on a silver eight-pointed star, a circle inscribed "Lincolnshire Regiment." Within the circle, on a raised ground of blue velvet, the Sphinx over Egypt, in silver.	As for the round forage cap.

BADGES OF TERRITORIAL REGIMENTS—*continued.*

Regiment.	On Buttons.	On Collar of Tunic.	On Helmet-Plates; Ornaments for Racoon-skin Caps and Highland Head-dress.	On the Waist-Plate.	On the round Forage Cap.	On Forage Cap for Active Service and Peace Manœuvres.
The Devonshire Regiment.	On an eight-pointed star a circle surmounted by the Crown. On the circle "The Devonshire Regt.," within, the Castle of Exeter.	In gilt metal, on a silver eight-pointed star, a circle surmounted by the Crown. On the circle "The Devonshire Regiment"; within, in silver, the Castle of Exeter with scroll inscribed *Semper fidelis*, on a ground of blue velvet.	The Castle of Exeter, with scroll inscribed *Semper fidelis*, in silver, on a black velvet ground. On the universal scroll "The Devonshire Regt."	As for helmet plate on a frosted gilt centre. On the circle "The Devonshire Regiment."	As for collar badge, except that the circle is pierced with the designation of the Regiment, the ground is of blue velvet, and the cap of the Crown is of crimson velvet.	In gilt metal, the Garter, with motto, surmounted by the Crown. Badge and ground as for helmet-plate.
The Suffolk Regiment.	Within a laurel wreath, the Castle and Key with scroll above inscribed "Gibraltar," and above the scroll, the Crown. Below the Castle and Key, two scrolls, the upper inscribed *Montis Insignia Calpe*, the lower "The Suffolk Regt."	The Castle and Key, in gold embroidery.	In silver, on a black velvet ground, the Castle and Key, with scroll above inscribed "Gibraltar," and scroll below inscribed *Montis Insignia Calpe*. On the universal scroll "The Suffolk Regiment."	In silver, on a frosted gilt centre, the Castle and Key with scroll above inscribed "Gibraltar," and scroll below inscribed *Montis insignia Calpe*. On the circle "The Suffolk Regiment."	In gold embroidery, on a raised blue cloth ground, the Castle and Key within a wreath of laurel; above the Castle the Crown; below, a scroll in blue velvet inscribed "Gib - raltar."	In silver, an oak-leaf wreath, within the wreath a circle surmounted by the Crown. On the circle *Montis Insignia Calpe*. Within the circle, the Castle and Key with scroll above, inscribed "Gibraltar."

The Prince Albert's (Somersetshire Light Infantry).	Within a laurel wreath, a circle surmounted by a mural crown. On the circle, "The Prince Albert's"; within, a bugle with strings.	In gold and silver embroidery, on a ground of green cloth, a bugle with strings, surmounted by a mural crown embroidered in silver; above the crown, in gold embroidery, a scroll inscribed "Jellalabad."	In silver, on a black velvet ground, a bugle with strings, surmounted by a mural crown with scroll above inscribed "Jellalabad"; the Sphinx over Egypt within the strings of the bugle. On the universal scroll, "Somersetshire Light Infantry."	On a frosted gilt centre, badge as for helmet-plate. On the circle, "The Prince Albert's" with two transverse twigs of laurel in the lower bend.	On a green cloth ground, in gold and silver embroidery, a bugle; within the strings on a convex surface, the Cypher of H. R. H. the late Prince Consort, in gilt metal. Above the bugle, embroidered in silver, a mural crown, surmounted by a gold embroidered scroll, inscribed "Jellalabad."	In gilt metal, the Garter, with motto, surmounted by the Crown. Badge and ground as for helmet-plate.
The Prince of Wales's Own (West Yorkshire Regiment).	The Tiger, within a circle, inscribed at the top, "India," and at the bottom, "Waterloo." Outside the circle, "Prince of Wales's Own, West Yorkshire."	The Prince of Wales's Plume, in gold and silver embroidery.	In silver, on a black velvet ground, the White Horse, with motto *Nec aspera terrent* on a scroll above. On the universal scroll "The West Yorkshire Regiment."	The Royal Tiger, in silver, on a frosted gilt centre. On the circle "West Yorkshire Regiment."	On a blue cloth ground, the White Horse in silver; above, the Prince of Wales's Plume, in gold and silver embroidery; below, a gold embroidered scroll, inscribed "West Yorkshire."	In gilt metal, a circle inscribed "Prince of Wales's Own, West Yorkshire"; within the circle, the White Horse in silver; and on a gilt scroll above, the motto, *Nec aspera terrent.* On and above the circle, the Prince of Wales's Plume in gilt and silver metal.
The East Yorkshire Regiment.	A laurel wreath on an eight-pointed star. The White Rose, in silver, within the wreath	In gilt metal, an eight-pointed star; on the star a laurel wreath; within the wreath, on a ground of black enamel, the White Rose, in silver.	In gilt metal, on a ground of black enamel, a laurel wreath on an eight-pointed star. Within the wreath the White Rose, in silver. On the universal scroll, "The East York shire Regt."	On a frosted gilt centre, badge as for helmet-plate. On the circle, "The East-Yorkshire Regiment."	In gilt metal, star etc., as for helmet-plate, but larger.	In gilt metal, the Garter, with motto, surmounted by the Crown. Badge and ground as for helmet-plate.

BADGES OF TERRITORIAL REGIMENTS—*continued.*

Regiment.	On Buttons.	On Collar of Tunic.	On Helmet-Plates; Ornaments for Racoon-skin Caps and Highland Head-dress.	On the Waist-Plate.	On the round Forage Cap.	On Forage Cap for Active Service and Peace Manœuvres.
The Bedfordshire Regiment.	On an eight-pointed star, a Maltese cross. On the cross, a circle inscribed "Bedfordshire." Within the circle, a Hart crossing a ford.	In dead gilt metal, a Hart crossing a ford; the water in silver. On a scroll below "Bedfordshire."	In silver, on a raised ground of blue enamel, an eight pointed star; on the star, in gilt metal, a Maltese cross. Within a gilt circle on the cross, a Hart, in silver, crossing a ford. On the universal scroll, "The Bedfordshire Regt."	On a frosted gilt centre, badge as for helmet-plate, except that the Garter, inscribed *Honi soit qui mal y pense*, is substituted for the gilt circle on the centre of the cross. On the circle "Bedfordshire Regiment."	In gilt metal, a Maltese cross on an eight-pointed star. On the cross, the Garter, with motto; within the Garter, on a raised ground of blue enamel, the Hart crossing a ford, in silver. A silver scroll inscribed "Bedfordshire" below the Garter.	In gilt metal, the Garter, with motto, surmounted by the Crown. Badge and ground as for helmet-plate.
The Leicestershire Regiment.	Within a laurel wreath, the Royal Tiger, with scroll above, inscribed "Hindoostan," and scroll below, inscribed "Leicestershire."	The Royal Tiger in silver, within a wreath in gilt metal.	On a black velvet ground, the Royal Tiger in silver, with silver scroll above, inscribed "Hindoostan." On the universal scroll, "Leicestershire Regiment."	In silver, on a frosted gilt centre, the Royal Tiger, with the Irish Harp below, and scroll above inscribed "Hindoostan." On the circle "Leicestershire Regiment."	An eight-pointed star in gilt metal: on the star, in silver, the Royal Tiger, with the Harp below. Above the Tiger, a scroll inscribed "Hindoostan" below, and at either side of the Harp, a scroll inscribed "Leicestershire Regiment."	In gilt metal, the Garter, with motto, surmounted by the Crown Badge and ground as for helmet plate.

The Royal Irish Regiment.	Within a shamrock wreath, a circle inscribed *Virtutis Namurcensis Premium*. Within the circle, the Harp: the circle surmounted by the Crown.	In silver, an Escocheon of the Arms of Nassau, with a silver scroll below, inscribed *Virtutis Namurcensis Premium*.	In silver, on a scarlet ground, the Harp and Crown within a wreath of shamrock. On the universal scroll "The Royal Irish."	On a frosted gilt centre, badge as for helmet-plate. On the circle "The Royal Irish Regiment.'	The Harp and Crown, in gold embroidery, on a blue cloth ground.	In gilt metal, the Garter, with motto, surmounted by the Crown. Badge and ground as for helmet-plate.
The Princess of Wales's Own (Yorkshire Regiment).	The Cypher of H.R.H. the Princess of Wales combined with a cross, and surmounted by the Coronet of the Princess. On the cross the figures 1875. On scroll below, "The Princess of Wales's Own."	The Cypher of H.R.H. the Princess of Wales, combined with a cross. The Cypher and Coronet in gold embroidery: the cross in silver.	On a black velvet ground, the Cypher of H.R.H. the Princess of Wales combined with a cross, and surmounted by the Coronet of the Princess. On the centre of the cross, the figures 1875. The Cypher and Coronet in gilt metal; the cross in silver. On the universal scroll "The Yorkshire Regiment."	On a frosted gilt centre, badge as for helmet-plate. On the circle "The Yorkshire Regiment.'	As for helmet-plate, but in embroidery; the Princess's Cypher, the Coronet, and the figures 1875, in gold embroidery; the cross in silver embroidery, edged with crimson. Blue cloth ground.	In gilt metal, the Garter, with motto, surmounted by the Crown. Badge and ground as for helmet-plate.
The Lancashire Fusiliers.	Within a wreath of laurel, the Sphinx over Egypt, with the Crown above.	A grenade, in gold embroidery.	A grenade in gilt metal; on the ball, in silver, the Sphinx over Egypt within a laurel wreath.	On a frosted gilt centre, badge as for the grenade on Racoon-skin cap, but smaller. On the circle "The Lancashire Fusiliers."	A grenade in gold embroidery, with badge in silver, as for waist plate.	A grenade in gilt metal, as for Racoon-skin cap, but smaller. Badge on the ball as for waist-plate.

BADGES OF TERRITORIAL REGIMENTS—*continued.*

Regiment.	On Buttons.	On Collar of Tunic.	On Helmet-Plates: Ornaments for Racoon-skin Caps and Highland Head-dress.	On the Waist-Plate.	On the round Forage Cap.	On Forage Cap for Active Service and Peace Manœuvres.
The Royal Scots Fusiliers.	The Thistle, surmounted by the Crown.	A grenade in silver embroidery; on the ball of the grenade, the Thistle, in silver metal.	A grenade in gilt metal; on the ball of the grenade, the Royal Arms.	Special pattern. In silver, on a frosted gilt rectangular plate, a wreath of thistles; within the wreath, the figure of St. Andrew with cross. On the wreath at the bottom, a silver scroll, inscribed "Royal Scots Fusiliers."	A grenade in gold embroidery. In silver metal, on the ball of the grenade, the Thistle.	As for Racoon-skin cap, but smaller.
The Cheshire Regiment.	On an eight-pointed star, a circle with acorn and oak-leaves in the centre. On the circle "The Cheshire Regiment."	Acorn with oak-leaves. The leaves and cup in dead gilt metal; the acorn in burnished silver.	In silver, on a black velvet ground, an eight-pointed star. Within a gilt circle on the star, the Prince of Wales's Plume on a burnished silver ground. On the universal scroll "The Cheshire Regiment."	On a frosted gilt centre, badge as for helmet-plate, but smaller. On the circle "Cheshire Regiment."	On a silver eight-pointed star, a gilt circle with a gilt acorn and oak-leaves in the centre on a ground of green enamel. On the circle "The Cheshire Regiment."	In gilt metal, the Garter, with motto, surmounted by the Crown. Badge and ground as for helmet-plate.
The Royal Welsh Fusiliers.	The Prince of Wales's Plume within the designation "The Royal Welsh Fusiliers."	A grenade, in silver embroidery.	A grenade in gilt metal; the Prince of Wales's Plume, in silver, on the ball.	In silver, on a frosted gilt centre, the Prince of Wales's Plume. On the circle "Royal Welsh Fusiliers."	A grenade in gold embroidery. The Red Dragon in silver, on the ball.	As for forage cap.

The South Wales Borderers.	The Welsh Dragon within a wreath of laurel.	The Sphinx over Egyyt in dead gilt metal.	In silver, on a black velvet ground, the Welsh Dragon, within a laurel wreath. On the universal scroll "The South Wales Borderers."	On a trosted gilt centre, badge as for helmet-plate. On the circle "The South Wales Borderers."	In silver, within a gilt laurel wreath, the Welsh Dragon on a raised ground of black velvet. The Crown in gilt metal above the Dragon.	In silver, the Garter, with motto, surmounted by the Crown Badge and ground as for helmet-plate.
The King's Own Scottish Borderers.	The Royal Crest, within the designation "King's Own Scottish Borderers."	On a dark blue cloth ground, the Castle of Edinburgh in silver embroidery. A flag in blue and crimson embroidery flies from each tower. The Castle rests on thistle leaves, etc., in gold embroidery. Beneath the gold embroidery a scroll, inscribed "The King's Own Scottish Borderers," on a ground of light blue silk.	In silver, a thistle wreath; within the wreath a circle pierced with the designation "King's Own Scottish Borderers." Above the circle a scroll surmounted by the Royal Crest. The scroll pierced with the motto, *In veritate religionis confido*. Over the circle, the Cross of St. Andrew in burnished silver. On the cross, the Castle of Edinburgh. On the wreath at the bottom of the circle, a scroll with the motto in relief, *Nisi Dominus frustra*.	On a frosted gilt rectangular plate with burnished edges, the Cross of St. Andrew in burnished silver; on the cross, a thistle wreath in silver; within the wreath and on the cross, the Castle of Edinburgh in silver.	In gilt metal, a thistle wreath; within the wreath a circle pierced with the designation "The King's Own Scottish Borderers." Above the circle, a scroll surmounted by the Royal Crest. The scroll pierced with the motto, *In veritate religionis confido*. Over the circle the Cross of St. Andrew in burnished silver, on the cross the Castle of Edinburgh in silver. On the wreath at the bottom, a scroll in gilt metal with the motto, in relief, *Nisi Dominus frustra*.	As for the centre of helmet-plate.

BADGES OF TERRITORIAL REGIMENTS—*continued.*

Regiment.	On Buttons.	On Collar of Tunic.	On Helmet-Plates; Ornaments for Racoon-skin Caps and Highland Head-dress.	On the Waist-Plate.	On the round Forage Cap.	On Forage Cap for Active Service and Peace Manœuvres.
The Cameronians (Scottish Rifles).	For the Great-Coat only. Within a thistle wreath, a bugle with strings; above the bugle, the Crown.	No badge.	A thistle wreath surmounted by a crown. On the leaves of the wreath, the battles of the regiment. Within the wreath, a mullet, and below the mullet, a bugle with strings. On a tablet to the right of the wreath, the Dragon of China; on a tablet to the left, the Sphinx. On the bottom of the wreath, a scroll inscribed "The Scottish Rifles."	Special pattern. In silver, on a frosted silver rectangular plate with burnished edges, a thistle wreath. Within the wreath, in burnished silver, a mullet surmounted by a crown. On the bottom of the wreath, a bugle with strings.	No badge.	The Thistle in silver, on a dark green cord boss.
The Royal Inniskilling Fusiliers.	A castle with three turrets with St. George's colours flying, superscribed "Inniskilling."	A grenade in gold embroidery; the Castle, in silver, on the ball.	A grenade in gilt metal; the Castle, in silver, on the ball.	Special Pattern. In gilt metal, on a round burnished gilt plate, a deep laurel wreath intertwined with a silver scroll bearing the battles of the Regiment. Within the wreath, in silver, on a ground of gilt metal, the White	A grenade in gold embroidery; the Castle, in silver, on the ball.	As for Racoon-skin cap, but smaller.

				Horse, with motto *Nec aspera terrent* on a scroll, in gilt metal below. Above the White Horse, a grenade, in gilt metal; on the ball of the grenade, in silver, the Castle of Inniskilling with scroll above, inscribed "Inniskilling." On the wreath, at the bottom, in gilt metal, the Sphinx over Egypt.		
The Gloucestershire Regiment.	Within a laurel wreath of single leaves, inclining inwards, the Royal Crest above the monogram G.R.	In dead gilt metal, on two twigs of laurel, the Sphinx over Egypt.	In silver, on a black velvet ground, the Sphinx over Egypt. On the universal scroll, "The Gloucestershire Regiment." Badge: for back of helmet—In dead gilt metal, the Sphinx over Egypt within a laurel wreath.	In silver, on a frosted gilt centre, the Sphinx over Egypt. On the circle, "Gloucestershire Regiment."	In gilt metal and red enamel, the Arms of the City of Gloucester surmounted by the Sphinx over Egypt on two twigs of laurel. Below the shield, a gilt scroll inscribed, in silver, "Gloucestershire Regiment."	In gilt metal, the Garter, with motto, surmounted by the Crown. Badge and ground as for helmet-plate.
The Worcestershire Regiment.	On an eight-pointed star, a circle surmounted by the Crown. The circle inscribed "The Worcestershire Regiment." Within the circle, a lion.	On a silver eight-pointed star, in gilt metal, the Garter with motto; within the Garter, in silver the Lion, pierced on a black velvet ground.	On a black velvet ground, a silver eight-pointed star. On the star, in gilt metal, the Garter with motto. Within the Garter, in silver the Lion, pierced on a	On a gilt frosted centre, a silver eight-pointed star. On the star, in gilt metal, the Garter with motto: within the Garter, in silver the Lion	In gold embroidery, an eight-pointed star. The Garter, in gilt metal, raised on the star, and pierced with the motto *Honi soit qui mal y*	In gilt metal, the Garter, with motto, surmounted by the Crown. Badge and ground as for helmet-plate.

BADGES OF TERRITORIAL REGIMENTS—*continued.*

Regiment.	On Buttons.	On Collar of Tunic.	On Helmet-Plates; Ornaments for Racoon-skin Caps and Highland Head-dress.	On the Waist-Plate.	On the round Forage Cap.	On Forage Cap for Active Service and Peace Manœuvres.
	Below the circle, a scroll, inscribed "Firm."	Below the Garter, in gilt metal, a scroll inscribed "Firm."	black velvet ground. Below the Garter, in gilt metal, a scroll inscribed "Firm."	pierced on a black velvet ground. Below the Garter, in gilt metal, a scroll inscribed "Firm." On the circle "The Worcestershire Regiment."	*pense*; the ground of black velvet. Within the Garter, in silver, the Lion pierced on a black velvet ground. Below the star, a scroll, in gold embroidery, inscribed "Firm;" the ground of blue cloth.	
The East Lancashire Regiment.	Within a circle inscribed "The East Lancashire Regiment," the Sphinx over Egypt; below the Sphinx, the ose of Lancaster.	The Rose of Lancaster, in red and gold embroidery.	In silver, on a black velvet ground, the Sphinx over Egypt. On the universal scroll, "The East Lancashire Regiment."	In silver, on a frosted gilt centre, the Sphinx over Egypt; below the Sphinx, the Rose in gilt metal. On the circle "The East Lancashire Regiment."	In red and gold embroidery, the Rose; above the Rose, in silver metal, the Sphinx over Egypt.	In gilt metal, the Garter with motto, surmounted by the Crown. Badge and ground as for helmet-plate.
The East Surrey Regiment.	On an eight-pointed star, a circle surmounted by the Crown. The circle inscribed "East Surrey," with two twigs of laurel in the lower bend. Within the circle, the Arms of Guildford.	The Arms of Guildford, in silver, on a shield in frosted gilt metal, with burnished edges.	In silver on a black velvet ground, an eight-pointed star; on the star, badge as for collar, but smaller. On the universal scroll, "The East Surrey Regiment."	On a frosted gilt centre, badge as for helmet-plate. On the circle, "East Surrey Regiment."	On a silver eight-pointed star, a raised gilt circle surmounted by the Crown. The circle pierced with the words "East Surrey," with two twigs of laurel in the lower bend: the ground of blue	In gilt metal, the Garter, with motto, surmounted by the Crown. Badge and ground as for helmet-plate.

					velvet. On a ground of blue velvet, badge as for collar, but smaller. The cap of the Crown is of crimson velvet.	
The Duke of Cornwall's Light Infantry.	Within the designation "Duke of Cornwall's Light Infy.," a bugle with strings, surmounted by the Coronet of the Prince of Wales, as shown on His Royal Highness's Great Seal as Duke of Cornwall.	In black enamel set in gilt metal, the badge of the County of Cornwall, surmounted by the Coronet, in gilt metal, of the Prince of Wales, as shown on His Royal Highness's Great Seal as Duke of Cornwall. On a scroll the motto *One and All*, pierced in gilt letters.	In gilt metal, on a ground of dark green velvet, a bugle with strings. On the strings of the bugle two red feathers set in gilt metal. On the stems of the feathers, in silver, a turreted archway. On the universal scroll, "The Duke of Cornwall's Lt. Infy."	Oak-leaf ends. In silver, on a frosted gilt centre, a bugle with strings. Above the bugle, the Coronet of the Prince of Wales, as described for the Collar badge, but in silver. On the circle, "The Duke of Cornwall's Light Infantry."	As for the centre of the helmet-plate, but larger. Below, but detached from the badge, a scroll in gilt metal, inscribed "The Duke of Cornwall's Lt. Infy."	In gilt metal the Garter, with motto, surmounted by the Crown. Badge and ground as for helmet-plate.
The Duke of Wellington's (West Riding Regiment).	Within the designation "Duke of Wellington's West Riding Regt.," the Elephant with howdah.	The Elephant in dead gilt metal, with howdah, in silver.	In silver, on a black velvet ground, the Crest of the Duke of Wellington, with motto on a scroll below, *Virtutis fortuna comes*. On the universal scroll "The West Riding Regiment."	On a frosted gilt centre, the Elephant with howdah, in silver. On the circle "The West Riding Regiment."	In gold embroidery, the Crest of the Duke of Wellington, with motto on scroll below. Blue cloth ground.	In gilt metal, the Garter, with motto, surmounted by the Crown. Badge and ground as for helmet-plate.

BADGES OF TERRITORIAL REGIMENTS—*continued.*

Regiment	On Buttons.	On Collar of Tunic.	On Helmet-Plates: Ornaments for Racoon-skin Caps and Highland Head-dress.	On the Waist-Plate.	On the round Forage Cap.	On Forage Cap for Active Service and Peace Manœuvres.
The Border Regiment.	The Dragon of China, with the word "China" above. In the 3rd and 4th Battalions the word "China" is omitted.	In gilt metal, a laurel wreath; within the wreath, on a burnished convex ground, badge as on button. In the 3rd and 4th Battalions the word "China" is omitted.	In silver, a laurel wreath: on the wreath a Maltese Cross with a Lion between each division. On the divisions of the Cross, the battles of the Regiment. On the centre of the Cross, a raised circle inscribed *Arroyo dos Molinos*, 1811. Within the circle, a ground of red and white enamel; the Dragon of China in gold on the red enamel and the word "China" in gold letters on the white. Below the wreath a scroll inscribed "The Border Regiment." In the 3rd and 4th Battalions, battles and the word "China" are omitted.	On a frosted gilt centre, the Garter in gilt metal on a silver eight-pointed star. The Garter pierced with the motto *Honi soit qui mal y pense*; the ground of blue enamel. Within the Garter, the Cross of St. George with the ground of red enamel. On the circle "The Border Regiment."	As for helmet-plate.	As for helmet-plate.

The Royal Sussex Regiment.	Within a circle inscribed "The Royal Sussex Regt.," a Maltese cross on a feather; on centre of cross a wreath; within the wreath a raised circle, within the circle, St. George's Cross.	A Maltese cross, in gilt metal, on a feather in silver, on the cross a wreath in silver and green; on the wreath a raised circle in blue enamel set with silver. Within the circle the Cross of St. George in red enamel, set with silver, on a silver ground.	On a black velvet ground, badge as for collar, but larger. On the universal scroll "The Royal Sussex Regiment."	On a frosted gilt centre, badge, as for the helmet-plate. On the circle "Royal Sussex Regiment."	In silver embroidery, an eight-pointed star, on a feather; the stem of the feather in gold embroidery. On the star, the Garter in gilt metal, with the motto, pierced; the ground of blue enamel. Within the Garter, the Cross of St. George with the ground of red enamel. A blue silk and gold embroidered scroll, inscribed "Royal Sussex Regiment," the word "Regiment" being in the centre of the scroll.	In gilt metal, the Garter, with motto, surmounted by the Crown. Badge and ground as for helmet-plate.
The Hampshire Regiment.	Within a laurel wreath, the Royal Tiger; below the Tiger, the Hampshire Rose.	The Hampshire Rose, in gold and red and green embroidery.	On a black velvet ground, the Royal Tiger, in gilt metal, within a laurel wreath, in silver. On the universal scroll "The Hampshire Regt."	In silver, on a frosted gilt centre, the Royal Tiger within a laurel wreath; below the Tiger, the Hampshire Rose in gilt metal and red and green enamel. On the circle, "The Hampshire Regiment."	In gold embroidery an eight-pointed star. On the star, the Garter in blue silk, surmounted by the Imperial Crown, as represented in the collar of the Order of the Star of India, in gold embroidery. The motto on the Garter embroidered in silver. Within the Garter, the Hampshire Rose, in red and gold embroidery.	In gilt metal, the Garter, with motto surmounted by the Crown. Badge and ground as for helmet-plate.

BADGES OF TERRITORIAL REGIMENTS—*continued.*

Regiment.	On Buttons.	On Collar of Tunic.	On Helmet-Plates: Ornaments for Racoon-skin Caps and Highland Head-dress.	On the Waist-Plate.	On the round Forage Cap.	On Forage Cap for Active Service and Peace Manœuvres.
The South Staffordshire Regiment.	The Staffordshire Knot with Crown above.	The Staffordshire Knot, in gold embroidery.	In silver, on a black velvet ground, the Sphinx over Egypt. On the universal scroll, "The South Staffordshire Regiment."	Special pattern with oak-leaf ends. In silver, on a burnished gilt centre, a laurel wreath. Within the wreath, in silver, Windsor Castle with the Sphinx over Egypt above, and the Staffordshire Knot below. On the wreath, at the bottom, "The South Staffordshire Regiment."	On a black cloth ground, the Staffordshire Knot in gold embroidery; above the Knot the Sphinx over Egypt in gilt metal.	In gilt metal, the Garter, with motto surmounted by the Crown. Badge and ground as for helmet-plate.
The Dorsetshire Regiment.	The Castle and Key. Above the Castle, a scroll inscribed "Gibraltar," and one below, inscribed *Primus in Indis*. Above the top scroll, "The Dorsetshire Regiment;" below the bottom scroll, the Sphinx on a tablet inscribed "Marabout."	The Sphinx in silver, on a gilt tablet. On the tablet "Marabout" in gilt letters on a ground of green enamel.	In silver, on a black velvet ground, the Castle and Key. A scroll above the Castle inscribed *Primus in Indis*, and one below, inscribed *Montis Insignia Calpe*. On the universal scroll "The Dorsetshire Regiment."	In silver, on a frosted gilt centre, the Castle and Key, with scroll above inscribed "Gibraltar." Below the Castle, the Sphinx on a tablet inscribed "Marabout." On the circle, "Dorsetshire Regiment."	The Castle and Key; the Castle in silver, the Key in gilt metal. Above the Castle, a scroll in gilt metal, with the words *Primus in Indis* in gilt letters on a ground of green enamel. Below the Castle, a gilt scroll, with the words *Montis Insignia Calpe* in gilt letters on a	In gilt metal, the Garter, with motto, surmounted by the Crown. Badge and ground as for helmet plate.

					ground of green enamel. Under this scroll, the Sphinx in gilt metal, on a gilt tablet, with the word "Marabout" in gilt letters on a ground of green enamel.	
The Prince of Wales's Volunteers (South Lancashire Regiment).	Within a scroll, and the laurel branch issuing from either end, a circle surmounted by the Crown. On the circle, "The South Lancashire Regiment;" within, the Prince of Wales's Plume above the Sphinx over Egypt.	The Prince of Wales's Plume, in gold and silver embroidery, on a blue cloth ground; the scroll in blue silk, with the motto in silver embroidery.	In silver, on a black velvet ground, the Sphinx over Egypt. On the universal scroll "South Lancashire Regiment."	Special pattern; oak-leaf ends. In silver, on a burnished gilt centre, a laurel branch at either side; at the top, a scroll, inscribed "South Lancashire Regt.;" at the bottom, a scroll, inscribed "Prince of Wales's Vols." In silver, within the scrolls and laurel branches, the Prince of Wales's Plume above the Sphinx over Egypt.	In silver, on a raised ground of blue cloth, the Sphinx over Egypt. Above the Sphinx, in gold and silver embroidery, the Prince of Wales's Plume; the motto in silver embroidery on a blue silk ground. On each side a laurel branch, in gold embroidery. A blue silk gold embroidered scroll, inscribed "The Prince of Wales's Volunteers."	In gilt metal, the Garter, with motto, surmounted by the Crown. Badge and ground as for helmet-plate.
The Welsh Regiment.	Within a laurel wreath, a Circle surmounted by the Crown. On the circle, "The Welsh Regiment;" within, the Prince of Wales's Plume.	The Welsh Dragon, in gilt metal.	In silver, on a black velvet ground, the Prince of Wales's Plume with scroll below inscribed *Gwell angau na Chywilydd.* On the universal scroll "The Welsh Regiment."	Oak-leaf ends. The Welsh Dragon, in silver, on a frosted gilt centre. On the circle "The Welsh Regiment."	In gold and silver embroidery, on a blue cloth ground, the Prince of Wales's Plume; the scroll in blue silk; the motto in gold embroidery. 1st Bn.—In metal.	In gilt metal the Garter, with motto, surmounted by the Crown. Badge and ground as for helme plate.

BADGES OF TERRITORIAL REGIMENTS—*continued.*

Regiment.	On Buttons.	On Collar of Tunic.	On Helmet-Plates: Ornaments for Racoon-skin Caps and Highland Head-dress.	On the Waist-Plate.	On the round Forage Cap.	On Forage Cap for Active Service and Peace Manœuvres.
The Black Watch (Royal Highlanders).	Within the designation "The Royal Highlanders, Black Watch," the Star of the Order of the Thistle, recessed. On the centre of the Star, a circle; within the circle, St. Andrew and Cross.	St. Andrew and Cross, in silver.	For Highland head-dress and white helmet. In silver, the Star of the Order of the Thistle; in gilt metal on the Star, a thistle wreath. Within the wreath, in gilt metal, an oval surmounted by the Crown. The oval inscribed, *Nemo me impune lacessit.* Within the oval, on a recessed *seeded* ground, St. Andrew and Cross, in silver. Below the wreath, the Sphinx, in gilt metal. In silver, a half scroll, to the left of the Crown, inscribed "The Royal;" another to the right inscribed "Highlanders." A half scroll to the left of the Sphinx, inscribed "Black;" another to the right, inscribed "Watch."	Special pattern. On a *seeded* gilt rectangular plate, with burnished edges, badge as for bonnet, but smaller.	This forage cap is not worn.	Glengarry—Badge as for Highland head-dress.

The Oxfordshire Light Infantry.	Scalloped edge; within a laurel wreath a bugle with strings; below the bugle "Oxfordshire."	Edgeless button; on the button, within a laurel wreath, a bugle with strings; above the bugle, the Crown; below the wreath "Oxfordshire." A piece of gold Russia braid 2½ inches long, attached to the button.	In silver, on a ground of black enamel, a bugle with strings. On the universal scroll, "The Oxfordshire Lt. Infy." The plate is of *gilding*, not of gilt metal.	In silver, on a frosted gilt centre, a bugle with strings. On the circle "Oxfordshire Light Infantry."	A bugle with strings, in gold embroidery, on a green cloth ground.	A bugle with strings, in silver.
The Essex Regiment.	Within an oak-leaf wreath, the badge of the County of Essex, with the Sphinx over Egypt above, and the Castle and Key below.	The County Badge. The shield in gilt metal; the blades of the seaxes in silver. 2nd and 3rd Bns.: the badge is in embroidery with the seaxes wholly in silver.	An oak-leaf wreath is substituted for the universal wreath. In silver, on a black velvet ground, the Castle and Key, with the Sphinx over Egypt above, and a scroll below, inscribed *Montis Insignia Calpe*. On the universal scroll "The Essex Regiment."	Special pattern with oak leaf ends. On a burnished gilt centre, an oak-leaf wreath, in silver. Within the wreath, a dead gilt circle, surmounted by the Crown, in silver. The circle inscribed, "The Essex Regiment." Within the circle, the County badge, on a shield of red enamel, set in gilt metal. The seaxes inlaid, the hilts in gilt metal, the blades in silver. The shield surmounted by the Sphinx over Egypt, in silver. On the wreath, at the bottom, the Castle and Key, in silver.	On a raised ground of blue cloth, a blue silk gold embroidered scroll inscribed "The Essex Regt." Within the scroll, the County badge surmounted by the Crown. The Crown and shield in gold embroidery; the seaxes in silver embroidery.	In gilt metal, the Garter, with motto, surmounted by the Crown. Badge and ground as for helmet-plate.

BADGES OF TERRITORIAL REGIMENTS—*continued.*

Regiment.	On Buttons.	On Collar of Tunic.	On Helmet-Plates; Ornaments for Racoon-skin Caps and High-land Head-dress.	On the Waist-Plate.	On the round Forage Cap.	On Forage Cap for Active Service and Peace Manœuvres
The Sherwood Foresters (Derbyshire Regiment).	A Maltese cross surmounted by the Crown; within an oak-leaf wreath on the cross, a Stag lodged. A half scroll on the left division of the cross, inscribed "Sherwood"; another on the right division, inscribed "Foresters." On the lower division, a scroll inscribed "Derbyshire."	A Maltese cross surmounted by the Crown, in silver. Wreath and scrolls, in gilt metal, as for buttons. Within the wreath, a Stag lodged, in silver, on a ground of blue enamel.	In the helmet-plate, the Garter, with motto, is omitted. Within the universal wreath, a Maltese cross, in silver. On the cross, in gilt metal, an oak-leaf wreath; within the wreath, on a ground of blue enamel, a Stag lodged, in silver. In gilt metal, on the left division of the cross, the word "The"; on the right division, "Regt.," and on a scroll on the lower division, "Derbyshire." A scroll of special pattern on the bottom of the universal wreath inscribed "Sherwood Foresters."	Special pattern: oak-leaf ends. On a burnished gilt plate, the badge as for collar, but larger.	As on Waist-plate.	As on Waist-plate.
The Loyal North Lancashire Regiment.	Within a circle inscribed "Loyal North Lancashire Regiment," the Arms of the City	In embroidery, the Arms of the City of Lincoln. The ground of the shield in silver,	In silver, on a black velvet ground, the Royal Crest. Below the Crest, the Rose of Lancaster in gilt	On a frosted gilt centre, the badge as for helmet-plate. On the circle "Loyal North Lan	In gold embroidery, the Royal Crest; below the Crest, the Rose of Lancaster.	In gilt metal, the Garter, with motto, surmounted by the Crown. Badge and ground as for

	of Lincoln, surmounted by the Royal Crest.	the Cross of St. George in red silk on the shield; the *fleur-de-lis* in gold on the cross.	metal and red and green enamel. On the universal scroll, "Loyal North Lancashire Regiment."	cashire Regiment."		helmet-plate.
!The Northamptonshire Regiment.	Within a scroll inscribed "The Northamptonshire Regiment," the Castle and Key with the Crown above.	In gilt metal, within a laurel wreath, a gilt circle pierced "Northampton-shire Regt."; the ground of blue enamel. In relief, within the circle, on a raised ground of blue enamel, the Cross of St. George, in silver. Below the cross, and on the circle, a horse-shoe in silver. The circle surmounted by a crown in gilt metal.	In silver, on a black velvet ground, the Castle and Key; on a scroll above, "Gibraltar," on a scroll below, "Talavera." On the universal scroll "The Northamptonshire Regiment."	In silver, on a frosted gilt centre, badge, and scrolls as for helmet-plate. On the circle "Northamptonshire Regiment."	In gold embroidery, the Castle and Key. Above the Castle, a blue silk gold embroidered scroll, inscribed "Gibraltar," and a similar scroll, below, inscribed "Talavera."	In gilt metal, the Garter, with motto, surmounted by the Crown. Badge and ground as for helmet-plate.
Princess Charlotte of Wales's (Royal Berkshire Regiment).	A circle inscribed "P. Charlotte of Wales's"; within the circle, the Dragon of China; above the Dragon, the Crown; below, "R. Berks."	The Dragon of China, in gold embroidery on a blue cloth ground.	In silver, on a scarlet cloth ground, a Stag under an oak. On the universal scroll "Royal Berkshire Regiment."	Oak-leaf ends. In silver, on a frosted gilt centre, the Dragon of China. On the circle "Royal Berkshire Regiment."	The Dragon of China, in gold embroidery.	In gilt metal, the Garter, with motto, surmounted by the Crown. Badge and ground as for helmet-plate.

BADGES OF TERRITORIAL REGIMENTS—*continued*.

Regiment.	On Buttons.	On Collar of Tunic.	On Helmet-Plates; Ornaments for Racoon-skin Caps and High-land Head-dress.	On the Waist-Plate.	On the round Forage Cap.	On Forage Cap for Active Service and Peace Manœuvres.
The Queen's Own (Royal West Kent Regiment).	The Royal Crest.	The Royal Crest, in gold embroidery.	In silver, on a black velvet ground, the White Horse of Kent on a scroll inscribed *Invicta*. Above the Horse, another scroll with motto *Quo fas et gloria ducunt*. On the universal scroll, "The Royal West Kent Regiment."	In silver, on a frosted gilt centre. the Royal Crest. On the circle "The Queen's Own Regiment."	In silver metal, the White Horse of Kent on a scroll, inscribed *Invicta*. Below, a blue silk gold embroidered scroll, inscribed "The Queen's Own Royal West Kent Regt."	In gilt metal, the Garter, with motto, surmounted by the Crown. Badge and ground as for helmet-plate.
The King's Own (Yorkshire Light Infantry).	A French horn surmounted by the Crown. In the centre of the horn the White Rose, in silver.	A French horn, in gold embroidery; in the centre of the horn, on a raised ground of dark green cloth, the White Rose, in silver metal.	In silver, on a black enamel ground, a French horn with the White Rose in the centre. On the universal scroll, "The King's Own Yorkshire Light Infantry."	In silver, on a frosted gilt centre, a French horn surmounted by the Crown. In the centre of the horn. the White Rose in silver. On the circle, "The Yorkshire Light Infantry."	As for the collar badge, but larger.	As for the round forage cap
The King's (Shropshire Light Infantry).	A circle surmounted by the Crown. On the circle, "Shropshire" with two twigs of laurel in the lower bend. Within the	A bugle with strings, in gold embroidery, on a ground of dark blue cloth.	In silver, on a ground of dark green velvet, a bugle with strings. In gilt metal within the strings of the bugle, the monogram K.L.I. On the	In silver, on a frosted gilt centre, a bugle with strings. Within the strings in gilt metal, the monogram K.L.I. On	In gilt metal, on a silver eight-pointed star, a raised circle, inscribed "Shropshire" with two twigs of laurel in	As for the round forage cap.

	circle, the monogram, K.L.I.		universal scroll, "King's Shropshire Lt. Infty."	the circle "Shropshire Light Infantry."	the lower bend. Within the circle, on a ground of dark green velvet, a bugle with strings, in silver. Within the strings, the monogram, in gilt metal.	
The Duke of Cambridge's Own (Middlesex Regiment).	Within a wreath of laurel, the Prince of Wales's Plume: on the bottom of the wreath, a scroll inscribed "Albuhera."	A laurel wreath in gilt metal; within the wreath, in silver, on a frosted gilt centre, the Prince of Wales's Plume; above the Plume, a scroll inscribed "Albuhera"; below the Plume, the Coronet and Cypher of H.R.H. the Duke of Cambridge.	In silver, on a black velvet ground. A laurel wreath; within the wreath, the Prince of Wales's Plume; below the Plume, the Coronet and Cypher of H.R.H. the Duke of Cambridge. On the bottom of the wreath a scroll inscribed "Albuhera." On the universal scroll "The Middlesex Regt."	In silver, on a frosted gilt centre, a laurel wreath; within the wreath the Prince of Wales's Plume; below the Plume, the badge of the County of Middlesex. A scroll on the bottom of the wreath, inscribed "Albuhera." On the circle "The Duke of Cambridge's Own."	In gold embroidery on a raised blue cloth ground, a laurel wreath; within the wreath, the Prince of Wales's Plume, the motto embroidered in silver on a ground of blue silk; below the Plume, in gold embroidery, the Coronet and Cypher of H.R.H. the Duke of Cambridge. On the bottom of the wreath, a light blue silk gold embroidered scroll, inscribed "Albuhera."	In gilt metal, a circle surmounted by the Crown. On the circle, "Duke of Cambridge's Own Middlesex Regiment:" within the circle, on a ground of blue enamel, the badges as for the helmet-plate except that the word "Albuhera" is on a scroll above the Plume.
The King's Royal Rifle Corps.	Within a laurel wreath, a bugle with strings: above the bugle, the Crown.	No badge.	In bronze, a Maltese cross surmounted by the Royal Crown resting on a tablet, inscribed *Celer et Audax*. On the Cross a circle, inscribed 'The King's	No badge.	No badge.	A bugle, in silver, on a scarlet cord boss.

BADGES OF TERRITORIAL REGIMENTS—*continued.*

Regiment.	On Buttons.	On Collar of Tunic.	On Helmet-Plates; Ornaments for Racoon-skin Caps and Highland Head-dress.	On the Waist-Plate.	On the round Forage Cap.	On Forage Cap for Active Service and Peace Manœuvres.
			Royal Rifle Corps"; within the circle, a bugle with strings on a scarlet cloth ground. On each division, of the cross, the battles of the Regiment. The dimensions are—from the top of the Crown to the bottom of the plate, back measurement, 4 inches; extreme width $2\frac{1}{2}$ inches.			
The Duke of Edinburgh's (Wiltshire Regiment).	The Cypher of H.R.H. the Duke of Edinburgh, with Coronet above, and "Wiltshire Regiment" below.	A Maltese cross in *lined* silver, with burnished edges. On the cross, a round convex plate, in burnished silver. On the plate, in gilt metal, the Coronet within the Cypher.	On a black velvet ground, the Maltese cross in *lined* gilt metal, with burnished edges. On the cross, a round convex burnished plate. On the plate, in silver, the Cypher surmounted by the Coronet. On the universal scroll, "The Wiltshire Regiment."	On a frosted gilt centre, badge as for helmet-plate. On the circle "The Wiltshire Regiment."	The Maltese cross in gold embroidery, surmounted by the Coronet. On the cross, a convex circle in blue velvet, edged with gold purl. On the circle, the Cypher in silver embroidery, with Coronet above in gold. Below the cross, a light blue silk gold embroidered scroll in-	A Maltese cross in dead gilt metal, with burnished edges. On each division of the cross, the battles of the Regiment in relief. The metal lined between each battle. On the cross a circle, inscribed "The Wiltshire Regiment." Within the circle, on a raised bur-

					scribed "The Wiltshire Regiment." 1st and 3rd Bns.: In gilt metal, the Cypher and Coronet in silver.	nished centre, the Coronet, within the Cypher in silver. 3rd Battalion: Battles omitted, but the word "Mediterranean" is inscribed on the upper division of the Cross."
The Manchester Regiment.	The Garter, with motto, *Honi soit qui mal y pense.* Within the Garter, the Sphinx over Egypt with the Crown above.	The Sphinx over Egypt in gold embroidery; the word "Egypt" embroidered in silver.	In silver, on a black velvet ground, the Arms with motto of the City of Manchester. On the universal scroll, "The Manchester Regiment."	In silver, on a frosted gilt centre, an eight pointed star; on the star, in dead gilt metal, the Sphinx over Egypt. On the circle "The Manchester Regiment."	The Sphinx over Egypt in gold embroidery; the word "Egypt" in silver embroidery. Below, on a blue cloth gold embroidered scroll "Manchester Regiment."	In silver, the Arms with motto of the City of Manchester. On scroll below, "The Manchester Regt."
The Prince of Wales's (North Staffordshire Regiment.)	Within a scroll inscribed "Prince of Wales's" and the laurel branch issuing from either end, a circle inscribed "The North Staffordshire Regiment;" within the circle, the Staffordshire Knot; above the circle, the Prince of Wales's Plume.	The Staffordshire Knot in gold embroidery.	In silver, on a black velvet ground, the Prince of Wales's Plume. On the universal scroll, "The North Staffordshire Regiment."	On a frosted gilt centre, badge as for helmet-plate. On the circle, "North Staffordshire Regiment."	On a blue cloth ground, the Staffordshire Knot in gold embroidery, surmounted by the Prince of Wales's plume in gold and silver embroidery. The motto in silver embroidery on a gold embroidered scroll.	In gilt metal, the Garter, with motto surmounted by the Crown. Badge and ground as for helmet-plate.

BADGES OF TERRITORIAL REGIMENTS—*continued.*

Regiment.	On Buttons.	On Collar of Tunic.	On Helmet-Plates; Ornaments for Racoon-skin Caps and Highland Head-dress.	On the Waist-Plate.	On the round Forage Cap.	On Forage Cap for Active Service and Peace Manœuvres.
The York and Lancaster Regiment.	A scroll inscribed "The York & Lancaster Regiment;" within the scroll, a laurel wreath; within the wreath the Royal Tiger: above the Tiger, a Coronet. On the wreath at the bottom, the Union Rose.	The Royal Tiger, in dead gilt metal.	In silver and gilt metal, on a black velvet ground, the Union Rose. On the universal scroll, "The York & Lancaster Regiment."	On a frosted gilt centre, the Union Rose in gilt and silver metal: below the Rose, the Royal Tiger, in silver. On the circle "York & Lancaster Regiment."	On a blue cloth ground, in gold embroidery, the Union Rose; below the Rose, the Royal Tiger.	In gilt metal, the Garter, with motto, surmounted by the Crown. Badge and ground as for helmet-plate.
The Durham Light Infantry.	Bugle, with the Crown above.	Bugle with strings, in gold embroidery.	In silver, on a black velvet ground, a bugle with strings. On the universal scroll, "The Durham Light Infantry."	On a frosted gilt centre, badge as for helmet-plate. On the circle, "Durham Light Infantry."	In gold embroidery, on a blue cloth ground, a bugle. Within the strings, on a blue cloth raised ground, the letters D.L.I.	In gilt metal the Garter, with motto, surmounted by the Crown. Badge and ground as for helmet-plate.
The Highland Light Infantry.	Star of the Order of the Thistle. On the star, a horn; in the centre of the horn, the monogram H. L. I. Above the horn, the Crown as represented in the collar of the Order of the Star of	In silver, the Star of the Order of the Thistle. On the star a silver horn. In the centre of the horn, the monogram H.L.I. in gilt metal. Above the horn, in gilt metal, the Crown as repre-	For Chaco. As for collar badge, except that the cap of the Crown is of crimson velvet. The scroll is detached from the Elephant, and the badge is larger.	Special pattern. Frosted gilt rectangular plate, with badge as for Chaco.	As for Chaco.	As for Chaco.

	India; below the horn a scroll, inscribed "Assaye," under the scroll, the Elephant.	sented in the collar of the Order of the Star of India; below the horn. a scroll, in gilt metal, inscribed "Assaye;" under the scroll, in gilt metal, the Elephant.				
Seaforth Highlanders (Ross-shire Buffs, the Duke of Albany's).	A stag's head, with the Cypher of H.R.H. the Duke of Albany above. A scroll below, inscribed "Seaforth Highlanders."	Two badges in gilt metal— I. The Cypher of H.R.H. the late Duke of York with scroll inscribed "Caber Feidh." II. The Elephant. Both badges to be worn on each side of the collar, the Cypher of the late Duke of York being nearest the end.	For Highland head-dress and white helmet. In silver, a stag's head; above, the Coronet and Cypher of H.R.H. the Duke of Albany; below, a scroll inscribed "Cuidich'n Righ."	Special pattern. Burnished gilt rectangular plate. Badge as for Highland head-dress, except that it is smaller, and that the motto on scroll is *Tolloch Ard.*	I. In gold embroidery, a thistle; on the thistle, the Star of the Order of the Thistle in silver metal; on the star, a circle in gilt metal; within the circle, on a ground of green enamel, the Cypher of the late Duke of York with Coronet above, in gilt metal. II. In dead gilt metal, the Elephant over a scroll, inscribed "Assaye." Both badges are worn at one time, the Elephant below the Thistle.	As for Highland head-dress.
The Gordon Highlanders.	The Cross of St. Andrew; on the cross a thistle wreath joined to a scroll let into the upper divisions of	The Royal Tiger, in gold embroidery.	For Highland head-dress and White Helmet. In silver, the Crest of the Marquis of Huntley within an ivy wreath.	Special pattern. Burnished gilt rectangular plate. In silver, badge as on buttons, but larger.	The Thistle, in gold embroidery.	As for Highland head dress.

BADGES OF TERRITORIAL REGIMENTS—*continued.*

Regiment.	On Buttons.	On Collar of Tunic.	On Helmet-Plates; Ornaments for Racoon-skin Caps and Highland Head-dress.	On the Waist-Plate.	On the round Forage Cap.	On Forage Cap for Active Service and Peace Manœuvres.
	the cross and inscribed "Gordon Highlanders." Within the scroll, on the upper divisions of the cross, the Sphinx over Egypt, within the wreath on the lower divisions of the cross, the Royal Tiger over India.		On the bottom of the wreath, *Bydand.*			
The Queen's Own Cameron Highlanders.	Within the designation "The Queen's Own Cameron Highlanders," the Thistle surmounted by the Crown.	The Thistle surmounted by the Crown, in silver embroidery.	For Highland head-dress and White Helmet. In silver, a thistle wreath; within the wreath the figure of St. Andrew with Cross.	Special pattern. Burnished gilt rectangular plate. In silver on the plate, a thistle wreath; within the wreath St. Andrew with Cross.	This forage cap is not worn.	Glengarry. As for Highland head-dress.
The Royal Irish Rifles.	Scalloped edge; within a scroll and the shamrock leaves issuing from either end, the Harp and Crown. On scroll, "Royal Irish Rifles."	No badge	In bronze, a shamrock wreath intertwined with a scroll bearing the battles of the Regiment; within the wreath, the Harp and Crown. Above the Harp, a	No badge	No badge	In silver, on a dark green cord boss, the Harp surmounted by a crown; on the Harp, a scroll, inscribed "Royal Irish Rifles."

			scroll, inscribed *Quis separabit*; below the Harp, the Sphinx over Egypt; below the Sphinx, a bugle with strings. Over the strings of the bugle, a scroll, inscribed "Royal Irish Rifles." No star behind.			
Princess Victoria's (Royal Irish Fusiliers).	Scalloped edge; an Eagle with a wreath of laurel; below the Eagle a small tablet inscribed with the figure 8.	A grenade in gold embroidery, with badge on ball as for buttons, but in silver. 2nd Badge—Coronet of H.R.H. the Princess Victoria in silver.	A grenade in gilt metal. In silver on the ball, the Eagle with a wreath of laurel. Below the Eagle a small tablet inscribed with the figure 8.	Special pattern; shamrock ends with harp. In gilt metal, on a frosted gilt centre, a grenade, with badge in silver, as for the Racoon-skin cap, but smaller. On the circle, a laurel wreath with the Crown at the top; on the wreath at the bottom, a scroll, inscribed "Royal Irish Fusiliers."	A grenade in gold embroidery. Above the grenade, the Coronet of H.R.H. the Princess Victoria. In silver, on the ball of grenade, the Prince of Wales's Plume over the Harp.	As for Racoon-skin cap, but smaller.
The Connaught Rangers.	Scalloped edge. Within a wreath of shamrock, the Harp over the Elephant.	The Elephant, in silver embroidery, on a ground of gold embroidery. Caparison in blue velvet edged with gold. Gold girths.	In silver, on a dark green velvet ground, the Harp, with scroll, inscribed *Quis separabit*. A sprig of laurel issues from either end of the scroll. On the universal scroll, "The Connaught Rangers."	In silver, on a frosted gilt centre, the Elephant with the Crown above. On the circle, "Connaught Rangers."	In gold embroidery, on a blue cloth ground, the Harp and Crown.	In silver, a circle surmounted by the Crown; the circle inscribed "The Connaught Rangers;" shamrock leaves in the lower bend. On a convex ground of dark green velvet, the Harp, in silver.

BADGES OF TERRITORIAL REGIMENTS—*continued.*

Regiment.	On Buttons.	On Collar of Tunic.	On Helmet-Plates; Ornaments for Racoon-skin Caps and Highland Head-dress.	On the Waist-Plate.	On the round Forage Cap.	On Forage Cap for Active Service and Peaee Manœuvres.
Princess Louise's (Argyll and Sutherland Highlanders).	A myrtle wreath interlaced with a wreath of butcher's broom. Within the myrtle wreath, a Boar's head on scroll, inscribed, *Ne obliviscaris*; within the wreath of butcher's broom, a Cat on scroll, inscribed *Sans peur*. A label of three points above the Boar's head and the Cat. Above the wreaths, the Coronet of H.R.H. the Princess Louise.	In frosted silver, a myrtle wreath interlaced with a wreath of butcher's broom. In gilt metal, within the myrtle wreath, the Boar's head on scroll, inscribed *Ne obliviscaris*; within the wreath of butcher's broom, the Cat on scroll, inscribed *Sans peur*. A label of three points in silver above the Boar's head and the Cat.	For Highland head-dress and White Helmet. In silver a thistle wreath: within the wreath, a circle, inscribed "Argyll and Sutherland." Within the circle, the double Cypher of H.R.H. the Princess Louise. To the left of the Cypher, the Boar's head; to the right the Cat. Above the Cypher, and on the circle, the Coronet of the Princess.	Burnished gilt rectangular plate. Devices as for collar badge, but *all* in silver. Above the wreaths, in frosted silver, a scroll surmounted by the Coronet of the Princess. The scroll inscribed "Princess Louise's," below the wreath, a silver scroll, inscribed "Argyll and Sutherland Highlanders."	This Forage cap is not worn.	Glengarry. Badge as for Highland head-dress.
The Prince of Wales's Leinster Regiment (Royal Canadians).	A Circle, inscribed "Prince of Wales's Leinster Regiment;" within the circle, the Prince of Wales's Plume.	The Prince of Wales's Plume, in silver; the Coronet in gilt metal.	In silver, on a black velvet ground, the Prince of Wales's Plume over two maple leaves. On a scroll, beneath the leaves, "Central India." On the universal scroll, "Prince	Special pattern, maple leaf ends. In silver, on a burnished gilt centre, a maple and laurel wreath. Within the wreath, a circle inscribed, "The Leinster Regt." Above the circle, the Crown; within, the Prince	In silver, the Prince of Wales's Plume, the scroll with motto, in gilt metal. Below the Plume a scroll, in gilt metal, inscribed "The Leinster."	In gilt metal, the Garter, with motto, surmounted by the Crown. Badge and ground as for helmet-plate.

			of Wales's Leinster Regiment."	of Wales's Plume; below, in dead gilt metal on the maple and laurel wreath, a scroll, inscribed "Central India."		
The Royal Munster Fusiliers.	Within the designation, "Royal Munster Fusiliers"; a grenade, with the Royal Tiger on the ball.	A grenade in gold embroidery, with the Royal Tiger, in silver, on the ball.	A grenade, in gilt metal. On the ball, a deep wreath of laurel intertwined with a scroll bearing the battles of the Regiment Within the wreath, the Heraldic device for the Province of Munster. the crowns in gilt metal, the shield in silver. On the bottom of the wreath. a scroll, in silver, inscribed "Royal Munster."	Special pattern: oak-leaf ends. On a burnished gilt centre, a deep laurel wreath intertwined with a silver scroll, bearing the battles of the Regiment. Within the wreath, a grenade, in gilt metal, with the Royal Tiger, in silver, on the ball. On the wreath at the bottom, a scroll, in silver, inscribed "Royal Munster."	A grenade, in gold embroidery, with the Royal Tiger, in silver metal, on the ball.	Grenade in gilt metal, with device for the Province of Munster, on the ball; the crowns in gilt metal, the shield in silver.
The Royal Dublin Fusiliers.	Within the designation "Royal Dublin Fusiliers," a grenade; on the ball of the grenade, the Crown	A grenade in gold embroidery; in silver, on the ball, the Royal Tiger; below the Tiger, the Elephant.	A grenade in gilt metal: on the ball, in silver, the Arms of the City of Dublin; below the shield—to the right, the Royal Tiger, on a silver tablet inscribed "Plassey," to the left, the Elephant, on a silver tablet inscribed "Mysore." Below the tablets a silver scroll inscribed *Spec-*	Special pattern; shamrock ends, with the Harp. In gilt metal, on a round burnished gilt plate, a grenade; in silver, on the ball, a circle inscribed "Royal Dublin Fusiliers;" within the circle, the Harp. Below the ball, in gilt metal, a scroll inscribed	A grenade, in gold embroidery; in silver, on the ball, the Royal Tiger; below the Tiger, the Elephant. Below, and detached from the grenade, a gilt scroll pierced "Royal Dublin Fusiliers;" the ground of blue enamel.	As for Racoon-skin cap, but smaller.

BADGES OF TERRITORIAL REGIMENTS—*continued.*

Regiment.	On Buttons.	On Collar of Tunic.	On Helmet-Plates; Ornaments for Racoon-skin Caps and Highland Head-dress.	On the Waist-Plate.	On the round Forage Cap.	On Forage Cap for Active Service and Peace Manœuvres.
			tamur agendo. In silver on either side of the shield, a rich mounting of shamrock leaves.	*Spectamur agendo.* Below the scroll, in gilt metal—to the right, the Royal Tiger on a scroll inscribed "Plassey," to the left, the Elephant on a scroll inscribed "Mysore." On either side of the grenade, a rich mounting of shamrock leaves, in gilt metal.		
The Rifle Brigade (The Prince Consort's Own).	Within a laurel wreath, and the designation Rifle Brigade, a bugle with strings; above the bugle, the Crown.	No badge	In bronze, a wreath of laurel intertwined with a scroll, bearing the battles of the Brigade. Within the wreath, a Maltese cross, with a Lion between each division. On each division, other battles of the Brigade. On the centre of the cross, a circle inscribed "Rifle Brigade;" within the circle, a bugle with	No badge	No badge	Bugle, in silver, on a black cord boss.

			strings, surmounted by the Crown. Above the cross, a crown on a tablet. inscribed "Waterloo;" below the cross, a scroll, inscribed "Peninsula," and another, on the bottom of the wreath, inscribed "The Prince Consort's Own."			
The West India Regiment.	A wreath of special pattern. Within the wreath, the letters, W.I.R.	No badge.	A wreath of special pattern in gilt metal. Within the wreath, the Garter, with motto. Within the Garter on a burnished ground, the letters, W.I.R. The battles of the Regiment on the larger rays of the star.	Special pattern. Oak-leaf ends. Badge as on helmet-plate, but smaller.	In gold embroidery, on a blue cloth ground, the wreath as on helmet-plate. Within the wreath, the Garter, with motto on a blue silk ground. Within the Garter, the letters, W.I.R.	As for the round forage cap.

INDEX.

Index.

Index.

Index.

Index.

Index.

www.ingramcontent.com/pod-product-compliance
Lightning Source LLC
Chambersburg PA
CBHW030403100426
42812CB00028B/2815/J

* 9 7 8 1 8 4 7 3 4 0 8 2 5 *